# All About
# MARKET
# TIMING

## THE EASY WAY TO GET STARTED

# All About
# MARKET
# TIMING

## THE EASY WAY TO GET STARTED

**Second Edition**

## LESLIE N. MASONSON

New York  Chicago  San Francisco  Lisbon  London  Madrid
Mexico City  Milan  New Delhi  San Juan  Seoul
Singapore  Sydney  Toronto

3 4 5 6 7 8 9 0   QFR/QFR   1 6 5 4 3

ISBN: 978-0-07-175377-7 (print book)
MHID:     0-07-175377-X

ISBN: 978-0-07-175378-4 (e-book)
MHID:     0-07-175378-8

This publication is designed to provide accurate and authoritative information in regard to the subject matter covered. It is sold with the understanding that neither the author nor the publisher is engaged in rendering legal, accounting, or other professional service. If legal advice or other expert assistance is required, the services of a competent professional person should be sought.
—*From a Declaration of Principles Jointly Adopted by*
*a Committee of the American Bar Association and*
*a Committee of Publishers and Associations*

**Library of Congress Cataloging-in-Publication Data**

Masonson, Leslie N.
  All about market timing / by Leslie N. Masonson. — 2nd ed.
      p. cm.
  Rev. ed. of: All about market timing : the easy way to get started. ©2004.
  Includes bibliographical references and index.
  ISBN 978-0-07-175377-7 (alk. paper)
  1. Investment analysis. 2. Stock price forecasting. 3. Speculation. I. Title.
  HG4529.M377 2011
  332.63'2—dc22

                                                      2010052730

To my parents and grandparents, who instilled in me
the appropriate values and a thirst for learning that
has helped me succeed in this challenging world.

To my beloved and incredible family.

And to all investors all across America: May you all benefit
from the research and strategies in this book to find a smarter and
safer way to invest and preserve your hard-earned money.

# CONTENTS

**Chapter 8**

**Chapter 9**

**Chapter 10**

**Chapter 11**

**Chapter 12**

# FOREWORD

**M**arket timing may be the most challenging approach to successful long-term investing. It can be tough and ugly. I know this well because I've been a market-timer in the trenches since 1983 both as an investor and as an advisor.

Timing requires thick skin and iron resolve. Because it is generally misunderstood, market timing is almost universally scorned on Wall Street.

Yet market timing can be an important tool for risk-averse investors. When it is used consistently over long periods of time, timing can improve returns dramatically while reducing risk, as Les Masonson has demonstrated repeatedly in this book.

If those in the establishment financial media were to study this book, they would be better able to reduce a tide of misguided negative articles about timing. Too many financial writers have discovered that they can easily "prove" that timing doesn't work and can't possibly work. However, those authors rarely specify any measurable definition of what would be necessary for a strategy to qualify as one that "works."

I've found that timing is 100 percent successful at reducing market risk by periodically getting investors out of the market. Every day that your assets are in a money-market fund is a day they are not at risk in the market. If timing keeps you on the sidelines 25 percent of the time, timing has reduced your risk by 25 percent.

Portfolios governed by timing often outperform buy-and-hold portfolios with similar assets during major market declines. To a long-term investor who holds some assets without timing—and this includes almost everyone—this lack of correlation amounts to a form of diversification.

However, timing will often underperform buy-and-hold during major market advances, sometimes for long periods. This can be disconcerting and upsetting to impatient investors.

Why do so many people believe that timing doesn't work? I believe the answer is twofold. First, most investors who undertake market timing are not prepared for the rigorous discipline it requires. Second, because they don't understand timing, they don't know what to expect from it.

Les Masonson's book will help to remedy this. He has put together the information and tools that investors need to make timing work for them. He has taken a complex topic and made it accessible for real people.

The biggest problem facing most investors is that they need the potential growth they can get from owning equities—yet equities are too volatile for most investors, as millions of buy-and-holders discovered in 2008 and early 2009.

As far as I know, there are only two solutions that make sense. One is to buy and hold a portfolio with an ample allocation of fixed-income funds. This brings stability, but at the same time, it reduces long-term returns. The second solution, the topic of this book, is to employ a disciplined market timing approach—which, by the way, can include fixed-income assets as well as equities.

As this book shows, mechanical market timing makes it possible for investors to achieve the returns they need at lower volatility. Investors who do this are much more likely to stay the course.

For various reasons that are detailed in this book, timing is not the best approach for every investor. Many people will be more successful with a buy-and-hold approach. However, most of my own investments are governed by market timing, and this suits me well. I have worked hard all my life to accumulate assets, and I'm most comfortable having an active defense against bear markets.

This book is for investors who share my conservative approach, who believe, as I do, that hanging onto their money is as important as making it grow. In this excellent guide, such investors will find everything they need to determine whether or not market timing is for them—and whether or not they have what it takes to be successful.

Paul Merriman
Founder, Merriman, Inc.,
Seattle, Washington, and author of
*Live It Up Without Outliving Your Money*

# ACKNOWLEDGMENTS

**W**riting a comprehensive book on market timing would not be possible without the expertise and assistance of many individuals and firms. Even with their help, I take full responsibility for any inadvertent factual errors in this book.

The following individuals provided significant input, and to them I first want to offer special thanks:

- Herb Weissman devoted many painstaking hours reviewing, editing, and providing critical input to the original manuscript. His clarity makes this a more readable book.

- Robert W. Colby, CMT and author of *The Encyclopedia of Technical Market Indicators*, Second Edition, provided the use of his research on timing strategies from his landmark book and also provided critical comments on the manuscript.

- Morgan Ertel, associate editor at McGraw-Hill Professional, and the entire McGraw-Hill publishing team for their hard work on producing this second edition.

- Nelson Freeburg, editor and publisher of *FORMULA RESEARCH*, provided the use of his research on calendar-based and presidential cycle strategies and insights on the subject of backtesting.

- Sy Harding, editor of *www.streetsmartreport.com* and president of Asset Management Research Corp., shared extensive information on his seasonal timing strategy using the MACD indicator.

- Paul Merriman, president of Merriman, Inc., wrote the Foreword and his firm provided market timing insights, research, and commentary.

I also want to thank the following organizations and individuals for their assistance, expertise, and information provided:

- *Active Trader* magazine and Mark Etzkorn, editor-in-chief
- *DecisionPoint.com* and Carl Swenlin, founder and publisher
- Eric Crittenden, research director, and Cole Wilcox, managing director at Blackstar Funds, LLC
- Hays Advisory Group, LLC, and Don R. Hays, president, and Mark Dodson
- The Hirsch Organization and *Stock Traders Almanac*, along with Jeffrey A. Hirsch, president, and Judd Brown, vice president
- Matt Hougan, president, ETF Analytics, global head of Editorial, Index Universe
- *Investor's Intelligence* and Michael L. Burke, editor, and John E. Gray, president
- Michael Johnston, ETF Database, for tables of ETF data
- Patrick Rygiel, president, MTR Investors Group
- David Korn's Advisory Service and David Korn
- Merriman, Inc., and Dennis Tilley, director of research
- Dr. Jerome Minton, president, Alpha Investment Management, Inc.
- Proshares
- Rydex-SGI
- Sam Stovall, chief investment strategist, Standard & Poor's
- *StockCharts.com*
- *Technical Analysis of Stocks & Commodities* and Jack K. Hutson, publisher
- *Timer Digest* and James Schmidt, editor and publisher
- Towneley Capital Management, Inc., and Wesley G. McCain, chairman, and Gretchen Hartman
- TradeStation (registered trademark of the TradeStation Group, Inc.) and Michael Burke, product manager

# All About
# MARKET
# TIMING

**THE EASY WAY TO GET STARTED**

# INTRODUCTION

*If you don't know who you are, the stock market is an expensive place to find out.*

—George Goodman

**D**id your investments get crushed in the last two stock market crashes in 2000–2002 but also the more recent one from October 2007 to early March 2009? If you are a buy-and-hold investor, you probably did get hit hard. I had no idea that we would witness a worse crash than the 2000–2002 crash just six years later. This is why the topic of market timing should be more in favor than ever. Sadly, this is not the case and probably will never be the case because of the Wall Street aversion to the topic. Moreover, the endless barrage of buy-and-hold banter continues unabated. Surprisingly, the *Wall Street Journal* had a November 13, 2010, article entitled, "How to Play Market Rally," written by Ben Levisohn and Jane J. Kim, whose first sentence was, "Forget 'buy and hold.' It is time to time the stock market." So maybe now financial journalists and perhaps financial advisors and others have realized that they need to promote a smarter way to invest instead of pushing the buy-and-hold mantra, which has failed investors big time.

Such well-known and well-respected individuals as John C. Bogle, founder and retired CEO of The Vanguard Group and author of *Common Sense on Mutual Funds*; Charles D. Ellis, consultant in investing, former managing partner of Greenwich Associates, and author of *Winning the Loser's Game*; and Burton G. Malkiel, Princeton economics professor and author of *A Random Walk Down Wall Street*, all believe that buy-and-hold is the most appropriate strategy for most investors. I respectfully disagree, and this book provides data and strategies that show that numerous market timing strategies can beat buy-and-hold with less risk.

Investors got a rude awakening when they opened their year-end 2008 brokerage statements (if they had the guts to do so) and viewed the devastation caused by the second bear market in the past decade. Investors who did not sell during the decline did make up much lost ground as the stock market bottomed on March 9, 2009, and rebounded about 90 percent by the end of 2010, but still below the prior highs of October 9, 2007.

Are you confused by the daily gyrations of the stock market and the contradictory financial, economic, and global news? Are you upset that you lost a bundle in those stock market crashes? Have you given up on the stock market? If so, then join the club, because almost all investors are in the same boat and diving for cover by diverting billions of dollars of their equity investments to low-paying money-market funds and all types of bond funds.

The vast majority of the "talking heads" on the business shows continually profess a bullish stance, no matter what the market is doing. Ignore their opinions. No one knows where the market is going tomorrow, let alone in the months and years ahead. Just because the stock market (as measured by the Standard & Poor's 500) has averaged an annual return of 10.1 percent from 1926 to 2010 (with dividends included) does not mean that you can count on that rate of return to continue in the coming year or the next five years. Just because you may not be retiring soon does not mean that you can afford to ignore what is going on in the stock market.

If you have been investing since 2003, you were probably ecstatic with your returns through the third quarter of 2007. However, the market plunged for the next 15 months, and it dropped at a much faster pace than it rose. Did you sell at or near the top in October 2007 and put the proceeds into cash? You probably did not. Did you sell after your stocks, mutual funds, or exchange-traded funds (ETFs) fell 10 percent, then 20 percent, then 30 percent, and perhaps 50 percent in some cases? Probably not, because you thought the market would come back, as it always has. Well, this time the market did came roaring back with a huge rally from the bottom through 2010, but it was still about 20 percent off the October 2007 high.

Most likely, you follow the widely touted buy-and-hold approach. And if you are like most investors, you have no game plan for cutting your losses or taking your profits. Lacking an investing strategy and blindly following the buy-and-hold approach can lead to financial ruin. It can wipe out years of investment profits in a short time, and it can take years for your portfolio to recover, if ever. Don't fall for the buy-and-hold ruse, even though 99.9 percent of financial professionals tout it as the only way to invest for the long term. This is the same crowd that tells you that dollar-cost averaging is a sound investment approach. This approach advocates investing equal amounts periodically, for example, monthly, no matter what the stock market is doing. The supposed logic is that you will buy some shares at market lows, thereby reducing your average cost of the investment and thus producing better overall returns.

Check it out for yourself. If you've used this approach, has it worked for you? The approach is great when stock prices are rising but not so great when they continue to fall. One of the most critical rules of smart investing is never average down in individual stocks. It is a loser's game. Think about all the unfortunate and uninformed investors who owned JDS Uniphase, Dell, Cisco, EMC, AT&T, Eastman Kodak, Xerox, AIG, Bear Stearns, Lehman Brothers, Citibank, General Motors, and many more. Those investors got killed by continually buying more shares on the way down—or by holding onto their original shares bought at much higher prices. Eventually, investors got nothing or very little back, and many lost most of their capital invested in many of these stocks.

## IS THERE A BETTER APPROACH THAN BUY-AND-HOLD?

Is there a smarter way to handle your investments, to protect your profits, and to steer clear of bear markets before they decimate your portfolio? Yes. That approach is called *market timing*, and it works, no matter what you've heard or read to the contrary. This book contains compelling data on successful market timing approaches that beat the market indexes over decades. The strategies are simple to follow and implement, so you can use them yourself. And for those of you who prefer to have a market-timer do the work for you, you'll be interested in the information provided on top-performing market timing newsletters and services that have been monitored by independent evaluation firms that have been around for decades.

After reading this book, you will understand the buy-and-hold myth and why market timing is a more sensible, risk-averse, and unemotional approach to investing.

*I do not recommend that the average investor buy individual stocks, ever!* Stocks are simply too risky for the average investor. With the continued accounting scandals, Securities and Exchange Commission (SEC) investigations, crooked corporate officers, and managed earnings, why should you take a chance on picking the wrong stock or the right stock at the wrong time and taking a big hit? It is much more prudent and far less risky to invest in appropriate index funds or ETFs to spread your risk within a larger basket of securities.

To give you a unique insight into the actual performance of individual stocks during a big bull market, consider the research performed by Eric Crittenden and Cole Wilcox of Blackstar Funds (refer to the Appendix on page 249 to see their full research paper). In a nutshell, they analyzed the price performance of all common stocks trading on the New York Stock Exchange (NYSE), the American Stock Exchange (AMEX), and the Nasdaq (National Association of Securities Dealers Automated Quotations System) from 1983 to 2006. There were approximately 8,000 securities in the sample. Here are their key findings for the lifetime return of stocks for the 23-year period:

- 39.4 percent of stocks had losses, and 60.6 percent had positive returns.
- 18.5 percent lost a minimum of three-quarters of their value, and about the same number gained an average of 300 percent or more.
- 64 percent of the stocks underperformed the Russell 3000 Index, and 36 percent had higher returns.

- 25 percent of stocks (about 2,000) provided 100 percent of all the stock market's gains; worst-performing stocks (75 percent) collectively had a total return of 0 percent.
- The average annualized stock's return was –1.06 percent compared with the median annualized return of 5.1 percent.

I'm sure you are astounded by the poor performance of the majority of stocks during one of the biggest bull markets in history. And the stocks that had the greatest performance (see the Appendix) cratered the most. In conclusion, stocks are riskier than you probably imagined, and I urge you to stay away from them unless you want to take the risk for the potential reward of the few real big winners.

## WHAT IS MARKET TIMING?

*market timing* is defined as making investment buy-and-sell decisions using a mechanical trading strategy with specific rules or indicators. The objective is to be invested in stocks during an uptrend and to be either in cash (or in a short position) when the stock market starts to decline. market timing can be applied to all types of investments, including stocks, stock and index options, mutual funds, ETFs, bonds, and futures. This book recommends using timing with index funds, sector funds, leveraged funds, and ETFs.

Market timing is aimed at taking your emotions out of the investing equation—or at least minimizing their impact. This objective is critical to your success. Investor psychology has been studied for years, and the "herd instinct" is rampant. The urge to follow the herd can play right into your hands because the crowd (whether individual investors or investment advisors) is characteristically wrong at *major* stock market tops and bottoms. This situation always will be with us because the emotions of dealing with investing—fear and greed—will never change. Therefore, we can invest opposite the crowd's actions.

Market timing is not a perfect investing approach; there is no such thing, just as there is no Holy Grail. Market timing cannot predict in advance when the market will change direction, but if you use a reliable, time-tested market timing system and follow *all* its signals, you will exit the market after it begins to turn down and you will reenter the market after it begins to turn up, all in time to make nice gains. Market timing will never pick the exact bottom or top of the market, but it will, nevertheless, provide useful signals after the trend has changed direction. Market timing signals are usually correct only 40 to 50 percent of the time, but that is good enough to make you money because small losses are more than made up for by the big gains. Anyone who claims 80 percent or more profitable trades should be checked out carefully because this is a very difficult feat to accomplish, especially with a timing approach that has many signals during a year.

My objective in writing *All About Market Timing* was fourfold. First, I wanted to provide the rationale and facts behind my assertion that market timing is a superior investment strategy to the ever-popular buy-and-hold strategy. Second, I wanted to provide a handful of easy-to-understand, easy-to-implement, and profitable market timing strategies. Third, I wanted to help you to avoid the brunt of future bear markets and protect your principal. And last, I wanted to provide additional insight into how difficult it is to make consistent profits in the stock market unless you have a specific time-tested approach that you engage in with discipline and patience.

## BEAR MARKETS ARE RECURRING—YOU MUST BE PREPARED TO DEAL WITH THEM

Future bear markets will arrive like clockwork, every three to six years, on average. Avoiding the brunt of these slumps is the key to protecting your hard-earned capital. Unfortunately, most investors have no clue as to how the stock market really works. Therefore, it is not surprising that they suffer the consequences when a bear market sneaks up and mauls them.

From 1950 to 1999, there were over a dozen bear markets, with the average one lasting 397 days, resulting in a loss in value of 30.9 percent based on the Standard & Poor's (S&P) 500 Index. The average recovery period to reach the previous high was about 622 days (1.7 years).[1] The first bear market of the past decade ended on October 9, 2002, when the S&P 500 Index dropped 49.1 percent from its peak on March 24, 2000, and lasted 941 days (2.6 years).

---

[1] "The Upside of Down Market: What Investors Can Learn From Volatility." *Of Mutual Interest* (Invesco Funds), Summer 2001.

Similarly, the Dow Jones Industrial Average dropped 37.8 percent (the actual top was January 14, 2000), and the Nasdaq Composite Index cratered a whopping 77.9 percent. In the most recent bear market from October 9, 2007, through March 9, 2010, the S&P 500 Index tanked 56.8 percent before recovering 23.4 percent in 2009, and 15 percent in 2010, but it was still 28 percent below its last market top.

There definitely will be future bear markets, and if we are in a secular (long-term) bear market, then this current bear market may not end until 2015 or 2016, based on the length of other secular bear markets. Therefore, the key to investing is to preserve your capital. This means that you should take prudent actions to avoid bear markets and not be invested in the stock market when they occur. If you do not exit the market, then your profits (if there are any) and even your principal will quickly shrink. How much can you lose in the next bear market? The crash of 1929 wiped out 86 percent of the value of investors' portfolios, and the investors required 25.2 years to break even (not counting dividend reinvestment).

The experts tell you that no one can time the markets with consistency. Guess what? The experts are wrong again, as you shall see when you read about newsletters and timing services that beat the market over decades in Chapter 12. This book also provides you with the strategies that work so that you don't have to guess or make an investing decision based on emotion or someone else's opinion of where the market is headed.

In late July 2002, Lawrence Kudlow, cohost of *Kudlow & Cramer* on CNBC, jokingly said that he and cohost Jim Cramer had called the 2001–2002 bear market bottom seven times and that they will eventually get it right! But this is no joke. You can't afford to depend on someone else's guesses. You need to make your own investment decisions, which you can do if you stick with the time-tested indicators and strategies presented in this book.

## FORGET ABOUT DOLLAR-COST AVERAGING IN A BEAR MARKET

Dollar-cost averaging is another popular investing strategy bandied about in the canyons of Wall Street. This approach advocates making investments of a fixed amount every month or quarter no matter what the stock market is doing. The rationale is that during bear markets, you are buying more shares at lower prices and thus will benefit when the market rises.

Catherine Voss Sanders wrote an article entitled "The Plight of the Fickle Investor" in the *Morningstar Investor* (December 1997), and she stated: "Because emotions and hype can get in the way of smart investing, systematic dollar-cost averaging is a sound strategy. . . . [I]n most cases, the dollar-cost averager is going to beat the willy-nilly investor."

On the contrary, *never* use dollar-cost averaging to buy stocks or equity ETFs in a bear market because it puts you on the wrong side of the trade when the market is tanking. It is the traders who are right when they say *never average down*. Take the advice of long-time market newsletter writer Richard Russell (*Dow Theory Letters*, 1984): "Averaging down in a bear market is tantamount to taking a seat on the down escalator at Macy's."

Imagine buying Corning at 113 (split-adjusted) on September 1, 2000, and buying more shares each month as it tanked so that you could lower your cost basis. Corning hit a low of $1.10 on October 8, 2002. Guess what? How in the world can you ever recoup that kind of a loss?

Dollar-cost averaging in a bear market is a strategy for dummies, not for intelligent investors. There is no guarantee that your stocks, mutual funds, and ETFs will return to their October 2007 highs any time soon, and throwing good money into a declining fund makes no sense to me. Remember that hundreds of mutual funds have gone out of existence or have merged into other funds simply because of their embarrassingly poor investment performance.

## MOST INVESTORS ARE NOT REALISTS

Most investors have a similar view of the investing scene. They hold the following beliefs:

- Buy a diversified basket of stocks and bonds or equivalent mutual funds and hold them for the long run.
- Buy-and-hold is the best approach to investing.
- Market timing is for losers.
- Dollar-cost averaging is a good strategy.

- Financial advisors, brokers, and so-called stock market gurus should be consulted or followed to obtain the best possible investment advice and investment results.
- Tax consequences are critical in making investment decisions.

Believe it or not, all these beliefs are false! Many intelligent individuals are not intelligent investors. In making their investment decisions, too many investors rely only on fundamental research and totally ignore the technical indicators of stock market investing. Investors must understand that their thinking may be neither realistic nor accurate and that they probably won't be successful investors by viewing the world through "rose-colored glasses."

Neither should investors let tax consequences interfere with sensible stock market strategies. Otherwise, they will end up paralyzed and confused, and they will never sell the small losers until they become big losers. Of course, market timing strategies can be used in tax-deferred retirement accounts because there are no tax consequences. However, don't assume that taking profits in regular accounts will work against you. It may or may not. Think about it for a minute. Would you rather let a profit of 50 percent on a stock stop you from selling it because of the taxes? A bear market can wipe out this entire profit if you never sell. *Your primary concern should be to protect your profits and preserve your capital.* Tax considerations are only a secondary concern, not a primary one.

You may be intrigued by some of the statements and findings presented in this book. This is to be expected because the financial media do not spend any time on these views. One of my major premises is that buy-and-hold is a loser's strategy—that's right, a loser's strategy. You won't see that statement very often in the financial media. During the past decade ending in 2009, the S&P 500 Index *lost* an annualized 0.95 percent. That's the result of buy-and-hold for 10 years—zilch! This is not the way to build wealth.

This is the reason that an entire chapter is devoted to debunking the buy-and-hold myth. Another one of my critical premises is that *the less time you stay invested in the stock market, the better.* The rationale is that the longer you're invested, the higher is the probability that the next bear market will take away your profits. Therefore, make your money in the shortest time frame possible, based on the strategy you are using, and then cash in and reside in the safety of cash until the next buying opportunity presents itself.

The safest way to invest in the stock market is to be *out* of the market (in a cash account or short the market) during declining periods and to be *in* the market only during the most favorable time periods. This completely contradicts what some experts will tell you. You will hear, "It's time in the market that counts, not timing the market." I will demonstrate that the opposite is true. It's the time out of the market that preserves your principal during bear markets that really puts you on the right track for building and keeping your wealth.

## BE AWARE OF LACK OF CANDOR IN SOME INVESTMENT AND BROKERAGE FIRM LITERATURE

Unfortunately, too many investment and brokerage firms do not provide fair and balanced investing information to the public. For example, I still come across incomplete information in investor material from Northwestern Mutual Financial Network, Merrill Lynch, Morgan Stanley, U.S. Global Investors, and Fidelity, to name a few. In the literature they send to investors, I've found a chart or table depicting the reduced annual returns if an investor had "missed the 10 best days" compared with buy-and-hold. Obviously, the return will be less if these days were missed. These firms use this argument to emphasize the virtues of buy-and-hold investing because they say that no one can predict when those days will occur.

However, they conveniently forgot to provide the counterargument that by missing the 10 *worst* days, the performance is much better if you had been out of the market. Therefore, you are only getting half the story because these firms want you to stay invested at all times. One reason is that it reduces their overhead expenses and costs of administering the fund to have you stay put. Second, it eliminates any liquidity problems for the fund that could be caused by a large number of fund holders liquidating at the same time. If this happens, it could force the fund to sustain unwanted market losses from selling off holdings in order to meet the redemption needs of exiting fund holders.

Your financial advisor or planner, if you have one, can help you with estate planning, retirement planning, asset allocation, insurance needs, and so on. In fact, almost 75 percent of investors use advisors to provide guidance in making sense of the market moves. But very few, if any, financial planners are market-timers; instead, they will counsel you on investing in a diversified group of stocks or mutual funds and some ETFs with annual rebalancing and then tell you to leave your portfolio alone. This is fine advice, as far as it goes. In a bear market, however, the equity holdings in your portfolio will decline in value. So it is entirely up to you to protect your own portfolio.

Over the years, I've attended many Money Show and Traders' Expos. I've listened to the investment experts at panel discussions give their market viewpoints and what they planned to cover in their sessions over the next few days. The experts were almost evenly split between bulls and bears. So, bottom line, as an investor or trader relying on these "experts" for advice, you were left in a quandary as to whether you should be buying or selling. Therefore, I consider such conferences to be sideshows for the uninformed. It is best for you to make your own investment decisions to protect your money.

To make money and be successful in the stock market, you need an action plan based on a solid strategy that works in bull markets and especially in bear markets. This is a daunting task for any investor because many studies have shown that most investors neither equal nor beat the market averages, nor do they equal the performance of the mutual funds that they've purchased because of their poor timing of purchases and redemptions. Investors act emotionally, and they swing between the fear of a market decline and the greed for making the most money during a market upswing. Eventually, investors tend to buy at the market top and sell at the market bottom because they invest with their stomachs instead of with their brains.

This pattern is repeated over and over again, usually resulting in underperformance—which is worse than just buying and holding. DALBAR, Inc. (a leading financial services research firm), studied the performance of mutual fund investors for the 20 years ending December 31, 2009. Company researchers found that the average equity fund investor earned an annualized 3.17 percent during that period compared with the benchmark S&P 500 Index performance of 8.20 percent. Investors using asset allocation earned an annualized 2.34 percent, which was even worse, and fixed-income investors earned only 1.02 percent, the worst of all. Clearly, individual investors have not been investing with their brains.

So how should investors participate in the roller-coaster stock market without getting heart palpitations, without losing all their profits or, worse, their initial capital, and without getting physically or mentally sickened by their losses? That is what this book is about. *All About Market Timing* will provide you, whether you're a beginner or a more advanced investor, with easy-to-understand, time-tested market timing strategies that work. Timing will help you to make more accurate buy-and-sell decisions. No longer will you sell out as the market bottoms or buy at the market tops. Keep in mind there is no Holy Grail—just a smarter way to invest.

## STICK WITH THE FACTS

This book provides the facts, information, and insights that you may not have seen elsewhere but that hopefully will put you on the profitable investing road. You will understand why the conventional wisdom on investing is dead wrong. Following bad advice actually can cause you great financial loss and emotional distress. The problem is that you have not been given the complete story on investing and on how difficult it is to succeed over the long term. In the long run, the only thing that matters is that you have protected your money and that you've helped it to grow. Letting bear markets devour your hard-earned cash does not make sense. Buy-and-hold does not make sense. It's like seeing a train come roaring down the tracks, and you decide to step in front of it. That's irrational and deadly because you know the outcome in advance.

My objective is to level the playing field and provide you with the knowledge you need to become a more informed, calm, and profitable investor. You have more important things to do than to be in constant turmoil about your investments as you listen to the financial news each day. You can manage your portfolio in a nonemotional, methodical manner if you put your mind to it. It is easy to do if you are a persistent, dedicated, calm, and patient person.

On the other hand, if you have none of those traits, then you probably won't make it as a self-directed investor.

Although this book was written for investors, it also provides usable strategies that financial advisors, financial planners, and brokers can use to protect and grow their clients' accounts. Hopefully, some of these professionals, after reading this book, will embrace timing strategies to use in their investment arsenal for the benefit of their clients.

## HOW THIS BOOK IS STRUCTURED

*All About Market Timing* is a "tell-it-like-it-is" book. There is no fluff, just the unvarnished truth. I am not a mutual fund manager, portfolio manager, or subscription-based newsletter writer. I am not selling any investment services. I am an individual investor, just like you, and I'm tired of being misled by not being given the full story on investing by the Wall Street crowd.

In writing this book, I have assumed that you have a basic knowledge of investing, stocks, and mutual funds. My emphasis is on the importance of market timing and how to use it to improve your investment performance while limiting your risk and protecting your principal.

The first three chapters set the groundwork for the remaining chapters. Chapter 1 focuses on how difficult it is for an investor to come out ahead in the stock market in the long run, when investors keep getting killed in the short run with periodic bear markets. In fact, in the aggregate, losses suffered in bear markets often exceed the gains earned in bull markets. Bull and bear market cycles are reviewed in detail, including secular bull and bear markets, where there are long periods of time when the market does nothing and you are biding your time. This is no way to make money. Also here, the poor record of the market experts is exposed for all to see.

Chapter 2 soundly debunks the buy-and-hold myth. Statistics and facts are provided to indicate that buy-and-hold is not a successful strategy in the long run because of intermittent bear markets and the continual impact of inflation. The complete story on missing the *best* days *and* missing the *worst* days will be provided. You'll be surprised by the outcome.

Chapter 3 covers the basics of market timing that you were never told by the Wall Street gurus, financial magazine articles, or financial radio and TV shows. The critical characteristics of successful market-timers are provided, as well as six key points about market timing that need to be understood. The distinction between classic market-timers and dynamic asset allocators is covered. Documented examples of specific market-timers who have been successful are provided to prove that market timing does work consistently in the real world.

Chapter 4 provides investors with useful insights on determining the market trend and detecting when it is changing. It covers a handful of technical market indicators with charts that can help you to determine the market's health and be on the right side of the market.

Chapters 5 and 6 review the most appropriate investment vehicles to use for timing the market. Chapter 5 focuses on the use of index funds, sector funds, and leveraged funds. Specific fund families are reviewed, as well as sourced for additional information. Regular mutual funds are not recommended because of their higher overall costs. Chapter 6 deals with the mushrooming and fast-growing ETFs and the substantial benefits they offer investors for timing the market. There is also a review of leveraged and inverse ETFs, when to use them and the risks involved.

Chapters 7 through 11 are the heart of the book. They provide specific market timing strategies that can be used to beat buy-and-hold with less risk—always a great combination. First, Chapter 7 reviews a simple, easy-to-use strategy focusing on the "best six months" of the year, where most of the stock market's gains are made. Certain months of the year consistently and significantly show better performance than others. For example, simply by *not* investing in September, you will improve your overall performance significantly. Imagine the beauty of investing only in the months that the market makes most of its gains and being in cash for the other months! Such a strategy alone would have saved your stock market retirement funds from being smashed in 2008.

Chapter 8 takes seasonal investing to a higher level by providing insight into the best and worst years of the four-year presidential cycle. You will find out that by investing in the pre-election and election years you can do much better than if you had invested in the post-election and midterm-election years. The performance over decades has proved this strategy's powerful results on a consistent basis. And by using margin, leveraged mutual funds or ETFs in the best months during the best years, the performance really skyrockets. Additionally, the best three-month periods are provided along with additional insights.

Chapter 9 uses a well-known, simple, time-tested strategy that has been used by many investors for decades. This is a simple moving average. It enables investors to view a major market index with a piercing of the moving average as the trigger market "buy" and "sell" signals. When the price of the index rises above the moving average, a "buy" signal is given, and when the index falls below the moving average, a "sell" signal is given. Studies of moving averages by independent researchers are presented to bolster the case for using moving averages. Also, a 20-day moving-average strategy and a 25-week moving-average strategy using the Nasdaq Composite Index are tested for performance over a long time frame with TradeStation. The detailed performance data are provided so that you have a complete picture of the risk versus reward.

Chapters 10 and 11 provide a market timing approach using a percentage filter to make buy-and-sell decisions. Chapter 10 provides a simple strategy of buying an ETF, for example, when a "buy" or "sell" signal is given on the Value Line Index using either a 4 or 3 percent filter. For example, you simply buy an ETF when that index rises 3 percent from its last bottom and sell when that index drops 3 percent from its last top. It's that simple, and this strategy has been profitable over decades. It certainly hasn't been perfect, but it has beaten buy-and-hold with less risk. Chapter 11 presents a similar strategy, but it uses a 6 percent filter with the Nasdaq Composite and the Nasdaq 100 Index. The Nasdaq strategy had large returns that were accomplished with more risk.

Chapter 12 provides useful information on market timing newsletters and services. *Timer Digest, TimerTrac, The Hulbert Financial Digest, FORMULA RESEARCH* (a newsletter that provides market timing models), and Web sites (*Sy Harding's Street Smart Report,* haysadvisory.com, fundadvice.com, decisionpoint .com, and David Korn's Advisory Service) are all covered.

## HOW TO USE THIS BOOK

If you are new to investing or are not familiar with market timing, then I recommend that you read this book chapter by chapter. On the other hand, if you are an experienced stock market investor, and if you are already convinced of the merits of market timing, then I recommend that you go directly to Chapters 5 through 11 for the recommended investment vehicles and market timing strategies. If you prefer subscribing to a market timing newsletter or service instead of using a self-directed timing strategy, then read Chapter 12 first.

Enjoy the road ahead, and get ready to consider changing the way you invest. Stay open-minded and be ready for change. I would like to hear from you with any comments about market timing or your comments on the value of this book. You also may be interested in another book I wrote that was published in 2010 entitled, *Buy DON'T Hold*, and its accompanying Web site and blog at www.buy donthold.com. Please e-mail me at lesmasonson@yahoo.com.

# PART 1

# Market Timing Basics

# The Stock Market = Bull Markets + Bear Markets

*The first rule is not to lose. The second rule is not to forget the first rule.*

—Warren Buffett

*In the battlefield that is the stock market, there are the quick and there are the dead! . . . The fastest way to take a bath in the stock market is to try to prove that you are right and the market is wrong.*

—William J. O'Neil (*How to Make Money in Stocks*, 2002, p. 54)

## ING DIRECT SHAREHOLDER SURVEY

Before covering the stock market's performance in bull and bear markets, let's first begin by reviewing the results of a survey of 1,021 young (ages 21 to 39 years) and old (ages 40 to 65 years) investors conducted by ING DIRECT to obtain their views about investing in the stock market. The study was conducted online from January 7 to 19, 2010, ten months after the market bottomed in March 2009. The survey questioned these investors on the following subjects: confidence and optimism, influencers, motives, barriers, and expected returns.

The key survey findings were as follows:

- 43 percent of those 21 to 39 years of age plan to invest more in 2010 compared with 33 percent of those 40 to 65 years of age.
- 26 percent of younger investors and 28 percent of older investors expect an annual return of between 10 and 20 percent.
- Older investors are leading the trend to become self-directed investors. Almost half (49 percent) of those 40 to 65 years of age have reduced or eliminated their reliance on financial professionals compared with 37 percent of investors aged 21 to 39 years.
- Younger investors currently rely more on financial Web sites and blogs (49 percent) and financial print publications (39 percent) than on financial planners or advisors (35 percent) or brokers (18 percent) for investing advice.
- Investors aged 40 years and older also rely more on financial Web sites and blogs (47 percent) and financial print publications (41 percent) than on planners or advisors (39 percent), brokers (36 percent), and family (19 percent).
- On average, investors think that they need $699 to get started investing.
- Almost half (48 percent) of younger investors think that they need more than $500 to start investing compared with 56 percent of older investors.
- Almost half (44 percent) of those with access to an automated platform that enables investing in small dollar amounts say that you can get started with just $100 or less.
- Almost one-third (30 percent) of the younger group say that their parents had the biggest influence in getting them started investing.
- 17 percent of investors 40 to 65 years of age say that their parents had the largest influence in getting them started investing.
- 81 percent of respondents who own a brokerage account and who are fully employed have a retirement account:

- • 34 percent are between 35 and 44 years of age, whereas 77 percent of those with no 401(k) account are older or younger than Generation X.
- • 47 percent earn at least $125,000 annually, compared with just 25 percent among those who do not own a 401(k).
- • 56 percent have at least a college degree or more education compared with 41 percent among those who do not own a 401(k).
- Over half (52 percent) of investors plan to invest about the same amount in 2010 as they did in 2009, and surprisingly, about 4 out of 10 (37 percent) plan to invest more.
- Just 11 percent say that they plan to invest less in 2010.
- Younger investors are even more optimistic. Forty-three percent of those 21 to 39 years of age plan to invest more in 2010 compared with 33 percent of those 40 to 65 years of age.
- More than 6 in 10 (63 percent) either plan to make no changes in their approach or plan to take a more aggressive approach to what they perceive as a buying opportunity.
- 22 percent say, "I think now is a great time to invest. I'm taking a more aggressive approach."
- Another 41 percent say, "I believe in a long-term view when it comes to investing, so I'm not making any changes to my investments."
- Just 5 percent indicate they have headed to the sideline with their choice of the statement, "It's too risky. I don't want to invest right now." Thirty-one percent say, "I'm more conservative than before, but it's still okay to invest."
- .61 percent of investors expect an annual return of between 5 and 10 percent on their money.
- 26 percent of younger investors and 28 percent of older investors expect an annual return of between 10 and 20 percent. The weighted-average return is 11 percent, considering all responses.

- 45 percent of investors have either reduced or eliminated their use of financial professionals for investing advice. Older investors are leading this trend. Almost half (49 percent) of those 40 to 65 years of age have reduced or eliminated their reliance compared with 37 percent of investors aged 21 to 39 years.
- 62 percent of younger investors indicate that the cost of advice was the reason they reduced or eliminated their reliance on financial professionals for investing advice. By comparison, 57 percent of investors 40 to 65 years of age feel that they can do just as good a job on their own.
- Family members (40 percent) are being used by more young investors for advice than brokers (18 percent). Investors aged 40 years and older also rely on financial Web sites and blogs (47 percent) and financial print publications (41 percent) more than planners (39 percent), brokers (36 percent), and family (19 percent).

## SURVEY OF AFFLUENT INVESTORS INDICATES CONCERNS

Let's look at another survey of investors that focuses only on more affluent investors. Merrill Lynch Affluent Insights Quarterly Survey results were based on interviews with 1,000 affluent investors with investable assets of at least $250,000 on June 11 and 29, 2010, and another 300 Americans in each of 14 target markets. The source of this information is a Bank of America press release dated July 28, 2010, sent over Business Wire.

The key findings of their survey are as follows:

- 70 percent of those surveyed do not believe that their retirement plans take into account the potential for unexpected family events (e.g., serious illness, divorce, caring for parents), but 35 percent have adjusted their priorities accordingly.
- 51 percent of couples disagree with each other on making investment decisions, how best to save and invest for retirement, sticking to family's budget, and paying off credit-card debt.

- 51 percent cited "financial know-how" when asked about important life lessons to impart to their children.
- 39 percent of parents were spending more time discussing financial matters with their children in light of current economic conditions.
- 74 percent of parents shared advice from their financial advisor to educate their children.
- 50 percent of respondents had a low risk tolerance and used conservative investment vehicles and strategies; this compares with 52 percent of younger persons (ages 18 to 34 years), who have a similar risk tolerance; 45 percent for 35- to 50-year-olds; 46 percent for 51- to 64-year-olds; and 55 percent for those age 65+.
- Both younger and affluent individuals (56 and 46 percent, respectively) are more conservative investors now than one year earlier.
- 45 percent of respondents are planning to delay their retirement compared with 29 percent in January 2010.
- 69 percent of the affluent want their financial advisor to be proactive with investment advice, and 68 percent want advice on how to maximize their 401(k).

## STOCK MARKET REALITY AND FORECASTS

In March 2000 and October 2007, investors had no idea that the next two to three periods would result in two horrendous bear markets. Just look at the massive devastation inflicted on investors during that combined period, where a total of $14 trillion in market value was erased in only 32 months from peak to trough in the 2000–2002 crash and in only 17 months in the 2007–2009 crash. The last crash has been the worst in percentage terms since the Great Depression.

During 1999 and 2000, the stock market and especially the "hot" Internet stocks were the topics of conversation at supermarkets, bowling alleys, bars, and hair salons all across America as the market soared to unprecedented heights. CNBC replaced the "soaps" as the most popular daytime entertainment medium, with its streaming stock quotes and never-ending procession of bullish market strategists, bullish financial analysts, and bullish CEOs.

Euphoria was in the air, and life was great for millions of retirees and regular folks who had started investing over the past 20 years, and especially day traders, who were racking up huge gains as stocks advanced day after day. That all came to a screeching halt, though, when the big bear started growling in April 2000, when the Nasdaq Composite dropped a jaw-dropping 25.3 percent during the *week* of April 14. The bear then unceremoniously clawed the market over the next few years.

The market's upswing finally began in October 2002, but there was another drop into March 2003 before the market started its slow rise to a recovery peak in October 2007, only to crash again to new lows by March 2009. At that point, a huge rally took place, vaulting the market by 90 percent from those lows by December 2010.

Many investors were so scared by the two most recent bear markets that they did not participate in the market's rise from the March 2009 lows; as they did not put money into equities but rather concentrated on building their cash and bond positions. Such a conservative approach allowed them to sleep better at night but cost them big gains, which don't come along very often.

## INVESTORS ARE TOO EMOTIONAL AND OVERCONFIDENT

Whether you believe it or not, the stock market is a very difficult place to consistently make money unless you have a strategy that works. This is not a new thought. Over the past 100 years, the stock market has been punctuated by sharp, uplifting bull markets, followed by swiftly plummeting bear markets. This cycle has happened in the past, and it will happen in the future—for, after all, the markets are driven by people's emotions and actions. Market cycles repeat themselves, just as history repeats itself. People are people, and where money is at stake, people react emotionally, which usually results in bad decision making. Investors have a poor track record of making money in the stock market.

Numerous surveys have shown that investors buy and sell at the wrong times, and they usually buy and sell the wrong investments at the wrong times. Behavioral researchers have found that the incorrect decisions that investors are prone to make are the result of overconfidence in their investment knowledge, overtrading, lack of diversification, and incorrect forecasting of future events based on recent history. Stock market success requires that investors act independently of the crowd and rein in their emotions. If fear and greed are not eliminated from the investing equation, the results can be catastrophic. Unfortunately, investors will continue to make the same mistakes over and over again. This is just the way it is.

Robert Safian in a January 2003 *Money* magazine article said: "All across America, millions of people are afraid to open their account statements, afraid to look at their 401(k) balances—afraid to find out what they've lost during this long bear market and where they stand today."[1] This is a pretty sad state of affairs. However, it did not have to be that way if investors would only have had an investment plan that forced them to take profits as stocks kept going up, and they had placed stop-loss orders on their stocks to protect their positions as prices collapsed. But most investors froze and did nothing until the market was well off its highs. Then, as the market hit subsequent lows in July and October 2002, investors took their billions of dollars out of equity mutual funds and began investing their money in bonds and money-market funds. Other investors just gave up and cashed in all their investments, having endured severe emotional and financial pain.

The vast majority of individuals are not savvy investors, even though many have above-average intelligence and consider themselves to be above-average investors. They do not have the time, background, or expertise to assess the market at key turning points (e.g., whether the bull market is beginning or ending). Moreover, the average investor's performance typically is worse than the appropriate market benchmark or even the actual performance of his or her mutual funds. This outcome is a result of poor timing on entry and exit points and lack of a coherent, well-researched strategy. Most investors buy and sell on a whim, or they take advice

---

[1] Robert Safian, "Taking Charge," *Money*, January 2003.

from a friend or CNBC, or they act based on hearing an "expert" giving his or her opinion on the market or a particular mutual fund or stock in the media.

Investors need a methodology to know when to buy and sell, but only a few investors have even thought about it, let alone have a methodology in place. Unfortunately, investors as a group invest and hope for the best. This approach is no way to build a nest egg for the future but rather is a recipe for financial disaster. You wouldn't leave your garden untended because you know that weeds will grow and kill your flowers and vegetables. The same logic applies to your investments. Being proactive is better than being nonactive. This is not to say that you should be an active trader or an aggressive investor but rather that investing is not a static endeavor. You should watch over your investments, making adjustments as necessary to weed out the dead wood and replacing it with more fruitful pickings. You are the best gardener for your investment patch. Don't let the experts tell you otherwise.

Just because you bought shares in high-quality companies doesn't mean that you made smart investments. Even the so-called blue chips had plummeted from their 2007 highs to much lower levels by March 2009. General Electric went from $42 to $6, Goldman Sachs went from $250 to $46, and AIG hit $1,400 before dropping to $0.35 (both prices split-adjusted). This type of devastation doesn't have to happen to you if you become a smarter investor going forward. Surely, by heeding the advice of the Wall Street intelligentsia, you can come out way ahead, right? Wrong!

## MARKET SEERS ARE AN EMBARRASSING LOT

> *If you ask five experts where to invest, there will be six answers: the five expert opinions, plus the right one.*
>
> —Jonathan Clements, "Need One Expert Opinion on Investing? Here's Five," *Wall Street Journal*, January 4, 2000

Think about all the stock market experts' market predictions you've read or heard about over the past few years. A handful of these characters have been let go or have changed firms. Even some well-known technicians do not have very good track records calling the market top. *BusinessWeek* published a year-end review for each year from 1999 through 2002 showing the market predictions of stock market experts for the upcoming year. In all the years, the experts had a poor track record because most were bullish, and their projections of the market's performance were way off. I haven't seen any surveys like this in the past few years. I wonder why?

*BusinessWeek* also published a list of the experts' individual predictions in its year-end issue. The number of prognosticators tracked by the magazine for the years 2000 through 2003 has varied between 38 to 65, with 50 being the average. This list represented a solid cross section of well-known market strategists at that time, including Joseph V. Battipaglia, Elaine Garzarelli, Edward Yardeni, Bernie Schaeffer, Edward Kerschner, Lazlo Birinyi, Jr., Hugh Johnson, Philip J. Orlando, and Jeffrey Applegate.

Table 1-1 shows the composite results of all their forecasts over four years for the Dow Jones Industrial Average (DJIA), the Standard & Poor's 500 Index (S&P 500), and the Nasdaq Composite Index. The table delineates for each year the high, low, and consensus forecast of all the forecasters for each of the three popular market averages. As you can see, starting with the first forecast for the 2000 stock market made at the end of 1999, the forecasters had a poor record. In fact, in each of the last three years their forecasts have gotten progressively worse. Forecasters, as a group, were simply overly optimistic. There are always a few bears around, but even the bears did not predict the actual lows of the market in 2002. The most inaccurate predictions were for the Nasdaq; the actual close compared with the consensus forecasts was off by 54 percent in 2000, 84 percent in 2001, and 67 percent in 2002. In conclusion, the "best and the brightest" appeared to be not so bright or right. To be fair, their actual stock picks for their clients could have been quite different and perhaps closer to the mark. For the sake of their clients, I hope that was the case.

## STOCK RETURNS VARY BY DECADE

Stock market yearly returns are not consistent; in fact, they vary all over the map. This fact is what drives investors crazy. They never

**TABLE 1-1**

*BusinessWeek* Fearless Forecasts, 2000–2003

| Year | DJIA Forecast | DJIA Close | % Diff. | S&P 500 Forecast | S&P 500 Close | % Diff. | Nasdaq Forecast | Nasdaq Close | % Diff. |
|------|---------------|-----------|---------|------------------|---------------|---------|-----------------|--------------|---------|
| 2000 | 14,000 H | | | 1,750 H | | | 5,000 H | | |
|      | 8,800 L | | | 1,000 L | | | 2,000 L | | |
|      | 12,154 C | 10,788 | −12.6 | 1,556 C | 1,320 | −17.9 | 3,805 C | 2,471 | −54.0 |
| 2001 | 13,050 H | | | 1,650 H | | | 4,300 H | | |
|      | 8,000 L | | | 1,000 L | | | 1,800 L | | |
|      | 12,015 C | 10,022 | −19.9 | 1,559 C | 1,148 | −35.8 | 3,583 C | 1,950 | −83.7 |
| 2002 | 13,250 H | | | 1,535 H | | | 2,626 H | | |
|      | 7,200 L | | | 920 L | | | 1,500 L | | |
|      | 11,090 C | 8,342 | −32.9 | 1,292 C | 880 | −46.8 | 2,236 C | 1,336 | −67.4 |
| 2003 | 11,400 H | | | 1,250 H | | | 2,500 H | | |
|      | 7,600 L | | | 800 L | | | 1,065 L | | |
|      | 9,871 C | 10,453 | +5.9 | 1,049 C | 1,112 | +6.0 | 1,703 C | 2,003 | +17.6 |

*Note:* H = high forecast; L = low forecast; C = consensus forecast.

*Source:* "Fearless Forecasts," *BusinessWeek*, last issue in December each year, 1999–2002. Only the forecasts, not the other comparative statistics, were provided by *BusinessWeek*. Issues used were as follows: December 30, 2002, pp. 110–111; December 31, 2001, p. 81; December 25, 2000, p. 75; and December 27, 1999, p. 123.

seem to know if they should be buying or selling. Listening to the advice and predictions of the Wall Street crowd further confuses investors. If investors are fully invested during uptrends, they can experience excellent returns. Unfortunately, the downtrends can take away a good portion of their gains if they just follow the buy-and-hold approach. Consider the wide variance in average annual stock market returns during the eight decades since the 1920s, as shown in Table 1-2.

The 1950s, the 1980s, and the 1990s produced above-average returns in the neighborhood of 18 percent, whereas on the flip side the 1930s, 1960s, and 1970s, and 2000s provided less-than-stellar returns. The 1940s provided a return close to the 9.89 percent annual return of stocks between 1926 and 2010. As you can see, the 1995–1999 period was an anomaly that produced abnormally high returns for those who stayed fully invested during that time period. Since the beginning of 1995, had those same investors been holding their stocks and mutual funds through October 9, 2002, they would have sustained substantial losses depending on their

## TABLE 1-2

S&P 500 Decade Performance Statistics*

| Decade | Average Annual Return Percentage† |
|--------|-----------------------------------|
| 1930s | −0.05 |
| 1940s | 9.17 |
| 1950s | 19.35 |
| 1960s | 7.81 |
| 1970s | 5.86 |
| 1980s | 17.55 |
| 1990s | 18.21 |
| 2000s | −0.95 |
| 1995–1999 | 28.76 |
| 2000–2002 | −14.65 |
| 2007–2010 | −0.96 |

*Data obtained from Ibbotson Associates (2000s and other data added by L. Masonson).
†Compounded, including capital gains and reinvested dividends.
Source: Taming a Bear Market: Investment Strategies for Turbulent Times (New York: American Century, 2001).

investment portfolio mix. (Remember that many investors had high exposure to the technology sector.)

## STOCK RETURNS FROM 2007 THROUGH 2009

The three major market averages performed horribly in the last bear market, each off by over 50 percent. Table 1-3 shows the widespread devastation from the highs to the lows. For just the year 2008 (not shown in the table), the Nasdaq Composite Index was down 38.5 percent, the S&P 500 Index was down 38.9 percent, and the DJIA fell 33.8 percent. To be fully invested in stocks, stock mutual funds, or equity exchange-traded funds (ETFs) during a severe bear market such as this one is a frightening experience and one that should be avoided. Based on what you hear from the so-called experts, there is no way to know when a bear market is coming or its duration. The "experts" keep professing that buy-and-hold is the way to go because in the long run you'll do fine. This ridiculous and costly advice will be tackled head-on in Chapter 2.

## THE STOCK MARKET CONFOUNDS MOST INVESTORS MOST OF THE TIME

The stock market confounds most investors most of the time, and it will continue to do so in the future. This is so because the markets are driven by investor psychology and perception of events. When good news comes out about a stock, sometimes its price rises, and sometimes it falls. When the Federal Open Market Committee (FOMC) of the Federal Reserve cuts interest rates, as

**TABLE 1-3**

Eighteen-Month 2007–2009 Bear Market Performance

| Index | High | Date | Low | Date | Percent Change |
|-------|------|------|-----|------|----------------|
| Nasdaq | 2,859.12 | 10/31/2007 | 1,268.64 | 3/09/2009 | −55.6 |
| DJIA | 14,164.55 | 10/09/2007 | 6,547.05 | 3/09/2009 | −53.8 |
| S&P 500 | 1,565.15 | 10/09/2007 | 676.0 | 3/09/2009 | −56.8 |

it has on many occasions in the past few years, sometimes the market rises and closes up for the day, and sometimes it falls and closes down for the day. In this respect, the market is unpredictable, and this confuses investors, as well as the so-called professionals, although they may not admit it.

The market is a discounting mechanism and is always looking ahead, not backward in the rearview mirror. Thus news, whether good or bad, will have an impact on the market in the short run. In the long run, though, growth in corporate earnings and dividends, coupled with a sound economy with low interest rates and low inflation, is what will drive stock prices much higher. Uncertainty caused by domestic and global political, economic, and social events will alter the market's course for days, weeks, or months, depending on the severity of the problem perceived. And when least expected by the vast majority of investors and professionals, the market will turn around and make a new bull run, with deceiving dips along the way to shake out the weak hands. And market bottoms usually occur when investor pessimism is at its highest, all the news is bad, and no one wants to own stocks, as in March 2009. Perception is what drives markets, not reality. Therefore, the market races ahead while investors are hoarding their cash.

## BULL AND BEAR MARKETS

Looking back, many middle-aged and older investors participated in the great bull run through 2000. From October 11, 1990, until January 14, 2000, the DJIA rose a cumulative 396 percent. From 1995 through 1999, the S&P 500 Index rose at a 28 percent annual compounded rate. In 1999 alone, the Nasdaq Composite Index jumped an astonishing 85.6 percent. This was its largest yearly increase since the index was created in 1971. Investors should have been extremely cautious in 1999 after such a huge unprecedented run-up, but they were net buyers of stock rather than net sellers right at the market top because of the unabashed euphoria, greed, and the bullish gurus.

Don't forget that a 50 percent loss in a stock requires a 100 percent gain, just to break even. And in the case of a 75 percent loss, a 300 percent gain is needed to break even. To recover from this magnitude of loss usually takes years. Fear and greed are factors that are at play when humans are involved, and this fact will never change.

## STOCK MARKET PERFORMANCE OVER 110 YEARS

How has the stock market performed over the past 110 years? To gain a perspective on the magnitude of bull and bear markets, consider Tables 1-4 and 1-5. The data were provided by the Hays Advisory Group, and the tables show all the bull and bear markets in the twentieth century, using the DJIA as the benchmark. Neither the S&P 500 nor the Nasdaq Composite Index had historical data that far back in time; therefore, the DJIA was used instead.

Market academicians define a bear or bull market as a decline or rise of 20 percent, respectively, in a major market index. Table 1-4 adheres to this classification, but Table 1-5 has six time frames in which the change in percentage was less than 20 percent. Since Hays provided the data, I did not adjust them.

As Table 1-4 indicates, there have been 29 bull markets from 1900 through 2009, with an average gain of 90.3 percent and an average duration of 29.9 months (2.49 years). The average gain is skewed by the superbullish May 1926–March 1937 time frame, in which the cumulative return was over 459 percent, and the November 1990 through July 1998 time frame, where the return was 300 percent. Be aware of this fact when comparing bull markets with each other.

Looking at the bear market scenario in Table 1-5, we find that there have been 29 bear markets, with an average drop of –30.8 percent. The largest decline ever was when the market tumbled 90 percent from September 1929 to July 1932. The next worst was the most recent bear market, with a drop of 54 percent. The previous bear market, ending on October 9, 2002, produced a drop of 38 percent for the DJIA, but the S&P 500 Index fell 49 percent during this time frame and the Nasdaq Composite got clobbered, dropping 78 percent.

The average bear market has lasted 17.3 months, with an average fall of 30.8 percent. But there have been some catastrophic bears, including the 35-month bear market from September 1929 to July 1932, the 13-month bear market from March 1937 to March

## TABLE 1-4

## Over a Century of Bull Markets

| | Dow Jones Industrial Average | | | | | |
|---|---|---|---|---|---|---|
| Start | | End | | Length (Months) | Starting Price | Ending Price | % Change |

| Start | | End | | Length (Months) | Starting Price | Ending Price | % Change |
|---|---|---|---|---|---|---|---|
| Sept | 1900 | June | 1901 | 10 | 54 | 78 | 44% |
| Nov | 1903 | Feb | 1906 | 27 | 44 | 100 | 127% |
| Nov | 1907 | Dec | 1909 | 26 | 54 | 100 | 85% |
| Sept | 1911 | Oct | 1912 | 14 | 73 | 94 | 22% |
| Dec | 1914 | Nov | 1916 | 24 | 54 | 110 | 104% |
| Dec | 1917 | Nov | 1919 | 24 | 68 | 115 | 69% |
| Aug | 1921 | Mar | 1923 | 20 | 65 | 105 | 62% |
| Jun | 1924 | Feb | 1926 | 21 | 90 | 170 | 89% |
| May | 1926 | Sep | 1929 | 41 | 150 | 390 | 160% |
| Jul | 1932 | Feb | 1934 | 20 | 40 | 110 | 175% |
| Sept | 1934 | Mar | 1937 | 31 | 85 | 190 | 124% |
| Mar | 1938 | Sept | 1939 | 19 | 100 | 160 | 60% |
| Apr | 1942 | June | 1946 | 50 | 95 | 210 | 121% |
| Jun | 1949 | Jan | 1953 | 43 | 180 | 295 | 64% |
| Sept | 1953 | Apr | 1956 | 32 | 270 | 510 | 89% |
| Oct | 1957 | Jan | 1960 | 27 | 410 | 690 | 68% |
| Oct | 1960 | Nov | 1961 | 14 | 580 | 720 | 24% |
| Jun | 1962 | Feb | 1966 | 45 | 540 | 1,000 | 85% |
| Oct | 1966 | Dec | 1968 | 27 | 750 | 975 | 30% |
| May | 1970 | Jan | 1973 | 32 | 550 | 1,050 | 91% |
| Dec | 1974 | Sep | 1976 | 22 | 570 | 1,025 | 80% |
| Mar | 1980 | Apr | 1981 | 13 | 750 | 1,020 | 36% |
| Aug | 1982 | Jan | 1984 | 18 | 790 | 1,300 | 65% |
| July | 1984 | Aug | 1987 | 37 | 1,100 | 2,750 | 150% |
| Oct | 1987 | Aug | 1990 | 33 | 1,620 | 3,025 | 87% |
| Nov | 1990 | Jul | 1998 | 92 | 2,350 | 9,367 | 300% |
| Sep | 1998 | Jan | 2000 | 16 | 7,400 | 11,750 | 59% |
| Oct | 2002 | Oct | 2007 | 60 | 7,286 | 14,165 | 94% |
| Mar | 2009 | TBD | TBD | TBD | TBD | TBD | TBD |

29 bull markets

Average length: 29.9 months

Average gain: 90.3%

TBD = to be determined.

*Source:* Don Hays, "Morning Market Comments," August 21, 2002. Reprinted with permission of Hays Advisory Group. Data from 2002 onward added by L. Masonson.

## TABLE 1-5

Over a Century of Bear Markets

| Dow Jones Industrial Average | | | | | | | |
|---|---|---|---|---|---|---|---|
| **Start** | | **End** | | **Length (Months)** | **Starting Price** | **Ending Price** | **% Change** |
| Dec | 1899 | Sep | 1900 | 10 | 75 | 54 | −28 |
| Jun | 1901 | Nov | 1903 | 30 | 78 | 44 | −44 |
| Feb | 1906 | Nov | 1907 | 22 | 100 | 54 | −46 |
| Dec | 1909 | Sep | 1911 | 22 | 100 | 73 | −27 |
| Oct | 1912 | Jul | 1914 | 22 | 94 | 72 | −23 |
| Nov | 1916 | Dec | 1917 | 14 | 110 | 68 | −38 |
| Nov | 1919 | Aug | 1921 | 22 | 94 | 72 | −23 |
| Mar | 1923 | Jun | 1924 | 16 | 105 | 90 | −14 |
| Feb | 1926 | May | 1926 | 4 | 170 | 150 | −12 |
| Sep | 1929 | Jul | 1932 | 35 | 390 | 40 | −90 |
| Feb | 1934 | Sep | 1934 | 8 | 110 | 85 | −23 |
| Mar | 1937 | Mar | 1938 | 13 | 190 | 100 | −47 |
| Sep | 1939 | Apr | 1942 | 31 | 160 | 95 | −41 |
| Jun | 1946 | Jun | 1949 | 37 | 210 | 180 | −14 |
| Jan | 1953 | Sep | 1953 | 9 | 295 | 270 | −8 |
| Apr | 1956 | Oct | 1957 | 19 | 510 | 410 | −20 |
| Jan | 1960 | Oct | 1960 | 10 | 690 | 580 | −16 |
| Nov | 1961 | Jun | 1962 | 7 | 720 | 540 | −25 |
| Feb | 1966 | Oct | 1966 | 9 | 1000 | 750 | −25 |
| Dec | 1968 | May | 1970 | 18 | 975 | 550 | −44 |
| Jan | 1973 | Dec | 1974 | 24 | 1,050 | 570 | −46 |
| Sep | 1976 | Mar | 1980 | 42 | 1025 | 750 | −27 |
| Apr | 1981 | Aug | 1982 | 16 | 1,020 | 790 | −23 |
| Jan | 1984 | Jul | 1984 | 7 | 1,300 | 1,100 | −15 |
| Aug | 1987 | Oct | 1987 | 2 | 2,750 | 1,620 | −41 |
| Aug | 1990 | Nov | 1990 | 4 | 3,025 | 2,350 | −22 |
| Jul | 1998 | Sep | 1998 | 2 | 9,367 | 7,400 | −21 |
| Jan | 2000 | Oct | 2002 | 30 | 11,723 | 7,286 | −38 |
| Oct | 2007 | Mar | 2009 | 18 | 14,164 | 6,547 | −54 |

29 bear markets

Average length (months): 17.3

Average loss: −30.8%

*Source:* Don Hays, "Morning Market Comments," August 21, 2002. Reprinted with permission of Hays Advisory Group. Data from 2007 forward provided by L. Masonson.

1938, the 24-month bear market from January 1973 to December 1974, and of course, the last two bear markets since 2000.

Bear markets drops are much faster than bull market rises. For example, from January 1, 1991, to March 31, 2000, a period of 9.25 years, the S&P 500 rose from 330.22 to 1498.50 points, a total gain of 1168.28 points, resulting in a gain of 353 percent. In stark contrast, from the end of June through the end of July 2002, the S&P 500 fell 266 points, a loss of approximately 23 percent of that entire gain over a period of just two months. That's volatility in a bear market! In the fourth quarter of 2008, the S&P 500 produced the worst quarterly results in 21 years, with a drop of 22.6 percent.

## BEAR MARKET RECOVERIES

Table 1-6 provides data on how long it takes to break even, assuming a buy-and-hold approach with the S&P 500 Index, once a bear market has reached bottom. Also shown is the combined time of the drop and the time to recovery. Unbelievably, it took over 25 years for buy-and-hold investors to break even from the ravages of the Great Depression. (*Note:* The 25 years does not include a calculation for reinvested dividends, which would have shortened the period.) Do you really want to wait this long just to get your money back, assuming that you didn't sell at the bottom and didn't get back in the market? Do you think the average investor was able to take the pain of an 86 percent drop and wait 25 years? I certainly don't.

From 1956 through March 2009, the average bear market lasted 341 days (0.98 year), resulting in an average loss of 34.3 percent. The average recovery period to reach the previous high was about 986 days (2.74 years).

Note that in every case it took more recovery time than the duration of the actual bear market itself. This last bear market was the worst since the Great Depression, but it had one of the best and fastest recoveries in history, as shown in Table 1-7. Investors should realize that these long bear markets will occur again in the future, so a strategy to protect principal must be in place in advance to avoid this ravaging of principal.

**TABLE 1-6**

Time to Recoup S&P Bear Market Losses

| Year Began | Percent Loss | Duration (Years) | Recovery Time (Years) | Combined Time (Years) |
|---|---|---|---|---|
| 1929 | −86 | 2.75 | 25.2 | 27.95 |
| 1933 | −34 | 1.7 | 2.3 | 4.0 |
| 1937 | −55 | 1.0 | 8.8 | 9.8 |
| 1938 | −48 | 3.4 | 6.4 | 9.8 |
| 1946 | −28 | 1.8 | 4.1 | 5.9 |
| 1956 | −22 | 1.2 | 2.1 | 3.3 |
| 1961 | −28 | 0.5 | 1.7 | 2.2 |
| 1966 | −22 | 0.7 | 1.3 | 2.0 |
| 1968 | −36 | 1.5 | 3.3 | 4.8 |
| 1973 | −48 | 1.75 | 7.5 | 9.25 |
| 1980 | −27 | 1.75 | 1.9 | 3.25 |
| 1987 | −34 | 0.33 | 1.9 | 2.23 |
| 1990 | −20 | 0.25 | 0.6 | 0.85 |
| 2000 | −49 | 2.6 | 4.4 | 7.3 |
| 2007 | −57 | 1.5 | TBD | TBD |

*Note:* The recovery time does not take into account dividends. L. Masonson adjusted the 2000 data through October 2009 to be up to date. TBD = to be determined.
*Source:* Paul J. Lim, "Staying Afloat," *U.S. News & World Report*, September 10, 2001. The data was obtained from InvesTech Research and B of A Sector Watch.

## PERCENT GAIN AFTER BEAR MARKET

The percentage gains after bear market bottoms have been substantial, as Table 1-7 illustrates. Rallies have been persistent even during the bear market of the 1930s. The S&P 500 experienced its best bear performance in the first 12 months from the recent bear market lows since 1949. And the recovery from the March 2009 lows has been phenomenal, with the two-month advance more than doubling the average for that time frame.

## SECULAR BULL AND BEAR MARKETS

Bull and bear markets occur over both short and long time frames. Table 1-8 shows two long-term (secular) bull and three long-term bear markets for the period 1929–2009. This table was prepared by

**TABLE 1-7**

Recoveries after Bear Markets: Percent Gain from S&P 500 Low

| Bear Market Ended | 2 Mos. After | 6 Mos. After | 9 Mos. After | 12 Mos. After |
|---|---|---|---|---|
| June 1949 | 13 | 23 | 26 | 42 |
| October 1957 | 1 | 10 | 19 | 31 |
| June 1962 | 14 | 21 | 27 | 33 |
| October 1966 | 12 | 22 | 25 | 33 |
| May 1970 | 12 | 23 | 40 | 44 |
| October 1974 | 8 | 31 | 52 | 38 |
| August 1982 | 31 | 44 | 60 | 58 |
| December 1987 | 13 | 19 | 18 | 21 |
| October 1990 | 11 | 28 | 28 | 29 |
| October 2002 | 15 | 11 | 29 | 33 |
| March 2009 | 37 | 52 | 61 | 68 |
| Average | 15 | 26 | 35 | 40 |

Source: "Patience Will Be Rewarded," Standard & Poor's *The Outlook*, September 24, 2002. L. Masonson added data for 2002–2010.

Dennis Tilley, director of research, Merriman, Inc. For the entire 81-year time frame, the S&P 500 Index had an average annual return of 9.1 percent. But it was not all smooth sailing over that period. The secular bull markets from 1942 to 1965 and 1982 to 1999 produced average annual gains of 15.7 and 18.5 percent, respectively. But the three secular bear markets produced much lower annual average returns. So, as you can see, there can be long periods of time when the market is flat or down.

Even in secular bull markets, there are cyclic bear markets, where prices rally and falter, rally and falter, but overall no progress or negative progress is made. There are numerous opportunities to make money, assuming that you have the ability and willingness to follow the markets and use a tried-and-true market timing approach that works.

The question to ponder now is whether we have entered another secular bear market that could last until the year 2017. No one knows the answer. This is why it is important to have a viable investing approach. Buying and holding in a secular bear market is

**TABLE 1-8**

Secular Bull and Bear Markets: Stock Market Returns (in Percent)

| Years | 1929–2009 | 1929–1941 | 1942–1965 | 1966–1981 | 1982–1999 | 2000–2009 |
|---|---|---|---|---|---|---|
| Type of market | Total period | Secular bear | Secular bull | Secular bear | Secular bull | Secular bear |
| Length in years | 81 | 13 | 24 | 16 | 18 | 10 |
| Annualized return of S&P 500 | 9.1 | –2.4 | 15.7 | 6.0 | 18.5 | –0.9 |
| Inflation index (CPI) | 3.2 | –0.8 | 3.1 | 7.0 | 3.3 | 2.5 |
| S&P 500 real return | 5.8 | –1.6 | 12.2 | –0.9 | 14.7 | –3.4 |

**Source:** Dennis Tilley, "Will the Bear Market Be with Us for a Long Time?" Merriman, Inc. Article written in November 2002. Updated in 2010 by Dennis Tilley.

not a money-making approach. And inflation always eats away at whatever returns you are able to obtain, although inflation has been minimal the last few years. After inflation, the two secular bear markets prior to 2000 had negative returns.

Michael Kahn, writing in the December 16, 2002, issue of *Barron's*, said: "Tired of waiting for a clear trend in the stock market? Get used to it. If an emerging pattern continues, the major indexes could be in for 15 years of bouncing around. That's right, 15 years. Since World War II, the market has seen an 18-year rally, followed by an 18-year flat period, followed by another 18-year rally—the one ending in 2000. That means we could be about three years into the next 18-year flat spell."[2]

## CONCLUSION

The stock market is not a place for amateur investors who think that they can sit back and rake in the profits, year after year, with little risk. As you just saw, secular bear markets follow secular bull markets. The stock market is a very risky place, where investors

[2] Michael Kahn, "Hold Your Fire," *Barron's*, December 16, 2002, p. 23.

need to be on their toes or their feet will get burned. Long-term financial success in the stock market is difficult to attain, if not impossible, unless investors use a solid investing plan, develop strict entry and exit strategies, and have the psychological makeup to make tough decisions when conditions look the bleakest. Buy-and-hold is an anachronism. As you learned in this chapter, bear markets occur often, take considerable time to come back to break even, and can result in significant financial loss and emotional distress. This is why investing in individual stocks, mutual funds, or ETFs at the wrong time can be deadly to your wealth.

# The Buy-and-Hold Myth

*It wasn't greed that killed America's retirement savings dream. It was an irrational belief in passive, buy-and-hold investment strategies.*
—William E. Donoghue

*"Buy and hold" is still valid, because 10-year intervals of stagnating stock prices are rare.*
—Knight Kiplinger

## BUY-AND-HOLD BASICS

*Buy-and-hold* is simply defined as buying a diversified portfolio of high-quality stocks and/or a diversified group of mutual funds or exchange-traded funds (ETFs) or a combination of all three and holding them for the long term—typically defined as 10 to 20 years or longer—and typically rebalancing at least once a year. This investing approach is well entrenched in books on investing, in the mutual-fund marketing literature, and in the verbiage of financial advisors, academicians, and financial journalists. As you know, it is almost impossible to change the conventional wisdom.

According to Chicago research firm Ibbotson Associates, based on the Standard & Poor's (S&P) 500 Index, there was a 29 percent probability from 1926 to 2001 that an investor would lose money in the market if he or she were investing for a one-year time frame. However, if he or she were to invest for a five-year period, the probability of loss dropped to 10 percent. For a 10-year period, it dropped to 3 percent, and for a 15-year period, there would be no loss whatsoever.

Translating these three numbers into actual dollar amounts, a $1,000 investment in stocks over the 76-year period would have been worth $2,279,000, whereas a bond investment of the same magnitude would have been worth $51,000, and T-bills would have been worth $17,000. Remember, now, these results apply only if you held for 76 years!

Moreover, if the investor restricted his or her investments to large-cap stocks for this 76-year period, then he or she would have realized a compounded annual return of 10.7 percent compared with 5.3 percent for U.S. Treasury bonds and 3.8 percent for T-bills.

Thus the argument for buy-and-hold is that a long-term investor makes out well, whereas those in the market for short periods of time have a higher probability of loss. This is true, but bear markets can reduce investors' capital significantly. Therefore, investors need a plan of action to limit those situations and preserve their capital. The last disastrous investing decade should give you enough reason to question the buy-and-hold approach going forward.

You would think that while investors were getting pummeled during a bear market they would have the common sense and the fortitude to cut loose from buy-and-hold and bail out. But this is not what a CNN/USA Today/Gallup poll found in a random sampling of 720 investors done on July 29–31, 2002 (when the market had already dropped by a substantial percentage for the year). Overall, according to that survey, 63 percent of the respondents felt that buy-and-hold was the best strategy for them, 30 percent felt that some other strategy they did not name was better, and 7 percent had no opinion. According to a CNBC/Associated Press poll conducted from August 26, 2010, through September 8, 2010, 78 percent of investors still think that buy-and-hold works (source: *Fortune Magazine*, October 18, 2010). Therefore, even after the terrible stock market performance as recently as March 2009, investors are still tilting heavily toward buy-and-hold. This is sad for many reasons.

The buy-and-hold strategy can't be used for all stocks because, in practice, it only works with specific stocks during specific time periods. Remember the research provided by the

Blackstar Funds in the Appendix pointing out the small percentage of stocks that really do well. Investors should diversify to insulate themselves from the risk of any particular stock going totally sour. Thus, if you own a portfolio of, say, 10 stocks, the odds that the buy-and-hold strategy will produce positive results for all your holdings over a period of time are probably nil—unless there is a bull market going on. Even a few bad apples with large losses can reduce your overall return to less than you could have earned in an index fund. There are a certain percentage of stocks in the universe for which buy-and-hold has worked well, but that is the short list, and those stocks are in the minority.

## BUY-AND-HOLD ARGUMENTS: PRO AND CON

Almost 100 percent of the Wall Street pros, including well-known financial authors, mutual fund managers, money managers, and others, speak convincingly about the wisdom of the buy-and-hold strategy. High-level Wall Street professionals and mutual-fund executives have put forth numerous arguments as to why buy-and-hold is a superior strategy to market timing, but their arguments lack sufficient detail or facts to back up their claims, or they produce backtest results with dubious assumptions. They may refer to one or two academic studies published in financial journals a few years ago to back themselves up. But I have read those studies, and I find that the key assumptions made by the authors are not always clearly spelled out or are not realistic. This leaves the investor with a problem as to the study's methodology, time frame, choice of investment vehicle, and hypothesis being tested. Let's first take some of the more popular buy-and-hold arguments and then present the flip side to that argument.

Common arguments in favor of buy-and-hold include

1. No one can predict the stock market's future performance. Therefore, it is best to buy and hold good-quality stocks and a bevy of diversified mutual funds because good companies always will persevere in the long run.
2. If you were out of the market and "missed the 10 or 20 best" trading days, then your average annual return would be

much lower than if you had been in the market and fully invested on those days. Therefore, you must be in the market all the time so that you don't miss the best time days.

3. There are no market timing strategies that work consistently or as well as buy-and-hold over long periods of time.

4. The famed Peter Lynch, money manager in the heyday of the Fidelity Magellan Fund, said, "There are no market-timers in the Forbes 400."

5. According to many academicians, stock prices are a "random walk," and future stock price movements cannot be predicted. They also argue the efficient-market hypothesis, which is another side of the coin and holds that all the information about a stock is "baked into" its stock price instantly, holds so that no one can consistently beat the market over the long term because the stock price has already taken it into account. Therefore, buy-and-hold is the only game in town.

6. I've never met a market-timer who, over the long term, has consistently equaled or beaten the results of buy-and-hold.

Let's take each one of these arguments and provide the counter-argument.

## No One Can Predict What the Market Will Do in the Future

It is true that no one can predict the market's future course. This does not mean that you just give up and keep your money invested 100 percent of the time when you know with 100 percent certainty that bear markets will occur and take away a major percentage or all of your profits every three to six years. Market timing has nothing to do with predicting the future but instead with providing you with a way to invest with the odds in your favor. Buy-and-hold is a defeatist attitude that only costs you money and grief. There is no reason to default into this defective strategy when a better one is available. It is true that most of the time a diversified portfolio will cushion the blow in bear markets, but in bear markets you still will have losses in the portion of your portfolio invested in equities. Moreover, diversification failed miserably in the latest bear market, where only Treasury bonds had gains.

Buy-and-hold has had disastrous returns, even for the well-known "nifty fifty" stocks of the 1970s. In the 1970s, the current vogue was to invest in the 50 largest blue chip growth companies with the expectation that they would continue to provide investors with substantial returns on their investments. Those who invested in Xerox under that theory saw their investment lose 72 percent of its market value in the 1973–1974 bear market, and it took them 24 years to recover their money. From October 1990 until May 1999, Xerox rose 1,100 percent but then dropped 93 percent from May 1999 through December 2000. Thus an investor buying $100 worth of Xerox stock in October 1990 saw the value of his or her stock rise to $1,200 by May 1999 and then saw it plummet to a value of $84, thus ending up with a loss of $16 over the 10-year period!

Polaroid Corporation lost 90 percent of its value from its peak price and took 28 years to break even again. Then it went into bankruptcy. Avon Products stock was stagnant for 24 years, and Black & Decker took 23 years to get back to its peak price. More currently, Enron peaked at $90 in August 2000 and then traded at $0.38 by year end 2002 and then went bankrupt. And hundreds of Internet and technology stocks lost 90 percent or more of their value three years after the market top in 2000. Even the stable stocks and growth stocks suffered substantial damage; witness what happened in the banking sector, Internet sector, automobile sector, and chemicals.

To look at the double speak of the mutual-fund managers, you only need to know that equity mutual-fund portfolio turnover, as measured by Morningstar, was around 15 percent in the 1950s through 1964, rose to 48 percent in the early 1970s, to 75 percent in 1983, to 111 percent in 1987, dropped back to 74 percent in 1993–1994, rose again to 90 percent in 2000 and 111 percent in June 2002, and was 90 percent in September 2010. Clearly, mutual-fund managers do not practice buy-and-hold with the funds entrusted to them but somehow inexplicably find it appropriate for individual investors to use that approach. I have already stated that the reason for this is that mutual funds cannot stay in business if the fund holders embark on large-scale redemptions of their funds.

By implementing specific market timing strategies, and by using a few technical market indicators, an investor can time the market successfully and avoid the major portion of downtrends while being fully invested during the major portion of uptrends. Chapters 4 and 7 through 11 cover this information in depth. After studying these chapters, you can make your own determination as to whether market timing or buy-and-hold is the preferred course.

## You Will Miss the 10 Best Days if You Are Not Fully Invested

The argument that you would have had much lower annual returns if you missed the best 10 days or months of the year is true. Keep in mind, though, that the 10 best days or months are not consecutive but occur randomly over the years. Second, the purveyors of that information rarely tell you the other side of the story—that you would have had an even higher annual return if you had missed the 10 *worst* days or months. And missing the worst days produces a far better overall return for you than missing the best days. For the actual statistics, see page 53 under the heading of "Missing the Best and Worst Days (Months) in the Market."

## There Are No Market Timing Strategies that Beat Buy-and-Hold over the Long Run

This statement is pure bunk. Of course, there are market timing strategies that beat buy-and-hold over the long run. *Timer Digest* and the *Hulbert Financial Digest*, covered in Chapter 12, provide performance data on actual market-timers that completely contradicts this assertion. But these types of results are not discussed very much in print or on the airwaves because of the vested interest in favor of buy-and-hold. There are more than five strategies presented in this book that have outperformed buy-and-hold over decades, and there are many more in print (such as in Robert Colby's classic book, *The Encyclopedia of Technical Market Indicators*, listed in the Bibliography) that do so by wide margins. The ones that I've chosen to present in this book have the advantage of being easy to put in practice, are simple strategies, and have shown profits over many years.

An illustration of a simple timing strategy that beats buy-and-hold is one that uses a moving average on an equity index price chart with price crossovers above and below the moving average giving the buy and sell signals. The details of this approach are covered in Chapter 9. Here's one example during the period 1929–1998. Had you used a 130-day moving average on the S&P 500 Index and bought that index or an equivalent portfolio when the price crossed above that moving average and sold it when the price penetrated below that moving average and remained in cash, you would have achieved an annual gain of 12.5 percent during that period. Compare that with a return of 10.3 percent for the same period for buy-and-hold with dividends reinvested. Over the 70-year period, the significant difference of 2.2 percentage points a year resulted in a huge difference in total return.

## There Are No Market-Timers Among the Forbes 400 Wealthiest People

True, there probably are no market-timers on the Forbes 400 list. So what? You still can get very rich without being on that list of billionaires. There are probably more than a few private individuals worth hundreds of millions of dollars who have developed and used market timing to become very wealthy. Except for a handful of hedge-fund managers (some of whom probably use a market timing component for their trade exit and entry points), the remainder of people on the Forbes list made their money by founding fledgling businesses that grew into stellar companies where they amassed millions of shares of stock. They have great wealth because they were the major shareholders in their own companies. Examples include Warren Buffett (Berkshire Hathaway), William Gates III (Microsoft), Michael Bloomberg (Bloomberg LP), and Lawrence Ellison (Oracle Corporation). These people have to buy and hold the majority of their shares for a number of reasons. It is interesting to note that when Peter Lynch was running Magellan Fund, his portfolio turnover in some of his best-performing years approached 300 percent—certainly not a buy-and-hold practitioner.

## Future Stock Prices Are Random and Cannot Be Predicted with Accuracy

You hear academicians profess the random-walk theory and the efficient-market hypothesis to bolster their case that no one can consistently outperform the market. If those two hypotheses were true, then only the lucky few investors would ever make any money in the market. Clearly, many individuals, hedge funds, and private investment firms do beat the buy-and-hold strategy by a long shot and with less risk over many years. Stock prices do stay in trends for weeks, months, and years, and this is not a "random walk." Chapter 12 has a listing of market-timers who have been top performers, as measured by *Timer Digest* and other sources.

## I Never Met a Market-Timer Who Has Beaten Buy-and-Hold over the Long Term

This statement by itself is ridiculous and insulting to successful market-timers. It implies that the individual who makes the statement knows *every* market-timer in the United States and has determined that none of them has a long-term track record of success. This is patently absurd.

I would not take at face value the statement of some stock market guru or famous investor who says that he or she has not met a successful long-term market-timer because there are many timers around. If such people really were interested in finding successful market-timers with long-term track records, they could subscribe to TimerTrac, *Timer Digest*, or the *Hulbert Financial Digest*. They also could contact the National Association of Active Investment Managers (NAAIM), which has hundreds of asset-allocators and market-timers as members. The Web site for NAAIM is www.naaim.org.

I suspect that individuals who profess that market timing does not work are either not being totally honest with you or have not researched the issue for themselves. As I have indicated, market timing is a threat to many people's business models. In most cases, failure to acknowledge the viability of market timing as a genuine investment strategy is all about the dollars and cents of the antagonist and not about anything else—and you can quote me on that!

# MORE NAILS IN THE
# BUY-AND-HOLD CASKET

You won't see the title of this chapter, "The Buy-and-Hold Myth," mentioned very often on financial shows or written about in the financial press. This is so because the buy-and-hold mantra has been pummeled into investors' psyches by the top Wall Street pros for decades. If the stock market rose 80 percent of the time, with corrections of 5 to 10 percent along the way, then perhaps the buy-and-hold strategy would make sense. But I will let the record speak for itself.

Many individuals believe that time is on their side in investing, and no matter what happens in the short run, they will come out fine in the long run. Nevertheless, cumulative short-term performance determines overall long-term performance. During 2002 and 2008, there were numerous stories of individual investors whose portfolios dropped by 50 percent or more. They had to go back to work or postpone their retirement. According to James Stack, editor of *InvesTech Market Analyst Newsletter* (October 1994), "The closer an investor is to retirement or needing his [or her] capital, the more dangerous a buy-and-hold strategy becomes." This certainly has been borne out in spades in the past decade.

Diversification through allocation of investments in a portfolio with, say, 60 percent stocks and 40 percent bonds can help to reduce market risk. Overall, you have less risk than the investor who is fully invested in stocks. But this didn't help much in this last market crash because all assets took a beating, except Treasury bonds. Thus diversification is not as good as it is cracked up to be.

For aggressive investors, the optimal scenario is to be 100 percent in investments such as equity ETFs in bull markets to capture the highest returns. Alternatively, such investors should be 100 percent in cash or cash equivalents (or to be short the market) during bear markets. By watering down their portfolios with bonds, they are denying themselves the incremental profits from equities. If bear markets are inevitable, then prepare for them, and sell your equity positions as the market trend begins to turn down. Consider using market timing to help you achieve this goal. This is what the heart of this book is all about—providing simple strategies to keep you on the right side of the market.

What leads to an investor's downfall in following a timing approach is the execution. When it is time to exit your position, you may rationalize that this time will be different, and you decide not to sell now. You say to yourself, "This year the decline in the market will not happen because of certain factors; therefore, I will stay put despite the historical record and the readings of the indicators." Or, you may say, "Even if the market should fall, the story behind my stock is so compelling that it cannot possibly decline." This is a gambler's approach, not a viable approach to investing. The odds are heavily against you, and you are bucking the odds. Far better to forego the profits you anticipate from that stock than for it to disappoint you and fall under the weight of the bear market. Preservation of capital is the ultimate consideration and is well worth the cost of foregone profits.

Look at Table 2-1, which provides a comparison of specific percentage allocations of stocks and bonds with their resulting risk and returns. Being 100 percent invested over the 76-year period from 1926 through 2002, each rolling 12-month period produced an average annual return of 13 percent with a risk of 22 percent. (Risk is the variability in return over the 76-year, 12-month rolling peri-

## TABLE 2-1

Percentage Mix of Stocks and Bonds, 12-Month Rolling
Periods: January 1926–September 2002

| Stocks/Bond Ratio | Annual Return | Risk |
| --- | --- | --- |
| 100 percent stocks | 13 percent | 22 percent |
| 90 percent/10 percent | 12.20 percent | 20 percent |
| 80 percent/20 percent | 11.50 percent | 18 percent |
| 70 percent/30 percent | 10.90 percent | 16 percent |
| 60 percent/40 percent | 10 percent | 14 percent |
| 50 percent/50 percent | 9.20 percent | 12.50 percent |
| 40 percent/60 percent | 8.50 percent | 11 percent |
| 30 percent/70 percent | 7.90 percent | 10 percent |
| 20 percent/80 percent | 7 percent | 9.10 percent |
| 10 percent/90 percent | 6.50 percent | 8.70 percent |
| 100 percent bonds | 5.80 percent | 9 percent |

Source: "Asset Allocation: Tips for Tending to Your Portfolio Mix," Of Mutual Interest, Invesco, Fall 2000, p. 5.

ods. In this example, with a return of 13 percent, the risk of 22 percent means that the return fluctuates between a high of 35 percent to a low of –9 percent.) A 60/40 percent split between stocks and bonds reduced the return to 10 percent from 13 percent, with risk falling from 22 to 14 percent. And at the other extreme, if you were all in bonds, your appreciation suffered greatly with a 5.8 percent return and a 9 percent risk factor.

As expected, the higher the return, the higher is the risk. What if I told you that you could obtain the returns of buy-and-hold (being 100 percent invested) but with half the risk? It is really simple. All you have to do is to use the "best six months" strategy, as explained in Chapter 7. You will see that you can beat buy-and-hold and be out of the market for six months in a money-market account. This means that you are getting a higher risk-adjusted return for your money. The sweetener is that you are accruing some interest income in a money-market account while almost everyone else's portfolio is most likely sinking in value.

## RISK MUST BE TAKEN INTO ACCOUNT

Investors usually do not consider the risk of investing until they've lost a big chunk of their money. Unfortunately, investors are fixated on how much money they are going to make in the market instead of "how do I protect my capital from eroding." Investors may not fully understand that all investments are risky. The alternative is to invest in a U.S. Treasury bill, note, or bond, all three of which are the safest investments there are—but the yield is pitiful compared with stocks or equity mutual funds over long time frames. Usually, the more risky the investment is, the greater the returns will be. However, in a down market, the added risk results in worse-than-average returns.

Every investor has to decide, before investing in any investment vehicle, what level of risk he or she is comfortable with. For example, can you withstand a drop of 20 percent in your equity portfolio in a 4- or 52-week time frame without feeling upset and concerned? If this level of risk is unacceptable, then you should consider a diversified portfolio of equity ETFs (composed of growth and value, domestic and international, small-cap and large-cap stocks) and a certain percentage of bond ETFs because they typically rise when stock funds decline so that there is a counterbalance.

Market timing can be used successfully with a diversified ETF portfolio to lower the risk of buy-and-hold even further. On a risk-adjusted basis, therefore, market timing used with a diversified portfolio should be able to equal or beat buy-and-hold.

## BUY-AND-HOLD IS VERY RISKY

Buy-and-hold exposes investors to every twist and turn in the market, and big drops in the market can devastate the value of their portfolios. Market timing usually underperforms buy-and-hold in long bull markets but will outperform it in bear markets. Investors who dismiss market timing as a viable investing strategy therefore are doing themselves a major disservice.

The last two bear markets are just examples over the last decade where buying and holding equities was not a wise, rational, or money-protecting strategy. Actually, it was financial suicide. Don't forget that there is something called the *opportunity cost* of money. It relates to the income foregone because an opportunity to earn income was not pursued. If you are not earning interest or capital gains on your money, then you are losing out. Had you sold in late 2007 instead of staying fully invested and losing over 50 percent by March 2009, and had you put your money into a money-market fund earning an average of 2 percent per year over the past few years, you would have been way ahead. By being fully invested, you gave up the opportunity to earn an average of 2 percent a year. Thus, in this case, you lost 50 percent of your money when you could have earned 6 percent over three years (not including compounding), so your opportunity cost was 0.6 percent.

Keep in mind the sage advice of Dan Sullivan, editor of *The Chartist Mutual Fund* newsletter:

> *Without a set of clear and concise rules to direct them, investors do not stand much of a chance. The investor without a feasible and simple plan will almost assuredly do things which are self-defeating. A disciplined approach to the market will protect us from making decisions based solely on emotion. The inexperienced investor falls prey to the demanding pressures exerted by investing one's own money. They will jump from one investment to another, hold a losing position too long or cut a winning position too soon. They will become greedy, or impatient, or after a few set-backs they become disheartened and throw in the towel.*

## MISSING THE BEST AND WORST DAYS (MONTHS) IN THE MARKET

Numerous articles and brokerage firm newsletters and information updates refer to the meager investment performance realized by the hypothetical investor who was unlucky enough to miss the best days or months in the stock market. The argument goes like this: Unless you are invested all the time using a buy-and-hold approach, you have no way of knowing when the market's best days or months will occur. Since these big up moves do not occur that often, an investor must be fully invested to take advantage of them. Unfortunately, this argument is only half the story.

The other half of the story should be told. And that is the very positive impact of missing the worst days or months in the market. This critical information is rarely mentioned in the financial press. The entire discussion of missing the best days is contrived for the benefit of the bogus buy-and-hold argument.

## RESEARCH ON MISSING THE BEST AND WORST TIME PERIODS

Interestingly, in 1994 and again in 2004, Towneley Capital Management, Inc., commissioned a study conducted by Professor H. Nejat Seyhun, Ph.D., at the University of Michigan School of Business Administration to research the effect of daily and monthly market swings on a portfolio's performance, initially from 1926 to 1993 and then from 1926 to 2004, respectively. Both studies analyzed the best and worst days' and months' performance.

These studies were titled, "Stock Market Extremes and Portfolio Performance." The two full studies can be accessed at the firm's Web site: www.towneley.com. A few of the critical findings of the earlier study are as follows:

- From 1926 through 1993, a capitalization-weighted index of U.S. stocks [New York Stock Exchange (NYSE) for the entire period, American Stock Exchange (AMEX) from July 1962, and the Nasdaq from December 1972] gained an average of 12.02 percent annually (buy-and-hold). An initial investment of $1.00 in 1926 would have earned a cumulative $637.30.

- From 1926 through 1993, missing the 48 *best* months, or only 5.9 percent of all months, decreased the annual return to 2.86 percent from 12.02 percent, and the cumulative gain amounted to only $1.60.
- From 1926 through 1993, eliminating the 48 *worst* months, or only 5.9 percent of all months, increased the annual return to 23.0 percent, and the cumulative gain swelled to a total to $270,592.80.
- From 1963 through 1993, missing the *best* 1.2 percent of all trading days resulted in missing out on 95 percent of the market's gains.
- From 1963 through 1993, missing the 10 *best* days lowered the annual return to 10.17 percent compared with 11.83 percent for buy-and-hold. However, missing the *worst* 10 days improved the annual return to 14.06 percent.
- From 1963 through 1993, missing the 90 *best* days lowered the annual return to 3.28 percent compared with 11.83 percent for buy-and-hold. However, missing the *worst* 90 days improved the annual return to 23.0 percent.
- The study clearly shows that "the returns from trying and failing to be an outstanding market-timer are highly likely to be less than simply owning Treasury bills."

The more recent study findings confirm the earlier study findings. Here are some of the key findings:

- The results from the more recent data were very similar to the prior study. Between 1926 and 2004, more than 99 percent of the market gains occurred during only 5.1 percent of all months. Also, a miniscule 0.85 percent of the trading days accounted for 96 percent of the market gains.
- From 1926 through 2004, a capitalization-weighted index of U.S. stocks gained an average of 10.04 percent annually (buy-and-hold). An initial investment of $1.00 in 1926 would have earned a cumulative $1,919.18.
- From 1926 through 2004, missing the 48 *best* months, or only 5.1 percent of all months, decreased the annual return to 7.01 percent, and the cumulative gain amounted to only $6.46.

- From 1926 through 2004, eliminating the 48 *worst* months, or only 5.1 percent of all months, increased the annual return to 20.26 percent, and the cumulative gain swelled to a total to $1,023,557.70.
- From 1963 through 2004, the results were similar, with an annual return of 10.84 percent. Missing the *best* 90 trading days, or 0.85 percent of the 10,573 trading days, an annualized return drops to 3.2 percent, and the cumulative gain drops to $1,693.68.
- From 1963 through 2004, missing the *worst* 90 days raised the annual return to 19.57 percent compared with 10.84 percent for buy-and-hold.

The study concludes: "The implications of this study could well be critical for the average investor. By being 'out of the market' for as few as even one or two of the best-performing months or days over several decades, a portfolio's return is significantly diminished. Since the study also shows that most of the damage to portfolio performance occurs during a very few months or days, if an investor could avoid such periods, the result would be to side-step losses and substantially grow one's portfolio."

Both studies clearly indicate that missing the worst days is critical to minimizing significant portfolio deterioration (Table 2-2). This is why I am recommending market timing. The odds are that you will miss many of the worst days by using any one of the strategies provided in this book.

Invesco AIM funds issued a report entitled, "Rethinking Risk: The Tale of 10 Days," in November 2009 analyzing the consequences of missing the best 10 days over an 81-year period from January 3, 1928, to March 31, 2009, using S&P 500 Index data. One key finding was that stock market returns more than tripled by missing the worst-performing days. There full study results are summarized in Table 2-3.

Interestingly, the research found that all 10 worst-performing days occurred during *bear markets*—six during October and one in July, September, November, and December. Also, seven of the best days also occurred during bear markets. The report says, "But who has 81 years to invest? Depending on your investment time horizon, it may be impossible to recover from losses of the bear

**TABLE 2-2**

Summary of Study Results

| Condition | Average Annual Return 1926–2004 |
|---|---|
| Missed 48 worst months | 20.26 percent |
| Missed 24 worst months | 16.27 percent |
| Missed 6 worst months | 12.33 percent |
| Market performance all months | 10.04 percent |
| Missed 6 best months | 8.05 percent |
| Missed 24 best months | 5.31 percent |
| Treasury-bill earnings | 3.84 percent |
| Missed 48 best months | 2.72 percent |

*Source:* "Stock Market Extremes and Portfolio Performance 1926–2004," Townley Capital Management, Inc.

**TABLE 2-3**

Telling Days: 81 Years Ending March 31, 2009

| Days | Growth of $1 | Cumulative Percent Return |
|---|---|---|
| Buy and hold best and worst 10 | $45.18 | 4,418 |
| Miss 10 best | 14.99 | 1,399 |
| Miss 10 worst | 143.47 | 14,247 |
| Miss 10 best and worst | 47.59 | 4,659 |

*Source:* Invesco Aim; Bloomberg LP.

market." Also, ". . . depending on your time horizon, a buy-and-hold strategy may not work either. . . . Your first investment priority should be to minimize risk, not maximize returns."

Will Hepburn of Hepburn Capital Management, LLC, has conducted research on the "best and worst" days over the past decade. According to his latest research, over a 25-year period ending in year 2008 (Table 2-4), he found that the average return of the S&P 500 Index was 7.06 percent. His research found that missing the worst days was much more valuable than missing the best days, and of course, missing the best and worst days resulted in a better performance by at least 1 percentage point a year than the buy-and-hold approach.

On November 5, 2001, *Barron's* published an article by Jacqueline Doherty entitled, "The Truth About Timing," that was based on a study of the five best and worst days by Birinyi Associates. The investment research firm evaluated the performance of the S&P 500 Index from 1966 through October 29, 2001, on an annual return basis each year (buy-and-hold) compared with missing the five best and worst days each year. A $1 investment at the beginning of the period held until the end of the period was worth $11.71 (a 1,071 percent gain). But missing just the five best days each year resulted in an astonishing ending value of $0.15 (an 85 percent loss) compared with a mind-boggling $987.12 (a 98,612 percent rise) by missing the worst five days each year.

This study puts another notch in the casket of the argument that missing the best days is more important than missing the worst days. It's amazing that 5 days out of 250 in the trading year, or 2 percent of the trading days a year, can have such a dramatic impact on the annual and compounded performance of investing. This is another reason why an investor should try to *minimize his or her time in the market* so that bad things do not happen to good people.

A study of the best and worst days (months) would show similar results no matter which stock markets were analyzed. For example, a study of the India stock market represented by the SENSEX and conducted by Munjunath Gaddi, research analyst, Fundsupermart, showed the value of a rupee and its annualized performance for almost a 30-year period (Table 2-5).

**TABLE 2-4**

Missing the Best and Worst Days: S&P 500, 1983–2008

|          | Missed Best Days | Missed Worst Days | Missed Both |
|----------|------------------|-------------------|-------------|
| 10 days  | 4.10 percent     | 11.23 percent     | 8.15 percent |
| 20 days  | 2.15 percent     | 13.80 percent     | 8.58 percent |
| 40 days  | −0.93 percent    | 17.59 percent     | 8.82 percent |

*Source:* Hepburn Capital Management, "Diversification by Strategy Reduces Risk, Study Shows," press release, January 15, 2009.

**TABLE 2-5**

Missing the Best and Worst Periods: SENSEX,
1980–October 2009

|                          | End of October 2009 | Annualized Return |
|--------------------------|---------------------|-------------------|
| SENSEX                   | Rs. 134.53          | 18.4 percent      |
| Missing top 10 months    | Rs. 13.41           | 9.4 percent       |
| Missing top 10 days      | Rs. 47.57           | 14.2 percent      |
| Avoiding worst 10 months | Rs. 812.58          | 26.0 percent      |
| Avoiding worst 10 days   | Rs. 354.99          | 22.4 percent      |

Rs. = rupees.
*Source:* Bloomberg, Fundsupermart.com.

## CONCLUSION

While watching CNBC on December 16, 2002, I saw an interview with Vern Hayden, certified financial planner at Hayden Financial Group. In the interview, Hayden said that buy-and-hold was no longer a viable strategy. He suggested that investors diversify their holdings and do their own asset allocation. I was encouraged to finally hear a financial advisor say this on the air. One can hope that he will not be the only voice of sanity on the airwaves in the future.

Buy-and-hold is a great strategy during long-term (secular) bull markets, but it is a very poor strategy during secular bear markets, where loss of principal can be extensive while inflation eats away at what's left.

Since history shows that bear markets follow bull markets, it is smart to sell at the end of the bull market and put your proceeds into money-market funds or other safe investment vehicles until the bear market is over. Alternatively, you may wish to short the market by shorting with inverse ETFs.

If investors were to sit down and really think about the frequency of bull and bear market cycles, they would realize that their inaction (e.g., adopting a buy-and-hold strategy) is not an intelligent move. Therefore, the only other choice is to have a solid, time-tested action plan for investing in the market. Market timing strategies fit the bill, as will be made clear in later chapters.

## CHAPTER 3

# Market Timing: What You Need to Know

*An investor needs to do very few things right as long as he or she avoids big mistakes.*

—Warren Buffett

*[Learn] how to make money in bear markets, bull markets, and chicken markets.*

—Conrad W. Thomas

If you were to mention the word *market timing* in an innocuous discussion with your broker, financial advisor, or friends, you shouldn't be surprised to see the conversation go downhill from there. Consider that probably 99.9 percent of the Wall Street professionals will tell you outright that market timing does not work, period. If you were to ask these people why they feel that way, they might cite a few academic studies performed a few years ago that have brought them to that conclusion. Or they might cite statistics from Ibottson Associates showing that over every 20-year rolling time period, the market has never gone down. Keep in mind what Aaron Levenstein said: "Statistics are like bikinis. What they reveal is suggestive, but what they conceal is vital." Even if this were true, you can't wait for five years or more to finally see your money come back from bear market lows. Long-term results cannot help you to invest for the here and now, which is when you need to see your money grow.

## WHAT IS MARKET TIMING?

In general, *market timing* is an investing or trading strategy that looks to be invested in the stock market when it is advancing and to be in cash and/or to be short when the market is declining. This definition applies to investing or trading in any investment vehicle, such as individual stocks, mutual funds, exchange-traded funds (ETFs), options, futures, gold, or bonds. Many individuals and professionals who use market timing focus on the two mutual-fund families (Rydex and ProFunds) and three ETF familes (Rydex, ProShares, and Direxion) geared specifically to market-timers as their timing vehicles.

The three main objectives of market timing are

- To preserve capital
- To avoid large market declines
- To equal or exceed the performance of a buy-and-hold portfolio on a risk-adjusted basis

The whole concept depends on limiting the risk when the market begins to decline by being defensive. Picture this: If you were in a leaking boat you'd have three choices:

1. Stay in the boat and stop the leak = Go short.
2. Get out of the boat = Switch to cash.
3. Go down with the ship = Buy-and-hold.

Do I have to ask you which is the worst choice? It's really easy to understand. What's not so easy is to execute the strategy. But we'll get to that later on.

A buy-and-hold approach in equities exposes 100 percent of the invested dollars to market risk. If an investor purchases an ETF for $50 a share, uses a buy-and-hold strategy, and then watches as the share price falls to $5 over a three-year time frame, the investor has lost 90 percent of his or her money. A market timing approach would have gotten the investor out of the ETF at a much higher price and placed the proceeds of the sale in a money-market fund or T-bill during the downdraft. Thus the risk is reduced because the time invested in the ETF is reduced. This is what timing is all about—*reducing your risk.*

As we know from experience, bear markets intercede every three to six years and cause investors to experience portfolio deterioration. An analysis of the Dow Jones Industrial Average (DJIA) from 1885 through 1993 found that bear markets consumed 32 percent of the investment timeline, getting back to breakeven took another 44 percent of the timeline, and only 24 percent of the timeline was spent in net bull territory.[1] This is the problem with buy-and-hold—long periods of negative or zero returns. And we haven't even factored in the opportunity cost of funds or the ravages of inflation, which are admittedly low in 2010.

## CLASSIC MARKET-TIMERS

There are two types of professional market-timers: the classic market-timers and the dynamic asset allocators. The former usually invest in mutual funds or ETFs as their investment vehicles, and they move their money into a money-market fund or T-bills when they are not invested in the market. A classic market-timer may decide to go from a cash position to a 100 percent invested position or possibly to a 25 percent invested position, in 25 percent increments, until fully invested based on a particular timing strategy. And he or she may decide to exit the same way, by selling 25 percent of the investment, in 25 percent increments. Also, some classic market-timers may go short instead of going into cash to take full advantage of a market decline. The market-timers who go short the market may use leveraged mutual funds such as Rydex Titan 500 and Rydex Tempest 500 to go 200 percent (because of the leverage) long the Standard & Poor's (S&P) 500 Index or 200 percent short the S&P 500 Index, respectively. Or they may use unleveraged funds (such as Rydex OTC Fund and Rydex Arktos) to go long the Nasdaq 100 Index or to go short the Nasdaq 100 Index, respectively. They also can use equivalent leveraged ETFs from Direxion, ProShares, and Rydex SGI funds.

---

[1] Jerry C. Wagner, "Why Market Timing Works," *Journal of Investing,* Summer 1997.

## DYNAMIC ASSET ALLOCATORS

Dynamic asset allocators, unlike classic market-timers, are typical-ly 100 percent invested in multiple asset classes, but they may spread their investments among ETFs, stocks, bonds, gold, alterna-tive investments, and cash in varying percentages. They either invest directly in those instruments or they use index mutual funds, sector mutual funds, leveraged mutual funds, or ETFs that represent these asset classes. For the investors who prefer to always be invested with wide diversification, the asset-allocation approach fits the bill nicely. And typically, the overall risk of the portfolio is less than that of investing in one specific investment vehicle such as equities.

## TIMING METHODS AND BENCHMARKS

Numerous methods are available to time the market. Typically, professional market-timers have developed strategies based on technical indicators aimed at price, volume, sentiment, or other variables to develop their timing models. Some professional timers disclose their model logic to their clients, whereas others keep it proprietary. Some market-timers use very simple market timing models (e.g., the 200-day moving average), whereas others may use multiple indicators. The main concern is how well the market timing strategy has performed against an appropriate benchmark and the amount of portfolio risk encountered, as measured by the standard deviation (volatility from the average price) or "ulcer index" (i.e., a measure of pain). For example, if a timer is investing in the XLK (the S&P Technology SPDR ETF), then the appropriate benchmark is the Nasdaq 100 Index.

The appropriate benchmark for dynamic asset allocators is more complicated than that for classic market-timers because the timers may invest in multiple asset classes. In such a situation, the benchmark should be a weighted average of individual bench-marks based on the asset allocation of the portfolio. For example, a portfolio composed of 25 percent equity large-cap mutual funds, 25 percent intermediate bond funds, and 50 percent gold funds would use three different benchmarks appropriately weighted to provide the composite benchmark.

## PERSONALITY CHARACTERISTICS OF PROFITABLE MARKET-TIMERS

You don't have to experience fear and greed over the inevitable and numerous market roller-coaster rides. Market timing can help you to develop a rational, time-tested, less risky investment methodology that will allow you to sleep at night and not worry about what tomorrow's news will bring. Is market timing perfect? Are you perfect? Of course not. No one in the market is perfect. However, by putting the odds in your favor, you can enhance your returns and minimize your losses. In the end, you will have more money in your pocket and be savvier than 98 percent of all investors who ignore reality and ride the emotional roller-coaster year in and year out.

The odds of using a market timing approach successfully depend greatly on your personality traits. If you are impatient, cannot stand to lose any money, expect perfection with regard to your timing system, or are always looking to change the way you invest (looking for the Holy Grail), then self-directed market timing will not work for you. The following are the personality traits necessary to have a solid chance at being a profitable self-directed market-timer:

- *Patience, determination, perseverance, and discipline.* Timing the market requires patience and discipline because you cannot afford to accept some of the timing signals and ignore others and you never know in advance which signals will lead to the most profitable trades. You must be able to sit tight and obey the timing signals after they are given, even though the market may go against you initially. You must have discipline to follow your timing rules, and you must be determined to let your timing system have sufficient time to work its wonders. Market-timers who persevere are the ones who survive.

- *Self-confidence.* If you believe in the market timing approach that you've selected and you're able to feel comfortable using that method, then you are better able to stay the course. Having a strong self-image and having your ego under control are critically important characteristics that lend themselves to a successful market timing outcome.

- *Independent thinker.* You must be able to think for yourself and not be swayed by your financial advisor, broker, friends, family, or popular opinion. You need to turn a deaf ear to all that noise and concentrate on your selected investment approach.

- *Realist.* Your market timing system will not beat the buy-and-hold strategy every year, especially during multiyear bull runs. This is why you need to give your timing strategy years to work. Using it for six months and then chucking it out the window is not the way. Moreover, you may feel concerned that only 40 to 50 percent of your trades are profitable. This is not a problem as long as the profits on your winning trades exceed the losses on your losing trading by at least a factor of 2 to 1. Moreover, you may experience runs of three to four losses in a row, and once in a while, you may have 14 losses out of 15 trades. Such an outcome can happen, but hopefully, it is rare, if ever. As you will see with one of the timing techniques discussed in Chapter 10, called the *Value Line 4 percent strategy*, such an unlucky streak did occur in the year 2000. Overall, market timing will minimize your loss of principal in bear markets. This is where market timing shines, and this is why you must realize that your strategy overall will beat or equal buy-and-hold with less risk.

- *Quick decision maker.* You must execute the timing signals quickly when they are triggered. This means that you need to act on every buy-and-sell signal with your investment vehicle the day the signal is given. At the very latest, you need to act by the next day if you cannot watch the market and anticipate the signal when it is close to triggering. If you question every signal for emotional reasons or because of extraneous outside influences (e.g., CNBC commentary, Fed meeting announcement, or unemployment report release), then you will not achieve satisfactory returns. If you rationalize your decision not to honor your signals or say that this time will be different, then you have compromised your timing system, and it won't work for you.

- *Emotionally stable.* If you are bothered by little things, are emotional about everything, hate to be wrong, and waver in dealings with people, then market timing will not suit your personality. A calm, self-controlled, emotionally stable personality is what you need to succeed. You cannot let your emotions enter the investing equation; otherwise, you will negate the benefit of using nonemotional, mechanical timing methods.

# SIX KEY FACTS ABOUT MARKET TIMING

You should understand the following facts about market timing.

## Market Timing Has Nothing to Do with Forecasting the Market's Future Direction

Samuel Goldwyn once said, "Never make forecasts, especially about the future." What you are trying to accomplish with market timing is to equal or exceed the buy-and-hold strategy's returns with much less risk while protecting your principal from erosion above all else. Just because you received a market timing buy or sell signal does not mean that the market will continue in that direction for an extended period of time. Nor does it mean that the signal will be successful all the time. Market timing has to do with putting the odds in your favor over multiple bull and bear market cycles. Overall, you will have satisfactory or better results without having to guess where the market is going. Your signals will tell you when to buy and when to sell. That's all you need to know. Don't listen to investment gurus, the vast majority of whom have been completely wrong in their calls on the market. Consider a *Barron's* article about stock market forecasting. Ten well-known market strategists from leading firms were interviewed by *Barron's* and were asked for their market predictions for the upcoming year. Nine of the 10 predicted a rising market and were proved wrong. And only one predicted a drop, but he was off by 75 points on the S&P 500. He predicted a close of 950 on the S&P 500, but it actually closed at 875.[2]

---

[2] Jacqueline Doherty, "How Now, Dow?" *Barron's*, December 30, 2002, p. 17.

## Market Timing Assumes that Stock Prices Are Not Random and that the Stock Market Is Not Efficient

These anomalies allow market-timers to take advantage of trends in the market. Of course, academicians have written extensively about the random nature of stock prices and the efficient-market hypothesis. In the practical world of professional investment management, however, academic theories are just that—academic theories that cannot usually be substantiated by what goes on in actual practice.

## Market Timing Should Be a Mechanical, Emotionless, and Boring Approach to Investing

Once you've decided to use a specific strategy that fits your personality, take *all* the signals, and monitor your performance. Once a signal is given, take it, and then get ready for the next one. If the last trade was a loss, so be it. Cut your losses short, and let your profits run. Small losses are good. But large losses are the killers. Ask anyone who stood pat with their investments from late 2007 to March 2009 how they would rate their investment skills. The answers would not be printable!

Unfortunately, most investors don't know when to sell, don't cut their losses short, and don't use a target price. An investor needs to set a fixed exit price (e.g., a fixed percent, such as 10 percent below his or her purchase price) to limit losses, and he or she needs to honor that exit price impeccably in the same way he or she honors his or her father and mother. Investors who don't use stop-loss or stop-limit orders to limit their losses and investors who are more worried about paying taxes on their gains than protecting their principal are asking for trouble, and sooner rather than later, they will find it. These shortcomings are mostly psychological in nature because taking a loss is basically admitting to yourself that your judgment was wrong and that you failed as an investor. Another common problem is that everyone is looking to get back to breakeven after a loss. If you bought Lucent at 70 and you still held onto it when it dropped by 99 percent, then you have emotional problems that you have to overcome. No market timing strategy is going to help you unless you rid yourself of your psychological baggage.

## With Market Timing, You Will Underperform in a Sustained Bull Market

This outcome is to be expected because there may be periodic sell signals in an uptrending market to take profits because the market is overbought. By using market timing, though, you will hit the gravy train in bear markets. Examples of the performance of actual market-timers are provided in Chapter 12, which shows that the majority exceeded buy-and-hold in the latest bear market.

## Market Timing Provides the Buy and Sell Signals to Tell You When to Go Long and When to Go Short on the Market

You should understand that going short the market is the exact opposite of going long. Either strategy has the same risk as long as you have the same tight exit rules for each one. With the availability of long and short (inverse) mutual funds such as the Rydex SGI funds family and ProFunds, as well as their ETF counterparts, you can easily go long or short the market without the need for margin. This is certainly a very useful alternative in self-directed retirement accounts.

## Market Timing Is Not Magic, Is Not 100 Percent Accurate, and Is Not for Everyone

The market timing strategies that will be presented in later chapters have all worked in the past, some better than others. They are all based on simple strategies, not complicated mathematical equations with numerous variables. Hopefully, they will continue to work in the future, but there is no guarantee that they will. Be aware that a strategy may be profitable less than 50 percent of the time and still be profitable overall. Market timing requires the critical characteristics mentioned earlier. Many individual investors do not possess them and therefore should not be self-directed market-timers. For those individuals, a market timing newsletter or timing service may be more appropriate.

## Market-Timers Have Succeeded
## in Beating Buy-and-Hold

There are market-timers and market timing advisors who have beaten buy-and-hold on a risk-adjusted basis for the last 10-year period and during subperiods within it, as Chapter 12 details. In that chapter there is documentation from the *Hulbert Financial Digest*, TimerTrac, and *Timer Digest* on timers who have beaten their benchmark. Table 12-1 indicates the performance of the top timers as measured by *Timer Digest* for the last 10 years and earlier time frames. During the past ten-, eight- five-, three-, and one-year periods, all 10 "Top Timers" beat the S&P 500 benchmark. So much for the critics of market timing who say with a straight face that it does not work. They don't want to be confronted with the facts.

# BEWARE OF THOSE KNOCKING
# MARKET TIMING

I caution you not to believe anything you hear or read about investing from anyone unless the statement is proven to you with verifiable facts and figures. Keep in mind the following statement Jonathan Clements made in his book, *25 Myths You've Got to Avoid If You Want to Manage Your Money Right: The New Rules for Financial Success* (Simon & Schuster, 1999):

> *Nobody on Wall Street has a monopoly on truth. Market strategists don't. Money managers and investment newsletter writers don't. Brokers, financial planners and insurance agents don't. Newspaper columnists don't. So treat all financial advice with caution. Look at every investment and every investment strategy with profound skepticism. Think long and hard about every financial myth. If you do that, you will do just fine.*

Financial con artists like Bernard Madoff have been known to misrepresent the true statistics on their performance records. The *Hulbert Financial Digest* provides the annualized return of many investment newsletters, as well as their buy and sell dates and total risk-adjusted performance. Many advertisements you see on television, on the Internet, or in print embellish or distort the truth in a dishonest attempt to gain your business. Don't trust anyone without first checking the claims and promises against the actual performance, their references, and the Better Business Bureau.

## MERRILL LYNCH CONSIDERS MARKET TIMING USELESS

Consider the full-page advertisement in the November 10, 1998, issue of the *Wall Street Journal* sponsored by Merrill Lynch. Here is the headline, which takes up one-third of the page: "Timing Is Nothing."
The ad goes on to say:

> *For as long as there have been markets, investors have tried to time them—to predict the precise moment when a down market turns upward or the legs give out on a bull. Sometimes it's hubris, sometimes it's fear: watching their investments fall, even seasoned investors can lose faith in the markets and, in a moment of panic, sell.*

I'll leave it up to you to decide if Merrill Lynch did well by its individual investors since this ad was printed. I think the company missed the point that timing *is* everything, especially with regard to investments.

## CONCLUSION

Market timing has long been a controversial subject, with strong views expressed on both sides of the argument. After the severe beating buy-and-hold investors have encountered in the past decade, I believe that there will be more and more individuals, financial advisors, stock brokers, and institutions using market timing because it reduces risk, protects principal, and *is* a conservative strategy. In contrast, even with diversification, buy-and-hold is a high-risk strategy, as many investors unfortunately have discovered.

## CHAPTER 4

# Determining the Market's Trend

*Spend at least as much time researching a stock as you would choosing a refrigerator.*

—Peter Lynch

*I measure what's going on, and I adapt to it. I try to get my ego out of the way. The market is smarter than I am, so I bend.*

—Martin Zweig

**W**ouldn't it be great to be able to discern a change in the market's trend and make money off of it? And wouldn't you like to be able to accomplish this feat yourself without having to rely on the advice of gurus, advisors, newsletters, or "talking heads" on Wall Street? Well, believe it or not, you can determine when a change in direction is taking place if you know what to look for and where to look. The market signals its intention to those who know how to read its vital signs.

This chapter will help you to become a skillful trend follower. Whether or not you plan to use the specific timing strategies that will be provided in later chapters, this chapter will provide guidance in determining the market's existing and changing trend so that you can make smarter investment decisions with your regular and retirement accounts. This ability will be very useful information no matter which investment vehicles you are investing in—stocks, equity mutual funds, or equity exchange-traded funds (ETFs). Remember that about 70 percent of the price changes of those investments depend on the market's direction. So knowing, watching, and obeying the trend ultimately will lead to more profitable investments with less risk than guessing whether the market will advance or decline.

To determine the market's current trend, you need to analyze specific market internals using charts with specific indicators. I suggest that you pick up a basic book on charting, such as John Murphy's *Visual Investor* or others listed in the Bibliography and get a handle on the basics when you have time. There are a number of technical indicators that have proven useful over a long time horizon in their ability to discern the current trend. There are hundreds of stock market indicators and methods that can be used to monitor the stock market. However, the vast majority of them either fail to provide the information that we are looking for, they duplicate the information from other indicators, or they do not have a high degree of historical reliability. I have selected four well-known, free and easy-to-use indicators that I've been using for decades that provide reliable market signals.

## WHAT THE INDICATORS NEED TO SHOW

Our objective is, first, to determine whether the market is in a major trend (an uptrend with increasing prices or a downtrend with decreasing prices) or in a *trading range*, where the price is essentially going nowhere. In a trading range, technicians call the lower price level *support* and the upper price level *resistance*. Prices will tend to bounce off support, hit the resistance level, and then bounce down to support again. However, once resistance is broken to the upside by increasing prices or support is broken to the downside, the new trend will be established, assuming that it is not a *false breakout*. We will use two moving averages to assess the intermediate- and long-term market trend.

Second, we want to know whether the market is in an extremely overbought or oversold condition. An *overbought* market is one in which the market indices are at a relatively high price level, where individual investors and market professionals are exuberantly bullish and some technical indicators are in over-bought territory. This condition can go on for an extended period of time, as indicated by the market's huge run-up into March 2000 and into December 2010. On the other hand, when the market is *oversold*, it is at a relatively low price level and individual investors and market professionals are excessively bearish; for example, this was the case in October 2002, March 2003, October 2008, and March 2009. This condition also can go on for some time before a change in trend occurs. It is critical that you invest with the major trend and not against it. This is why you have to stay alert to an impending change in the market's over-bought/oversold condition.

No one can accurately forecast when the market will change direction, but you can be on the lookout for *extreme* readings on certain indicators because when such a reading occurs, the market usually reverses direction. If we, as investors, can take advantage of such a situation, then we are well on our way to investing profitably. This is what this chapter is all about—taking the pulse of the market. Either an overbought or oversold condition can be turned to your advantage if you put yourself on the right side of the market's new direction.

First, I will focus on simple moving-average indicators to show you how to detect the overall market trend. Second, I will cover the New York Stock Exchange (NYSE) bullish percentage to show you how to measure the market's overbought or oversold condition. And third, I will cover the percentage of stocks above their 200-day moving average (200-dma) to allow you to detect the strength of the trend. I will not be covering the use of basic trend lines and support and resistance, which you can learn easily by going to the "Chart School" on www.stockcharts.com or reading a basic charting book. These two basic tools should be drawn on all charts as an added visual aid.

These market indicators normally should be checked weekly. However, during periods of market extremes and high volatility (e.g., October 2002, September 2008, and March 2009), they should be checked daily so that you can ascertain a better entry/exit point for your investments.

# INTERNAL MARKET INDICATORS

*Be fearful when others are greedy and greedy only when others are fearful.*

—Warren Buffett

The key to profitable investing is to be on the right side of the market. This is when market timing strategies excel. Too many investors do not pay attention to what the market is saying. Instead, they prefer to read financial and investment magazines, newspapers, and newsletters and watch financial shows that transmit the market hype instead of the objective facts they need. These spin stories are misleading because all the information they impart is just "noise." It has no value to the average person in terms of what he or she needs to know to be a more informed investor.

Instead, every investor should use a more systematic analytical approach and learn to understand what the market itself is telling him or her to determine if it is time to buy or sell. This goal can be accomplished easily by "putting your ear to the ground" and "listening carefully" to what the market is telling you. The market speaks loudly and clearly, not softly and surreptitiously. After reading about the market indicators in this chapter, you will come away with solid information to judge whether the market trend is changing. This information alone is very useful in making your investment decisions.

No one indicator should be used alone to make your buy and sell decisions. They should be used as a group. When you find that a majority of the indicators line up in a bullish or bearish direction, then that is the time to carefully consider making your move. Remember that an extreme reading on an indicator (except the moving average, which has no extreme points) first must reverse direction before you invest your money.

## Indicators 1 and 2: 200-Day and 50-Day Simple Moving Averages

Moving averages are one of the most well-known and time-tested tools used by investors and professionals to determine the market's overall long-term trend. This tool shows you where you've been; thus it is a lagging indicator, but it is still a very useful one. Market technicians use various moving averages, but the ones used most often to determine the market's intermediate- to long-term trend, respectively, are the 50- and 200-day moving averages (50-dma and 200-dma).

Figure 4-1 shows a 200-dma (the line that begins in February 2009 at that top left of the chart) and a 50-dma (the lower line that is tighter to the index line) on the Standard & Poor's (S&P) 500 Index from November 2008 through October 20, 2010. In simple terms, the 200-dma depicts the average price of that index over the last 200 days. This moving average is plotted as a line on the daily price chart of the index in this example. Each day, the last 200 days of prices are added together and divided by 200 to calculate today's moving-average price point. In our example, the last price for the 200-dma is 1181.73 compared with the last closing index price of 1181.23, so this means that the trend is positive because the price of the index is above the moving-average line. The moving average smoothes out the daily prices, so the trend is easily discernible.

How is the moving average used? Looking at Figure 4-1, if the price of the S&P 500 Index is above its 200-dma, then the market is considered in an uptrend. This was the case from August 2009 through May 2010. As you can see, there were a number of

## FIGURE 4-1

S&P 500 with 50- and 200-day simple moving averages.

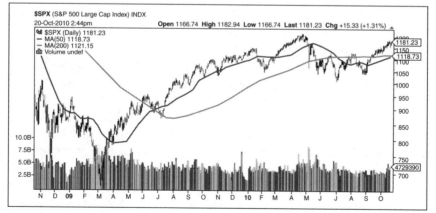

Source: Courtesy of StockCharts.com.

crossovers of the index and the moving-average line in June, July, August, and September because the index was in a trading range.

If the S&P 500 Index price is below the 200-dma, and if the moving-average line is slanting downward, then that is a declining trend, as was the case from December 2007 (not on chart) through late May 2009—a downtrend lasting 18 months. Being out of the stock market during that frightful period saved astute investors a great deal of financial and emotional pain because the market dropped 50 percent from top to bottom. There are rare occasions when the index price fluctuates by as much as 20 to 30 percent above or below the 200-dma. Consider that level to be an extreme reading, and look for the index to most likely reverse its direction because such a strong trend is never sustainable.

The faster-moving 50-dma provides a quicker way of gauging the market's direction than the 200-dma because it provides earlier signals as to the market's direction on both the buy and sell sides. Figure 4-1 also includes the 50-dma, which is the line directly underneath the index beginning in late March 2009. There are more crossovers of the index with the 50-dma, as you will notice, between December 2008 and February 2009, as well as in July through September 2010. You will note that the 50-dma had a crossover in middle to late March 2009 for a buy signal compared with the 200-dma crossover that occurred much later in early July. You would have about 10 percent more money in your pocket had you acted on this earlier signal.

Intelligent investors should not necessarily wait for any of the market averages (such as that of the DJIA, the S&P 500, or the Nasdaq Composite Index) to penetrate its 200-dma on the downside before deciding to sell their investments or make new purchases. Such an approach can be financially ruinous because by the time the moving average gets penetrated to the downside, for example, the portfolio already could be down 10 to 20 percent from the highs, especially if high-flying issues are held in the portfolio.

Price penetration of the moving averages in either direction should not by itself warrant a buy or sell decision on your investments. Rather, it needs to be used in conjunction with the other indicators mentioned in this chapter to obtain a consensus reading on the market. You will find a profitable moving-average strategy in Chapter 9.

## Indicator 3: New York Stock Exchange Bullish Percentage

*Investor's Intelligence,* a well-known and long-standing newsletter, developed a unique market sentiment indicator called the *NYSE Bullish Percentage* ($BPNYA symbol on StockCharts.com) in the 1950s. The firm uses point-and-figure charts instead of the more traditional bar charts to track the $BPNYA percentage changes. Point-and-figure charts are used by the firm to monitor individual stocks, mutual funds, sectors, industries, and ETFs. In addition, the charts are also used to measure a stock's relative strength and other market measurements. A simple point-and-figure chart is provided in Figure 4-2. A point-and-figure chart is composed of columns of X's and O's corresponding to increasing and decreasing prices, respectively. Neither a security's daily volume nor its daily prices are shown on the chart. You can find more information about these unique charts from the Web sites and books listed in the Bibliography.

The $BPNYA measures the percentage of NYSE stocks that have bullish point-and-figure chart patterns. This is comparable with looking at regular bar charts that have just formed bullish patterns (e.g., breaking through double and triple tops). Figure 4-2 contains over seven years of data from January 2003 through October 20, 2010. The numbers in the chart represent the months of the year in each year's data (October through December are represented by the letters A, B, and C, respectively). As you can see, low-percentage $BPNYA readings below 30 that then turned up into a column of X's turned out to be excellent times to get into the market. The high-percentage readings of 70 or over were excellent times to get out of the market, after they'd turned down into a column of O's from 70. The lowest readings occurred in October 2008 at an unbelievable reading of 4 percent. Interestingly, at the bear market low of March 2009, the $BPNYA reading was higher at 14 percent.

Conversely, the high readings of the bullish percentage occurred in January 2004, April 2007, May 2009, September 2009, and April 2010, all at relative market highs. Remember to wait for extreme $BPNYA readings to reverse direction before investing, as well as waiting for a consensus from the other indicators in this chapter.

**FIGURE 4-2**

NYSE Bullish Percent Index.

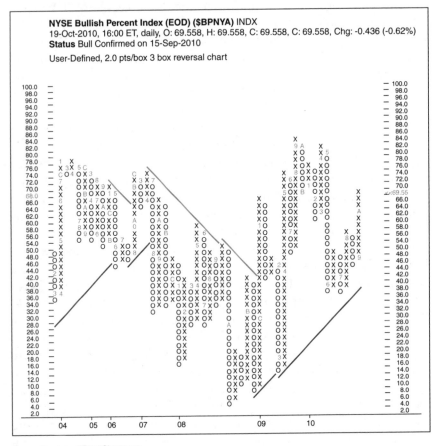

*Source:* Courtesy of StockCharts.com.

## Indicator 4: Percentage of Stocks above Their 200-dma ($NYA200R)

Figure 4-3 is a chart from StockCharts.com of the NYSE Composite Index on the upper graph and the percentage of those stocks above their 200-dma on the larger lower graph. As we know from our prior discussion, the 200-dma is a long-term moving average, and stocks tend to stay above or below it for extended periods during bull or bear runs. When the market is in a strong rally mode, it is

## FIGURE 4-3

NYSE percent of stocks above their 200-dma.

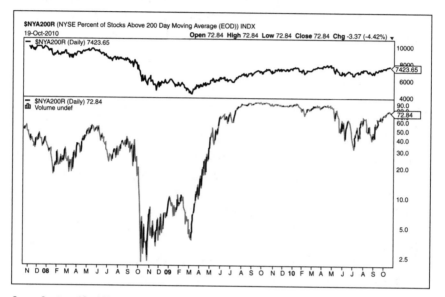

*Source:* Courtesy of StockCharts.com.

common to find that an increasing percentage or more of all stocks on the NYSE trade above their own 200-dma. An unusual and rare situation occurred from July 2009 through early May 2010, when the market was in a strong uptrend. During that entire 11-month period, the percent of stocks above their 200-dma stayed well above 75 percent or higher as the market kept rising. Only in May did the market begin to drop, and it finally bottomed at 32 percent in early July 2010. When the $NYA200R begins to turn down from its peak and *drops below 70 percent*, that is usually a potential market top and is considered a sell signal on this indicator.

Likewise, when the stock market bottoms or becomes very oversold, you will find that only about 20 percent or fewer of all stocks are trading above their 200-dma. This situation occurred in mid-January 2008, twice in March 2008, and in early October 2008. Astoundingly, from September 2008 through late April 2009, the $NYA200R stayed below 20 percent, bottoming at 1.5 percent in October 2008 and 3.75 percent in March 2009, levels not seen before on this indicator. In comparison, at the market bottom on October 9, 2002, only about 20 percent of stocks were trading above their 200-dma. Therefore, when the $NYA200R reaches 20 percent or lower and then advances above 20 percent in the opposite direction, that is typically a buy signal on this indicator.

## CONCLUSION

By tracking the four market indicators covered in this chapter, you will be able to determine the market's trend and be able to observe an impending trend change. It is only when three out of four indicators have a signal in the same direction that you can assume with a high probability that a trend change is occurring. Therefore, it is important to view all the indicators (daily data are used) weekly and especially daily during potential turning points based on how close the index is piercing its two moving averages (200-dma and 50-dma) and the extreme readings on the other two indicators. If you want to go long the market or short the market with a basket of stocks, mutual funds, or ETFs, make sure that the trend has been confirmed; otherwise, you are risking losses if you try to go against the trend. Never fight the trend, or you may not have any principal left to invest in the future. Do not assume that you are smarter than the market because you nor anyone else has ever been that lucky.

Table 4-1 is a summary of the four indicators with their key buy and sell readings. By reviewing all the indicator readings, you will ascertain the market's trend. When three or four indicators are positive, that would indicate a buy signal. When three or more indicators are negative, that would indicate a sell signal. Any readings less than three in either direction are ignored. Keep in mind that this is just an example of how to view the indicators and not an exact science. You may personally want to weight the indicators differently than I have done and come up with your own scoring system. Remember that being on the right side of a trending market and minimizing your risk are both critical elements in building wealth.

Make sure that once the indicators change to a market buy signal that you make your investment, and remember to place stop-limit orders in the range of 7 to 10 percent, for example, to protect your principal from a market reversal. Once the price starts

## TABLE 4-1

Market Trend Indicators

| Indicator Name | Ticker Symbol | Key Levels | Trend Up or Down |
|---|---|---|---|
| 200-dma on S&P 500 Index | $SPX on StockCharts.com | Price crossover above or below moving average | *Up*—when index crosses from below<br>*Down*—when index crosses from above |
| 50-dma on S&P 500 Index | $SPX on StockCharts.com | Price crossover above or below moving average | *Up*—when index crosses from below<br>*Down*—when index crosses from above |
| NYSE Bullish Percentage | $BPNYA on StockCharts.com | <30 and turns up above 30 to column of X's<br>>70 and turns down below 70 to column of O's | *Up*<br><br><br>*Down* |
| Percent of stocks above their 200-dma | $NYA200R on StockCharts.com | <20 and turns up above 20<br>>70 and turns down below 70 | *Up*<br><br>*Down* |

advancing, you should consider using trailing stop-limit orders for the same reason. The first indication of a market that may be changing direction is if the S&P 500 Index falls below its 50-dma, so be aware of such an occurrence, and be ready to take the necessary action if two other indicators also deteriorate. The penetration of the 200-dma will take a longer time to occur.

## CHAPTER 5

# No-Load Mutual Funds: Index, Sector, and Leveraged Funds

*Warren Buffett says that indexing is the best approach to the stock market for 99 percent of all investors.*

—Lewis Schiff and Douglas Gerlach,
*The Armchair Millionaire*, 2001, p. 125.

**S**uccessfully picking stocks that consistently make money is not easy. The odds are heavily stacked against the average investor. One major difficulty is determining exactly what stocks to buy, but more important is when to buy and when to sell them. Moreover, if your stock portfolio is not diversified because you decided to load up stocks from one industry, then you are exposing yourself to more risk than perhaps you intended to take.

Bad news about your stock, its industry group, or even a competitor's stock can result in large down moves that can decimate the stock's price by 25 to 50 percent almost overnight. To avoid potential losses that can occur at any time for any reason, the astute investor will steer clear of individual securities entirely. Simply put, the risks are too high with respect to the rewards. If the majority of professional money managers with impeccable financial credentials and vast experience cannot consistently select a stock portfolio that does better than a comparable benchmark index, then how do you expect to do it? Consider the fact that only 31 percent of actively managed large-cap mutual funds beat their benchmark over the 15-year period ending June 2009.[1]

Instead of investing in individual stocks, consider investing in a few no-load mutual funds such as index, sector, and leveraged funds. These represent a wide range of investment choices. Make sure that you understand the components, details, and costs of each of these investment vehicles before deciding to invest. And make sure that you take into account your risk tolerance. This chapter covers the key features and choices available for index, sector, and leveraged funds, whereas Chapter 6 covers the popular and ever-growing exchange-traded funds (ETFs). If you decide on one of the market timing strategies provided in Chapters 7 through 11, then your best choice, from a risk-reward standpoint, is to select investment vehicles covered in this chapter and Chapter 6 rather than individual stocks.

## INDEX FUNDS

An *index fund* is a unique type of mutual fund that holds stocks that exactly mirror the makeup of an existing stock market index. The index fund's performance will replicate the performance of the index it is mimicking minus the fund's internal operating expenses. In 1971, Wells Fargo Investment Advisors marketed the first index fund to institutional investors. In 1976, John C. Bogle, founder of the Vanguard Group, marketed the Vanguard Index 500 Trust to retail investors. This index replicates the Standard & Poor's (S&P) 500 Index. Almost 40 percent of mutual-fund assets, as of year end 2009, were invested in S&P 500 Index funds. The total assets in index funds at year end 2009 were $837 billion in 359 index funds. Also, 27 percent of households own at least one index fund.[2] A sampling of the least expensive S&P 500 Index funds, as measured by the annual expense ratio, is provided in Table 5-1.

Equity index funds represent 13.7 percent of all mutual-fund assets. In 2009, of all equity fund inflows, almost 60 percent of new

---

[1] "Good News About Index Funds," *Kiplinger's Personal Finance*, September 2009, p. 37.

[2] *2010 Investment Company Fact Book*, 5th ed. New York: Investment Company Institute, 2010, p. 33.

## TABLE 5-1

S&P 500 Index Funds: Least Expensive

| Fund Name | Ticker | Annual Expense Ratio (%) | Fund Minimum |
|---|---|---|---|
| Schwab S&P 500 Index | SWPPX | 0.09 | $100 |
| Fidelity Spartan 500 Index | FUSEX | 0.10 | $10,000 |
| Columbia Large Cap Index Fund | NEIAX | 0.14 | $2,500 |
| E*TRADE S&P 500 Index Fund | ETSPX | 0.16 | $5,000 |
| Vanguard 500 Index Fund | VFINX | 0.18 | $3,000 |
| SSgA S&P 500 Index | SVSPX | 0.18 | $10,000 |
| DFA U.S. Large Company | DFUSX | 0.10 | $0 |
| Vantagepoint 500 Stock Index II | VPSKX | 0.26 | $0 |
| DWS Equity 500 Index Fund | BTIEX | 0.32 | $2,500 |
| T. Rowe Price Equity Index 500 | PREIX | 0.35 | $2,500 |

investor money, went into index funds. Index funds slightly under-perform the index they are replicating because, unlike the index itself, the funds incur operating and administration costs that slightly reduce their performance.

Fidelity Spartan 500 Index (FUSEX) holds stock in the same proportion as the S&P 500 Index. If the S&P 500 moves up or down 15 percent, this Fidelity fund will move in lockstep with it and go up or down close to 15 percent. For example, for the year 2009, FUSEX increased by 23.61 percent compared with the S&P 500's rise of 23.45 percent, the 0.15 percentage point difference being the result of inter-nal operating expenses (0.10 percent) and administrative fees.

Index funds are available from many mutual-fund families. They cover major indexes such as the Wilshire 5000, Russell 2000, Morgan Stanley Capital International (MSCI), Europe, Australasia, Far East (EAFE), and 10-year bonds. Index funds are managed pas-sively, and portfolio changes are rare. As a result, administrative and internal costs are minimal.

Compare this situation with that of standard equity mutual funds that are actively managed. They have annual operating expenses ranging between 1.19 and 1.97 percent and an average annual portfolio turnover of between 60 percent (e.g., conservative allocation funds) and over 100 percent (e.g., aggressive funds)

depending on the fund type. The average balanced domestic mutual fund has portfolio turnover averaging 62 percent per year, with a
1.25 percent annual expense ratio (AER), according to Morningstar.[3]
All this trading eats into the performance of such funds because
trading fees mount up. Interestingly, trading costs are not included
in the annual expense ratio numbers. Investors would like to see
these trading costs embedded in the AER to show the full cost, but
such a change will need approval by the mutual funds themselves
and initiative from regulators.

## Key Factors in Selecting an Index Fund

When investing in an index fund, make sure you obtain the following information:

- *Minimum initial investment amount.* Some funds have
  minimums of $1,000, whereas others may require $5,000,
  $10,000, or even higher amounts.
- *Annual expense ratio.* A ratio below 0.20 percent is desirable.
  A number of funds have a ratio below 0.10 percent. Sector
  funds have an average expense ratio of about 1.60 percent.
  This means that 1.60 percent of your investment is going
  toward paying the fund's overhead each year, in addition
  to any load or commissions you pay on purchasing or
  exiting the fund. The lower the ratio, the better.
- *Trading deadline.* Each fund family has a specific deadline
  for making an exchange or a trade the same day. Typically,
  the time ranges between 3:30 and 3:59 p.m. to get today's
  closing price. Calling and placing your order after 4 p.m.
  will result in getting the next day's closing price.

The later in the day the trade deadline, the better, because you
have more time to make the decision. Trades can be made online
through the fund's Web site if you bought the fund directly,
through your brokerage account if bought through that venue, or
via a phone call. Keep in mind that mutual funds do not trade during the day like ETFs, so the price you receive is the closing price,
even if you want to sell the fund at 1 p.m. that day. This is one of

---

[3] *Morningstar Mutual Funds*, September 19, 2010, p. S12.

the negatives of owning mutual funds compared with ETFs, which trade throughout the day.

- *Maximum number of trades permitted over a 12-month period.* Most funds are very stringent about the number of trades permitted, and almost all fund families do not cater to market-timers. Make sure that you can make at least four transactions a year at a minimum. The optimal situation is being permitted to have unlimited trades with no restriction during a 30-day period. The more trades allowable, the better.
- *Redemption fees.* Some funds levy charges of approximately 0.5 to 1 percent if a fund is redeemed within 30 to 180 days of purchase. Each fund has its own policy. Try to select a fund that does not have these fees.

If you subscribe to Morningstar online (www.morning star.com) or its *Morningstar Mutual Funds* publication (available in most libraries), you can check out and compare all index funds at once instead of going to each Web site or receiving the material in the mail. Another comprehensive resource is www.indexfunds.com.

## Market Timing with Index Funds

You can invest in any index fund when using market timing to make buy and sell decisions. For example, if you are interested in investing in large-cap stocks or the market as a whole, you can select an index fund that tracks the S&P 500 or the Wilshire 5000 (total stock market).

Of course, if you prefer to invest in other market indexes, such as a small-cap or value fund index, that's easy to do too. To spread your risk, you may want to select a few different index-style funds (e.g., large-, mid-, or small-cap growth; large-, mid-, or small-cap value; or international funds) with different weightings (e.g., 60 percent in small-cap growth fund, 20 percent in international, and 20 percent in large-cap value). This approach is similar to building a diversified stock portfolio, except that in the case of index funds there could be thousands of stocks represented in the index.

Morningstar offers a tool called *Instant X-Ray* to provide the total portfolio composition of an investor's mutual fund holdings.

The objective is to minimize overlapping positions of multiple funds and to provide the necessary diversification. All you have to do is key enter the ticker symbols of your funds, and the program provides the analysis.

There are two mutual fund families that cater directly to traders and market-timers: Rydex SGI funds and ProFunds. Their annual expense ratios and minimum investments are typically higher than those of other mutual-fund families for index funds, but they provide a wide selection of sector, index, and leveraged funds without restrictions or penalties for frequent trading. More detailed information about these funds is provided in the upcoming sections, and their respective Web sites contain comprehensive fund information.

You can use the technical indicators covered in Chapter 4 to obtain a consensus reading on the market and obtain a chart of the index funds to see if the trend is positive. If all the key factors are in place, then you can go long the market in a no-load fund of your choice.

## SECTOR FUNDS

Only a few mutual-fund families offer sector funds. As the name implies, *sector funds* purchase stocks in a particular industry sector. Typical sectors include technology, biotech, consumer cyclicals, financial services, precious metals, real estate, natural resources, and medical equipment. Sector funds replace the need to purchase a group of individual stocks in a particular industry, which thereby avoids multiple brokerage commissions. Having a large number of stocks in a sector fund portfolio offers some degree of diversification. However, if the entire sector is having financial difficulties or is out of favor, then its performance will suffer. Investing in a sector fund is much riskier than investing in a broad index fund; therefore, you need to have specific defensive rules in place to exit the fund if it declines.

Typically, sector funds have higher volatility and portfolio turnover and usually higher returns and losses than a diversified stock fund because of their highly focused stock selection. Only more experienced and venturesome investors with a higher risk tolerance should use these funds. Make sure to have mental stop-loss orders to protect your principal because placing automatic stops on mutual funds is not possible. Keep in mind that some industry sector funds usually excel in bear markets, such as natural resources, and precious metals. Thus, depending on the market's trend, the right sectors need to be chosen; otherwise, large losses may result. Interestingly, in 2002 and 2008, not one of the 10 S&P sector categories had positive returns. This is a rare occurrence, but it can and has happened.

Fidelity is the pioneer in sector fund offerings, and it has named its funds *Fidelity Select Portfolios*. The company's first few sector funds came out in July 1981, with additional funds being launched in the mid-1980s and a few more added in the last few years. Currently, there are 41 sector funds, including one sector money-market fund. This large selection makes Fidelity the largest sector fund player in the mutual-fund industry.

Fidelity Select Portfolios have no load and a minimum $2,500 investment for regular accounts and $500 for SEP-IRAs or Keoghs. There is also a 0.75 percent redemption fee when a fund is sold within 30 days of purchase. Fidelity does not encourage market timing, and it will restrict your trading if you exceed a certain number of trades in a given time period.

According to the Fidelity Prospectus:

*Shareholders with two or more roundtrip transactions in a single fund within a rolling 90-day period will be blocked from making additional purchases or exchange purchases of each fund for 85 days. Shareholders with four or more roundtrip transactions across all Fidelity funds within any rolling 12-month period will be blocked for at least 85 days from additional purchases or exchange purchases across all Fidelity funds. Any roundtrip within 12 months of the expiration of a multifund block will initiate another multifund block. Repeat offenders may be subject to long-term or permanent blocks on purchase or exchange purchase transactions in any account under the shareholder's control at any time.*

Complete information about the Select Portfolios is available at www.fidelity.com or by calling Fidelity at 800-343-3548. Other mutual-funds families that offer sector funds include Vanguard (www.vanguard.com), Rydex-SGI (www.Rydex-sgi.com; 17 sectors), and ProFunds (www.profunds.com; 23 leveraged and inverse sector funds). Check their Web sites for the latest statistics and fund information.

## Market Timing with Sector Funds

Sector funds offer the experienced and aggressive investor a way to capture significant profits, but only when these funds are purchased and sold at the right time. Timing is extremely critical with these funds; otherwise, you could suffer losses from which you might take years to recover. Bad earnings or a killer bear market can decimate any sector fund, even if it contains so-called high-quality stocks. In bear markets, most sectors get hit hard, except for the precious metals sector, which usually excels, but not always. Thus sector funds should be used only with specific buy-and-sell rules and market timing strategies to protect your principal. After reviewing the timing strategies presented in Chapters 7 through 11, you can select one that you feel will work with a group sector.

# LEVERAGED FUNDS

*Leveraged* mutual funds amplify the performance of the indexes they track. Prior to the inception of the Rydex Funds in 1993, an investor had no way of obtaining leverage on mutual-fund investments without resorting to margin (if offered on mutual funds by the brokerage firm). And margin interest would be accruing every day, eating into any gains. Retail investors, traders, and market-timers therefore were delighted when Rydex offered leveraged funds without margin. Rydex currently offers 81 funds in different categories, as well as many leveraged and unleveraged funds. Table 5-2 provides a snapshot of just Rydex's leveraged/inverse broad market equity funds. Rydex also offers four leveraged/ inverse fixed-income funds and leveraged inverse international funds.

## Rydex Funds: First Inverse and Leveraged Funds

Leveraged funds provide magnified returns that are between 25 and 200 percent greater than those of nonleveraged funds. These funds have betas between 1.25 and 2.00. This means that the risk rises as well. For bullish investors who want leverage, the Rydex Nova fund tracks the S&P 500 Index with a beta of 1.5. Thus every 1 percentage point move in the S&P is equivalent to a 1.5 percentage point move in Nova. If the S&P 500 rises 10 percent, then Nova theoretically would rise 15 percent. I use the word *theoretically* because the percentage may not be exactly 15 percent, although it should be very close to it. That is so because there could be a *tracking error*, which is the difference between the price behavior of the leveraged fund and the price behavior of the index.

If the S&P falls instead of rises, this fund will lose money 1.5 times as fast. Thus timing the purchase and sale of these funds is critical to capital preservation. Nova's annual expense ratio is 1.28 percent, and the minimum investment to open an account for a self-directed investor or for a retirement account is $25,000.

## TABLE 5-2

Target Beta—Leverage/Inverse—Domestic Equity/Broad Market A Class

| Product | Ticker | Total Assets ($Mil) |
|---|---|---|
| Dow 2× Strategy | RYLDX | 3.38 |
| Inverse Dow 2× Strategy | RYIDX | 1.81 |
| Inverse Mid-Cap Strategy | RYAGX | 0.38 |
| Inverse Nasdaq-100 2× Strategy | RYVTX | 1.41 |
| Inverse Nasdaq-100 Strategy | RYAPX | 0.98 |
| Inverse Russell 2000 2× Strategy | RYIUX | 1.91 |
| Inverse Russell 2000 Strategy | RYAFX | 1.84 |
| Inverse S&P 500 2× Strategy | RYTMX | 8.84 |
| Inverse S&P 500 Strategy | RYARX | 10.64 |
| Mid-Cap 1.5× Strategy | RYAHX | 0.78 |
| Nasdaq-100 | RYATX | 11.02 |
| Nasdaq-100 2× Strategy | RYVLX | 7.65 |
| Nova | RYANX | 3.82 |
| Russell 2000 | RYRRX | 1.28 |
| Russell 2000 1.5× Strategy | RYAKX | 2.50 |
| Russell 2000 2× Strategy | RYRUX | 2.22 |
| S&P 500 | RYSOX | 9.21 |
| S&P 500 2× Strategy | RYTTX | 10.52 |

*Note:* Inverse and leveraged funds are not suitable for all investors. These funds should be used only by investors who (1) understand the risks associated with the use of leverage, (2) understand the consequences of seeking daily leveraged investment results, (3) understand the risk of shorting, and (4) intend to actively monitor and manage their investments.

*Source:* www.rydex-sgi.com

For bears, the Rydex Inverse S&P 2× Strategy fund tracks the inverse of the S&P 500 with a beta of 2.0. Thus every 1 percentage point drop in the S&P means a 2 percentage point rise in the fund. If the S&P 500 Index falls 10 percent, then the fund should *rise* about 20 percent. This fund's annual expense ratio is 1.43 percent. If the Inverse 2× Strategy fund is held by a financial intermediary, the minimum investment is $15,000, and if it is opened with a brokerage firm, the minimum is $2,500 for regular accounts and $1,500 for retirement accounts.

For additional information on Rydex Funds, call 800-820-0888 or access the company Web site at www.Rydex-SGI.com. Some investment firms offering access to the Rydex family include Fidelity, TD Ameritrade, Charles Schwab, Vanguard Brokerage Services, T. Rowe Price, and Scottrade, among others.

## ProFunds

ProFunds opened its doors in 1997, in direct competition with Rydex Funds. ProFunds offers 64 index-based funds, more than any other mutual-fund firm. The funds offered include:

- 11 Classic ProFunds
- 10 Ultra ProFunds
- 13 Inverse ProFunds
- 22 Sector ProFunds
- 5 Non-Equity ProFunds
- 1 Money Market ProFund
- 2 Access High Yield–Flex Funds

ProFunds' minimum initial investment for all types of accounts is $15,000 for self-directed individual investors or $5,000 for investors working through an affiliated financial professional. To provide leverage, ProFunds not only invests in securities but also may invest in futures contracts, options on futures contracts, swap agreements, options on securities and indices, U.S. government securities, repurchase agreements, or combinations of these instruments.

The performance statistics of each of the ProFunds is provided on its Web site at www.profunds.com. ProFunds can be purchased directly from the firm or through the following firms: Accutrade, TD Ameritrade, Charles Schwab, Fidelity Investments, and Scottrade. Table 5-3 provides information on ProFunds Ultra sector funds. Other data in this format can be found on the company Web site.

## Market Timing with Leveraged Funds: Be Very Careful

Initially, investors just starting out with market timing strategies should not jump into leveraged funds. Once an investor feels comfortable with his or her market timing strategy, his or her rules for cutting loses (including the use of stop-limit orders), and his or her performance against a suitable benchmark, that investor can consider leveraged funds—but only after he or she first acquires a complete understanding of leveraged funds, how they work, and their inherent risks. A novice market-timer using leverage can get destroyed in a week if the market declines, assuming mental stops are not used to get out with a small loss. Losses of 50 percent and higher can occur easily with the double-leveraged (2.0-beta) funds.

After investors have used market timing profitably for a few years, they may want to invest in leveraged funds, but they should begin with a minimal dollar amount to get real-world experience before putting more money at risk. After six months of experience, additional positions can be taken. Slow and steady wins the race with these enhanced funds. Your main concern is minimizing your losses and protecting your capital, not maximizing your profits. The profits will come if you have the proper timing model in place and if you follow your game plan.

Leveraged funds offer market-timers who get on the right side of the market a powerful vehicle for participating in both bull and bear markets. For aggressive investors who are able to control their risk, leveraged funds can lead to significant returns in short time frames. However, leveraged funds can be deadly in the wrong hands. So make sure that you are aware of all the nuances before getting involved in these rocket-propelled funds.

Since both Rydex and ProFunds offer leveraged ETFs, most investors will use them instead of their mutual-fund counterparts

## TABLE 5-3

ProFunds Ultra Sector and Inverse Sector Funds

| Investor Class | Annualized as of 9/30/2010 (%) | | | | | | | Gross expense ratio (%) | Net expense ratio with contractual waiver (%) | Inception Date |
|---|---|---|---|---|---|---|---|---|---|---|
| | YTD as of 10/18/2010 (%) | 3 mos. as of 9/30/2010 (%) | 1 year | 3 years | 5 years | 10 years | Since inception | | | |
| **Sector ProFunds—Ultra Sector** | | | | | | | | | | |
| Banks | −7.74 | 2.95 | −18.87 | −46.50 | −29.46 | | −15.09 | 1.98 | 1.68 | 9/4/2001 |
| Basic Materials | 19.48 | 31.86 | 24.60 | 13.32 | 3.29 | | 3.59 | 1.56 | | 9/4/2001 |
| Biotechnology | 6.13 | 17.1 | −3.40 | −2.88 | −1.36 | −7.15 | −6.02 | 1.60 | | 6/19/2000 |
| Consumer Goods | 16.78 | 16.60 | 18.97 | 5.06 | 1.17 | | 2.87 | 2.47 | 1.68 | 1/30/2004 |
| Consumer Services | 18.19 | 20.47 | 24.27 | 8.66 | 2.91 | | −2.01 | 3.53 | 1.68 | 6/19/2000 |
| Financials | 2.33 | 7.11 | −4.37 | −38.16 | −22.15 | −11.83 | −9.59 | 2.02 | 1.68 | 6/19/2000 |
| Health Care | 2.35 | 13.38 | 10.48 | 7.52 | 1.92 | 4.08 | 3.62 | 1.76 | 1.68 | 1/30/2004 |
| Industrials | 17.93 | 19.44 | 21.54 | 16.26 | 2.66 | | 0.04 | 2.18 | 1.68 | 1/30/2004 |
| Internet | 33.12 | 39.46 | 43.19 | 0.44 | 6.25 | 19.78 | −19.74 | 1.67 | | 6/19/2000 |
| Mobile Telecommunications | 26.90 | 22.64 | 23.81 | 50.39 | 33.70 | 31.42 | 34.32 | 1.92 | 1.68 | 6/19/2000 |
| Oil, Equip., Srv.,and Dist. | 2.79 | 27.95 | −0.89 | −28.47 | | | −13.59 | 1.54 | | 6/5/2006 |
| Oil and Gas | 3.99 | 19.34 | 0.52 | −19.72 | −3.98 | 3.91 | 4.29 | 1.50 | | 6/19/2000 |
| Pharmaceuticals | 5.29 | 16.21 | 15.92 | −5.36 | −0.09 | 7.46 | −7.29 | 2.02 | 1.68 | 6/28/2000 |
| Precious Metals | 30.97 | 14.77 | 28.16 | −6.35 | 5.24 | | 5.18 | 1.46 | | 6/3/2002 |
| Real Estate | 33.67 | 18.99 | 38.50 | −24.80 | −11.32 | 2.66 | 3.68 | 1.78 | 1.68 | 6/19/2000 |

## TABLE 5-3

ProFunds Ultra Sector and Inverse Sector Funds (continued)

| | | | | | | | | | |
|---|---|---|---|---|---|---|---|---|---|
| Semiconductor | -6.75 | 6.99 | 3.24 | -17.89 | -10.37 | -20.27 | -23.99 | 1.77 | 6/19/2000 |
| Technology | 6.71 | 17.65 | 13.95 | -8.52 | 0.37 | -15.98 | -17.79 | 1.82 | 6/19/2000 |
| Telecommunications | 12.06 | 31.27 | 21.40 | -19.19 | -0.68 | -12.56 | -15.17 | 1.84 | 6/19/2000 |
| Utilities | 9.19 | 17.73 | 15.06 | -11.49 | -2.68 | 3.18 | -0.07 | 1.62 | 7/26/2000 |
| **Sector ProFunds—Inverse Sector** | | | | | | | | | |
| Short Oil and Gas | -11.30 | -13.67 | -11.38 | -8.99 | -11.83 | | -12.38 | 1.62 | 9/12/2005 |
| Short Precious Metals | -25.88 | -11.07 | -28.71 | -30.22 | | | -25.09 | 1.55 | 1/9/2006 |
| Short Real Estate | -26.64 | -14.09 | -31.21 | -26.22 | -19.52 | | -19.07 | 1.53 | 9/12/2005 |

*Source:* www.profunds.com.

because there are no restrictions on minimum account size, they have lower annual expense ratios and they can be traded through-out the day like a stock.

## CHAPTER 6

# Exchange-Traded Funds

*Quite often, when someone says something won't work, what they really mean is, "I can't make it work!"*
—John K. Sosnowy, SAAFTI Conference, May 1996

## ETF BASICS

In the first edition of this book, which was published in late 2003, this chapter was six pages long. Based on the profound impact on the investment world of exchange-traded funds (ETFs), this chapter has been greatly expanded. This chapter will provide the basic information to understand ETFs and how to use them. It is not meant to be an exhaustive review of the subject. The Bibliography lists excellent ETF books, Web sites, and other useful resources.

In 2003, only 1.9 percent of investor assets owned ETFs compared with 6.6 percent in 2009. Most of the players are frequent traders, institutions, and hedge funds rather than buy-and-hold investors or the common retail investors. However, as investors, financial advisors, and brokers become more familiar with the advantages of investing in or trading ETFs, these individuals will rely less on conventional mutual funds, sector mutual funds, leveraged mutual funds, and index funds.

In the United States, at year end 2009, there were 797 ETFs valued at $777.1 billion, which comprised 6.6 percent of all investment company assets (includes mutual funds, ETFs, closed-end funds, and unit investment trusts).[1] This compares with 102 ETFs valued at $102.1 billion at year end 2002. According to BlackRock and Bloomberg, by October 31, 2010, there were 1,040 ETFs valued at $940 billion. Almost all ETFs are listed on the Nasdaq and New York Stock Exchange (NYSE) Arca. A listing of NYSE-listed ETFs can be found at www.nyse.com/screener/, along with other useful information.

An *exchange-traded fund* (ETF) is an investment company, typically a mutual fund or unit investment trust, whose shares are traded intraday on stock exchanges, similar to stocks. ETFs are baskets of securities, usually set up as indexes, that trade throughout the day based on the net asset value of their underlying assets. Typical ETFs include major stock indexes, sectors, metals, commodities, international, fixed income, currencies, and other vehicles.

In 1993, the American Stock Exchange (AMEX) listed the first ETF: The Standard & Poor's Depositary Receipt (SPDR), pronounced "spider." It exactly mirrors the movement of the Standard & Poor's (S&P) 500 Index, and its ticker symbol is SPY. There are also ETFs that track the Dow Jones Industrial Average (DJIA), called *Diamonds*; the Nasdaq 100 (QQQQ), called *Cubes*; the largest 1,000 U.S. incorporated companies, known as the *Russell 1000* (IWB); and many other industry sectors and indexes. For example, there are nine select sector SPDR funds corresponding to specific sector indexes.

ETFs have been developed for the following types of portfolios:

- Broad stock indexes (total stock market, Russell 3000)
- Well-known indexes (DJIA, S&P 500, Nasdaq 100)
- Styles and market capitalization (e.g., small-cap, mid-cap, and large-cap; value, and growth). Table 6-1 lists ETFs with the largest market caps.
- Sectors (e.g., technology, financials, information technology, energy, consumer staples, health care, industrial, telecommunications, and consumer discretionary).

---

[1] *2010 Investment Company Fact Book*, 50th ed. 2010, p. 136.

## TABLE 6-1

### Top 25 ETFs by Market Capitalization

| Symbol | Name | Market Cap* | Average Volume |
|---|---|---|---|
| SPY | SPDR S&P 500 | $83,604.38 | 213,008,000 |
| GLD | SPDR Gold Shares | $55,344.15 | 14,858,000 |
| EEM | iShares MSCI Emerging Markets Index | $47,547.92 | 65,711,100 |
| VWO | Vanguard Emerging Markets Stock ETF | $40,329.09 | 14,348,800 |
| EFA | iShares MSCI EAFE Index | $36,272.47 | 21,474,100 |
| IVV | iShares S&P 500 Index | $23,105.47 | 3,594,560 |
| QQQQ | PowerShares QQQ | $22,567.60 | 83,867,100 |
| TIP | iShares Trust Barclays TIPS Bond Fund | $20,835.79 | 817,934 |
| VTI | Vanguard Total Stock Market ETF | $15,184.68 | 1,999,450 |
| LQD | iShares iBoxx $ Invest Grade Corp Bond | $14,643.63 | 1,030,380 |
| IWM | iShares Russell 2000 Index | $13,589.72 | 64,939,700 |
| AGG | iShares Barclays Aggregate Bond Fund | $12,591.05 | 784,815 |
| EWZ | iShares MSCI Brazil Index | $11,750.44 | 18,095,700 |
| IWF | iShares Russell 1000 Growth Index | $11,328.73 | 2,781,000 |
| MDY | SPDR S&P MidCap 400 | $10,665.36 | 3,644,360 |
| BND | Vanguard Total Bond Market ETF | $9,143.30 | 726,285 |
| FXI | iShares FTSE/Xinhua China 25 Index | $9,114.96 | 22,202,300 |
| IWD | iShares Russell 1000 Value Index | $8,860.85 | 1,884,210 |
| SHY | iShares Barclays 1–3 Year Treasury Bond | $8,448.00 | 1,118,440 |
| IJH | iShares S&P MidCap 400 Index | $7,958.17 | 963,152 |
| GDX | Market Vectors Gold Miners ETF | $7,810.62 | 9,990,730 |
| DIA | SPDR Dow Jones Industrial Average | $7,733.71 | 8,898,750 |
| SLV | iShares Silver Trust | $7,590.24 | 11,538,600 |
| XLE | Energy Select Sector SPDR | $6,811.51 | 17,094,500 |
| XLF | Financial Select Sector SPDR | $5,709.95 | 93,438,000 |

*Market cap is shown in millions of dollars. Volume is daily. October 2010 data.
Source: ETF Data Base, www.etfdb.com. Printed with permission.

- International and country-specific equity indexes (e..g., Chile, Canada, Sweden, France, Israel, Brazil, China, Russia, and Australia) and international style.
- Fixed-income indexes (e.g., short- and long-term Treasury bonds, corporates, municipals, and Treasury Inflation Protected).

- Specialty indexes (e.g., commodities, currency, real estate).
- Leveraged and inverse (e.g., 2× to 3× leveraged long and short).

## MERRILL LYNCH HOLDRS

Another instrument similar to ETFs in most respects, called *HOLDRS* (*Hol*ding Company *D*epositary *R*eceipts), was created by Merrill Lynch. According to www.holdrs.com, "HOLDRS are securities that represent an investor's ownership in the common stock or ADRs of specified companies in a particular industry, sector or group. HOLDRS allow investors to own a diversified group of stocks in a single investment that is highly transparent, liquid and efficient." They have features similar to ETFs. Almost all 18 HOLDRS are either sector funds, concentrated in one industry, or a country— Europe or Spain—and they contain 2 to 54 stocks, with most having an average of 15 stocks. Such a concentration can be risky if you are long a sector when it is declining in price. Of course, if you are short the ETF, you will reap the rewards of a bearish price trend. Detailed information about HOLDRS and their portfolio composition, performance, and price charts can be found at www.holdrs.com.

The following is a listing of the current HOLDRS with their ticker symbols:

- Biotech (BBH)
- Brazilian Telecom (TBH)
- Broadband (BDH)
- B2B Internet (BHH)
- Europe 2001 (EKH)
- Internet (HHH)
- Internet Architecture (IAH)
- Spain IBEX 35 (IIH)
- Market 2000+ (MKH)
- Oil Services (OIH)
- Pharmaceutical (PPH)
- Regional Bank (RKH)
- Retail (RTH)

- Semiconductor (SMH)
- Software (SWH)
- Telecom (TTH)
- Utilities (UTH)
- Wireless (WMH)

## TABLE 6-2

### Top 25 ETFs by Average Daily Trading Volume

| Symbol | Name | Average Volume | Market Cap* |
|--------|------|----------------|-------------|
| SPY | SPDR S&P 500 | 213,008,000 | $83,604.38 |
| XLF | Financial Select Sector SPDR | 93,438,000 | $5,709.95 |
| QQQQ | PowerShares QQQ | 83,867,100 | $22,567.60 |
| EEM | iShares MSCI Emerging Markets Index | 65,711,100 | $47,547.92 |
| IWM | iShares Russell 2000 Index | 64,939,700 | $13,589.72 |
| FAZ | Direxion Daily Financial Bear 3× Shares | 55,463,800 | $1,177.49 |
| FAS | Direxion Daily Financial Bull 3× Shares | 49,268,400 | $1,695.29 |
| SDS | ProShares UltraShort S&P500 | 37,486,800 | $2,982.38 |
| UNG | United States Natural Gas | 23,637,400 | $2,406.48 |
| VXX | iPath S&P 500 VIX Short-Term Futures ETN due 1/30/2US | 23,467,200 | $1,948.32 |
| FXI | iShares FTSE/Xinhua China 25 Index | 22,202,300 | $9,114.96 |
| EFA | iShares MSCI EAFE Index | 21,474,100 | $36,272.47 |
| EWJ | iShares MSCI Japan Index | 20,176,300 | $4,042.10 |
| SSO | ProShares Ultra S&P 500 | 18,715,500 | $1,439.48 |
| TZA | Direxion Daily Small Cap Bear 3× Shares | 18,426,100 | $862.94 |
| EWZ | iShares MSCI Brazil Index | 18,095,700 | $11,750.44 |
| XLE | Energy Select Sector SPDR | 17,094,500 | $6,811.51 |
| XLI | Industrial Select Sector SPDR | 17,046,700 | $3,220.60 |
| QID | ProShares UltraShort QQQ | 15,840,800 | $802.00 |
| SMH | Semiconductor HOLDRs | 14,932,600 | $1,199.07 |
| GLD | SPDR Gold Shares | 14,858,000 | $55,344.15 |
| VWO | Vanguard Emerging Markets Stock ETF | 14,348,800 | $40,329.09 |
| IYR | iShares Dow Jones US Real Estate | 13,959,800 | $3,028.42 |
| XRT | SPDR S&P Retail | 12,839,600 | $462.14 |
| TNA | Direxion Daily Small Cap Bull 3× Shares | 12,570,500 | $435.46 |

*Market cap is shown in millions of dollars. October 2010 data.
*Source:* ETF Data Base, www.etfdb.com. Printed with permission.

One unusual limitation of HOLDRS is that they can be bought or sold only in 100-share lots, whereas ETFs can be purchased in odd lots. Also, the HOLDRS portfolios never add or delete stocks unless the company disappears in an acquisition or goes bankrupt. This may not contribute to price stability. The opposite could be true. We need price stability and predictability, not just *portfolio* stability.

## ETF BENEFITS

ETFs are viable and useful investment vehicles for the following reasons:

- *Transparency.* The portfolio composition is known. Since there is no active management (except for a few dozen actively managed ETFs), you always know what you are buying.
- *Liquidity.* Trades can be made instantaneously any time during the day including pre-market and after-market with small bid-ask spreads. Thus the investor is not at the mercy of the market for the entire day (as is the case with mutual funds) and can liquidate a position at any time for any reason. This flexibility is critical in times of volatile, panicky, or news-driven markets that are more frequent than ever before. Refer to Table 6-2 for ETFs with the largest daily trading volumes.
- *Low cost.* Annual expense ratios and management fees are much lower than with regular mutual funds and usually a few basis points (0.01 = 1 basis point) lower than index funds. No analysts or investment managers need to be paid; however, there is a brokerage commission each time an ETF is bought or sold. A discount or online broker can be used to keep the commission well below $10 for each trade. The Standard & Poor's SPDRs, for example, have an annual expense ratio of just 0.09 percent, and Barclay's iShares S&P 500 has a ratio of 0.18 percent. The Vanguard 500 Index Fund annual expense ratio is 0.18 percent per year. On a $10,000 initial investment, that works out to an annual cost of $18. Remember that among mutual-fund families, Vanguard is known to have extremely low fees,

whereas other fund families may have significantly higher expense ratios. See Table 6-3 for the least expensive ETFs.

Active traders pay commissions whenever they trade an ETF. Thus, having an index fund with low expenses and the ability to do active trading could be comparatively

## TABLE 6-3

Least Expensive ETFs

| Symbol | Name | Expense Ratio | ETF Db Category |
|--------|------|---------------|-----------------|
| VOO | Vanguard S&P 500 ETF | 0.06% | Large-cap blend equities |
| SCHB | Schwab U.S. Broad Market ETF | 0.06% | All-cap equities |
| VTI | Vanguard Total Stock Market ETF | 0.07% | All-cap equities |
| SCHX | Schwab U.S. Large-Cap ETF | 0.08% | Large-cap blend equities |
| SPY | SPDR S&P 500 | 0.09% | Large-cap blend equities |
| IVV | iShares S&P 500 Index Fund | 0.09% | Large-cap blend equities |
| TUZ | PIMCO 1–3 Year U.S. Treasury Index Fund | 0.09% | Government bonds |
| SCHR | Intermediate-Term U.S. Treasury ETF | 0.12% | Government bonds |
| SCPB | SPDR Barclays Capital Short-Term Corporate Bond ETF | 0.12% | Corporate bonds |
| WFVK | Wilshire 5000 Total Market ETF | 0.12% | All-cap equities |
| VONE | Russell 1000 ETF | 0.12% | Large-cap blend equities |
| SCHO | Short-Term U.S. Treasury ETF | 0.12% | Government bonds |
| SCHG | Schwab U.S. Large-Cap Growth ETF | 0.13% | Large-cap growth equities |
| VV | Vanguard Large-Cap ETF-DNQ | 0.13% | Large-cap blend equities |
| ITE | SPDR Barclays Intermediate-Term Treasury ETF | 0.13% | Government bonds |
| LAG | SPDR Barclays Aggregate Bond ETF | 0.13% | Total bond market |
| MGC | Vanguard Mega Cap 300 ETF | 0.13% | Large-cap blend equities |
| TLO | SPDR Barclays Long-Term Treasury ETF | 0.13% | Government bonds |
| MGK | Vanguard Mega Cap 300 Growth | 0.13% | Large-cap growth equities |
| MGV | Vanguard Mega Cap 300 Value | 0.13% | Large-cap value equities |
| SCHA | Schwab U.S. Small-Cap ETF | 0.13% | Small-cap blend equities |
| SCHV | Schwab U.S. Large-Cap Value ETF | 0.13% | Large-cap value equities |
| SCHF | Schwab International Equity ETF | 0.13% | Foreign large-cap equities |
| BIL | SPDR Barclays 1–3 Month T-Bill ETF | 0.13% | Money market |
| BIV | Vanguard Intermediate-Term Bond ETF | 0.14% | Total bond market |

*Source:* ETF Database, www.etfdb.com. Printed with permission. October 2010 data.

cheaper. But most mutual fund families (except Rydex and ProFunds) do not allow more than four exchanges a year. Still, four exchanges could work fine for some of the less active market timing strategies recommended in Chapters 7 through 11. A number of brokerage firms are offering investors free ETFs with certain restrictions on limited universes of ETFs. These firms include Fidelity (25 ETFs), Vanguard (62), Schwab (11), and TD Ameritrade (100).

- *Tax efficiency.* ETFs are more tax-efficient than a comparable mutual fund because they involve lower capital gains and minimal portfolio turnover. With mutual funds, you have to declare capital gains on your tax form whenever they are declared by the fund, even though you may not sell the fund during that year. Owners of ETFs have capital gains or losses only when an ETF is sold. If there are no closing trades, then there are no capital gains or losses to be paid. By contrast, mutual funds pass on the capital gains and losses realized within the fund to their shareholders, who must declare these gains and losses.

- *Flexibility for implementing trading strategies.* ETFs can be purchased on margin and sold short. And options are available for purchase on many ETFs. Also, the usual types of orders such as limit and stop orders can be placed with your brokerage account. These capabilities are not present with mutual funds. An ETF is considered a passive investment like an index fund. Portfolio turnover is minimal, except when certain issues are replaced when they are replaced in the underlying index. Investors can buy and sell ETFs at any time during trading hours.

  A short sale is the opposite of buying a stock or EFT. The seller, in effect, borrows the stock or ETF from the brokerage firm, hoping to repurchase it later at a lower price and repaying the broker with the stock purchased at the lower price. The objective in short selling is to make money when the price drops. If a stock sold short drops in price, the shares are bought back at a lower price, generating a profit for the investor. But if the share price rises instead of falls, the investor suffers a loss because he or she has to buy back the shares at a higher price.

For investors who want to short the market, the inverse and leveraged ETFs offered by Rydex SGI, ProShares, and Direxion also can be used. The ETFs are bought long, and no margin is required.

- *Diversification.* Equity ETFs are composed of a portfolio of stocks. Investing in this type of ETF substantially reduces overall risk compared with buying a portfolio of 10 individual stocks. Of course, the specific ETF purchased may be more risky than another ETF depending on its portfolio mix and volatility.
- *Favorable interest income and dividends.* Dividends declared on stocks or interest paid on bonds held in the ETF will be passed on to shareholders.

The ETFs with the most assets under management are shown in Table 6-4.

## ETF RISKS

Of course, like any investment, ETFs have specific risks:

- *Market risk.* Like stocks and mutual funds, the price fluctuates throughout the day, sometimes with wide price swings, depending on many variables.
- *Net-asset-value risk.* The price may not trade at exactly the net asset value; instead, it may be a bit higher or lower depending on conditions of the market. This is called *tracking error.* In the case of the most active ETFs, there is a minimal, if any, difference between the net asset value and the market price. Any wide differences would be observed, and big institutional traders and hedgers would step in to take advantage of the situation, thereby rapidly closing any price gap.
- *Bid-ask price spread.* Depending on the volume of transactions, some ETFs may have higher price spreads between the bid and ask prices, thereby resulting in higher transactions costs. The spread is minimal (e.g., a few

## TABLE 6-4

### ETF Assets under Management

| Name | Ticker | Exp. Ratio | Assets under Management | Average Daily Share Volume |
|---|---|---|---|---|
| SPDR S&P 500 | SPY | 0.09 | 78,013,974,338 | 280,800,258 |
| SPDR Gold Shares | GLD | 0.4 | 54,809,778,373 | |
| iShares MSCI Emerging Markets | EEM | 0.72 | 45,093,472,503 | 90,382,163 |
| Vanguard Emerging Markets | VWO | 0.27 | 36,199,053,910 | 16,744,872 |
| iShares MSCI EAFE | EFA | 0.35 | 34,937,138,576 | 20,512,654 |
| iShares S&P 500 | IVV | 0.09 | 22,685,982,794 | 5,652,908 |
| PowerShares QQQ | QQQQ | 0.2 | 22,140,062,670 | 105,807,348 |
| iShares Barclays TIPS Bond Fund | TIP | 0.2 | 20,345,690,572 | 713,427 |
| iShares iBoxx $ Investment-Grade Corporate Bond Fund | LQD | 0.15 | 14,864,475,735 | 700,945 |
| Vanguard Total Stock | VTI | 0.07 | 14,583,124,597 | 3,098,330 |
| iShares Russell 2000 | IWM | 0.28 | 12,895,412,727 | 64,653,785 |
| iShares Barclays Aggregate Bond Fund | AGG | 0.24 | 12,715,622,433 | 626,584 |
| iShares Russell 1000 Growth | IWF | 0.2 | 10,831,365,461 | 2,448,085 |
| SPDR S&P MidCap 400 | MDY | 0.25 | 10,399,854,021 | 7,871,596 |
| iShares MSCI Brazil | EWZ | 0.65 | 10,386,379,266 | 25,810,901 |
| Vnguard Total Bond Market | BND | 0.12 | 9,065,054,601 | 488,764 |
| iShares Russell 1000 Value Index Fund | IWD | 0.2 | 8,758,528,157 | 2,045,412 |
| iShares Barclays 1–3 Year Treasury Bond | SHY | 0.15 | 8,606,221,643 | 757,450 |
| iShares FTSE Xinhua China 25 | FXI | 0.73 | 8,530,162,190 | 29,460,217 |
| Dow Diamonds | DIA | 0.17 | 8,053,718,384 | 9,279,674 |
| iShares S&P 400 MidCap | IJH | 0.22 | 7,811,538,785 | 1,281,478 |
| Market Vectors Gold Miners | GDX | 0.53 | 7,405,295,924 | 16,843,886 |
| Barclays 1–3 Year Credit Bond | CSJ | 0.2 | 7,313,925,518 | 351,586 |
| iShares Silver Trust | SLV | 0.5 | 6,941,185,000 | 30,868,400 |
| iShares iBoxx $ High-Yield Corporate Bond | HYG | 0.5 | 6,864,534,961 | 617,442 |

*Source:* www.indexuniverse.com. Printed with permission. October 2010 data.

pennies) on the more active ETFs. On the less liquid ETFs, the spreads can be much larger, so make sure that you check the trading volume of any ETFs you plan to purchase and look for at least 100,000 shares a day, and preferably one million shares a day.

- *Sector risk.* Buying a sector EFT has added risk because any news that affects companies in that sector will affect the ETF's price, either positively or negatively.

## ETF Families

Since the introduction of ETFs, many more players have entered the marketplace. There are currently over a dozen families offering 815 different ETFs. The following is a list of the families, their Web sites, and the number of funds they offer:

- Direxion (www.direxion.com; 38 funds, all of which are 2× and 3× bear and bull)
- First Trust (www.ftportfolio; 43 funds)
- Guggenheim, formerly Claymore (www.guggenheimfunds.com; 38 ETFs)
- HOLDRS (www.holdrs.com; 18 funds)
- iShares (www.us.ishare.com; 218 funds)
- Market Vectors (www.vaneck.com; 29 funds)
- PowerShares (www.invescopowershares.com; 128 funds)
- ProShares (www.proshares.com; 111 funds, many leveraged and inverse)
- Rydex SGI (www.rydex-sgi.com; 19 funds, mostly leveraged and inverse)
- State Street Global Advisors (www.spdrs.com; 93 funds)
- Barclays iPath (www.ipathetn.com; 25 funds)
- Vanguard (www.vanguard.com; 62 funds)
- WisdomTree (www.wisdomtree.com; 44 funds)

## Leveraged and Inverse ETFs

Similar to leveraged mutual funds, leveraged ETFs amplify the *daily* returns of their benchmarks by as much as two to three times (200 to 300 percent), before fees and expenses. They are also referred to as *2.0-beta* and *3.0-beta funds*. For example, the ProShares Ultra S&P 500 ETF (ticker symbol SSO) doubles the daily price performance of the S&P 500 Index benchmark, so if the latter rises 1 percent today, the SSO rises 2 percent. Of course, the opposite is also true. When the S&P 500 Index falls 1 percent, the SSO will fall twice as fast, or 2 percent. Leveraged funds also have inverse varieties similar to inverse mutual funds, also referred to as *bear* or *short funds*. The same principle applies in how returns are calculated for those ETFs that are 3.0 beta. Examples of regular and leveraged ETFs offered by RydexShares™ Exchange Traded Funds and ProShares are listed in Tables 6-5 and 6-6.

**TABLE 6-5**

### RydexShares™ ETFs

| Rydex Fund Name | Fund Type |
|---|---|
| Rydex S&P Equal Weight ETF | Large cap |
| Rydex S&P Equal Weight Consumer Discretionary ETF | Consumer discretionary |
| Rydex S&P Equal Weight Consumer Staples ETF | Consumer staples |
| Rydex S&P Equal Weight Energy ETF | Energy |
| Rydex S&P Equal Weight Financials ETF | Financials |
| Rydex S&P Equal Weight Health Care ETF | Health care |
| Rydex S&P Equal Weight Industrials ETF | Industrials |
| Rydex S&P Equal Weight Materials ETF | Materials |
| Rydex S&P Equal Weight Technology ETF | Technology |
| Rydex S&P Equal Weight Utilities ETF | Utilities |
| Rydex S&P 500 Pure Growth ETF | Large growth |
| Rydex S&P 500 Pure Value ETF | Large value |
| Rydex S&P MidCap Pure Growth ETF | Midgrowth |
| Rydex S&P MidCap Pure Value ETF | Midvalue |
| Rydex S&P SmallCap Pure Growth ETF | Small growth |
| Rydex S&P SmallCap Pure Value ETF | Small value |
| Rydex 2× S&P 500 ETF | Large cap |
| Rydex Inverse 2× S&P 500 ETF | Large cap |

*Source:* www.rydex-sgi.com.

## TABLE 6-6

Ultra ProShares ETFs

| Ultra ProShares | Index/Benchmark | Daily Objective* | Trading Symbol |
|---|---|---|---|
| **Ultra MarketCap** | | | |
| Ultra QQQ | Nasdaq-100 | 200% | QLD |
| Ultra Dow30 | Dow Jones Industrial Average | 200% | DDM |
| Ultra S&P500 | S&P 500 | 200% | SSO |
| Ultra Russell3000 | Russell 3000 | 200% | UWC |
| Ultra MidCap400 | S&P MidCap 400 | 200% | MVV |
| Ultra SmallCap600 | S&P SmallCap 600 | 200% | SAA |
| Ultra Russell2000 | Russell 2000 | 200% | UWM |
| UltraPro QQQ | Nasdaq 100 | 300% | TQQQ |
| UltraPro Dow30 | Dow Jones Industrial Average | 300% | UDOW |
| UltraPro S&P500 | S&P 500 | 300% | UPRO |
| UltraPro MidCap400 | S&P MidCap 400 | 300% | UMDD |
| UltraPro Russell2000 | Russell 2000 | 300% | URTY |
| **ULTRA Style** | | | |
| Ultra Russell1000 Value | Russell 1000 Value | 200% | UVG |
| Ultra Russell1000 Growth | Russell 1000 Growth | 200% | UKF |
| Ultra Russell MidCap Value | Russell Midcap Value | 200% | UVU |
| Ultra Russell MidCap Growth | Russell Midcap Growth | 200% | UKW |
| Ultra Russell2000 Value | Russell 2000 Value | 200% | UVT |
| Ultra Russell2000 Growth | Russell 2000 Growth | 200% | UKK |
| **ULTRA Sector** | | | |
| Ultra Basic Materials | Dow Jones U.S. Basic Materials | 200% | UYM |
| Ultra Nasdaq Biotechnology | Nasdaq Biotechnology | 200% | BIB |
| Ultra Consumer Goods | Dow Jones U.S. Consumer Goods | 200% | UGE |
| Ultra Consumer Services | Dow Jones U.S. Consumer Services | 200% | UCC |
| Ultra Financials | Dow Jones U.S. Financials | 200% | UYG |
| Ultra Health Care | Dow Jones U.S. Health Care | 200% | RXL |
| Ultra Industrials | Dow Jones U.S. Industrials | 200% | UXI |
| Ultra Oil & Gas | Dow Jones U.S. Oil & Gas | 200% | DIG |
| Ultra Real Estate | Dow Jones U.S. Real Estate | 200% | URE |
| Ultra KBW Regional Banking | KBW Regional Banking | 200% | KRU |
| Ultra Semiconductors | Dow Jones U.S. Semiconductors | 200% | USD |
| Ultra Technology | Dow Jones U.S. Technology | 200% | ROM |

(continued on next page)

**TABLE 6-6**

Ultra ProShares ETFs (continued)

| Ultra ProShares | Index/Benchmark | Daily Objective* | Trading Symbol |
|---|---|---|---|
| Ultra Telecommunications | Dow Jones U.S. Select Telecommunications | 200% | LTL |
| Ultra Utilities | Dow Jones U.S. Utilities | 200% | UPW |
| **ULTRA International** | | | |
| Ultra MSCI EAFE | MSCI EAFE | 200% | EFO |
| Ultra MSCI Emerging Markets | MSCI Emerging Markets | 200% | EET |
| Ultra MSCI Europe | MSCI Europe | 200% | UPV |
| Ultra MSCI Pacific ex-Japan | MSCI Pacific ex-Japan | 200% | UXJ |
| Ultra MSCI Brazil | MSCI Brazil | 200% | UBR |
| Ultra FTSE/Xinhua China 25 | FTSE/Xinhua China 25 | 200% | XPP |
| Ultra MSCI Japan | MSCI Japan | 200% | EZJ |
| Ultra MSCI Mexico Investable Market | MSCI Mexico Investable Market | 200% | UMX |
| **ULTRA Fixed-Income** | | | |
| Ultra 7–10 Year Treasury | Barclays Capital 7–10 Year U.S. Treasury | 200% | UST |
| Ultra 20+ Year Treasury | Barclays Capital 20+ Year U.S. Treasury | 200% | UBT |
| **ULTRA Commodity†** | | | |
| Ultra DJ-UBS Commodity | Dow Jones-UBS Commodity | 200% | UCD |
| Ultra DJ-UBS Crude Oil | Dow Jones-UBS Crude Oil Sub-Index | 200% | UCO |
| Ultra Gold | London PM Gold Fixing | 200% | UGL |
| Ultra Silver | London Silver Fixing | 200% | AGQ |
| **ULTRA Currency†** | | | |
| Ultra Euro | EUR/USD 4:00 p.m. ET exchange rate | 200% | ULE |
| Ultra Yen | JPY/USD 4:00 p.m. ET exchange rate | 200% | YCL |

*Before fees and expenses.
†Generates a K-1 Tax Form.
*Source:* Reprinted with permission of ProShares.

Leveraged ETFs can be used by investors for specific purposes:

- To benefit from the beginning of or continuation of a market uptrend or downtrend, investors buy leverage long and short ETFs to provide double or triple the returns in both directions.

- To act as a hedge on an existing portfolio by buying an inverse ETF, where the investor believes that a market correction may be imminent but wants to protect the portfolio's principal.

- To take a long or short position using less cash than buying a full position. For example, if an investor has only $3,333 to invest but wants to buy $10,000 worth of S&P 500 EFT (SPY ticker symbol), he or she could buy the ProShares Ultra Pro S&P 500 (3.0-Beta) Fund and invest only $3,333 because he or she will be obtaining the same performance as if he or she had invested $10,000.

## Compounding of Daily Returns
## Needs to Be Understood

Investors need to be extremely careful using leveraged products because they can move very quickly in either direction. They have higher than normal volatility, and some may not have adequate daily volume to keep the spread between the bid and ask prices reasonable. They are more complex than traditional mutual funds in their portfolio composition because a certain percentage of the underlying stocks are purchased along with index futures contracts and equity index swap agreements to obtain the compounding.

Each day the price of each leveraged ETF is reset so that it tracks its benchmark index. Over time, the ETF may drift in price owing to the impact of compounding from its benchmark, especially when there is abnormally high volatility. Let's use two examples to show how compounding affects the price of an unleveraged ETF and a leveraged ETF with a beta of 2.0 under normal circumstances.

- *Example 1:* In a bull market, assume an investor owns an ETF valued at $100 a share (with no leverage) that increased 10 percent each day for two consecutive days. At the end of the second day, the share price is $121 ($100 × 1.1 = $110; $110 × 1.1 = $121).
- *Example 2:* Now take the same scenario, but assume that the investor owns a double-beta fund (200 percent). At the end of day 1, it is worth $120 a share, and at the end of day 2, it is worth $144 a share, which is greater than the expected $142.

When the stock market has high volatility with swings of 500 points or more a day in the DJIA, then the leveraged ETFs can get out of whack with their benchmark owing to the compounding effect. This is why ProShare and Rydex Shares™ ETF shares warn investors about this situation on their Web sites and indicate that investors and traders need to completely understand how these ETFs work and the risks involved.

### FINRA Warning Buy-and-Hold Investors on Use of Leveraged and Inverse ETFs

The Financial Industry Regulatory Authority (FINRA) is the largest independent regulator for all securities firms doing business in the United States. FINRA's mission is to protect America's investors by making sure the securities industry operates fairly and honestly. FINRA has evaluated leveraged and inverse ETFs for buy-and-hold investors and has made the following comment:

> *The best form of investor protection is to clearly understand leveraged or inverse ETFs before investing in them. No matter how you initially hear about them, it's important to read the prospectus, which provides detailed information related to the ETFs' investment objectives, principal investment strategies, risks, and costs. The SEC's EDGAR system, as well as search engines, can help you locate a specific ETF prospectus. You can also find the prospectuses on the websites of the financial firms that issue a given ETF, as well as through your broker.*
>
> *You should also consider seeking the advice of an investment professional. Be sure to work with someone who understands your investment objectives and tolerance for risk. Your investment profes-*

*sional should understand these complex products, be able to explain whether or how they fit with your objectives, and be willing to monitor your investment.*

For complete information on the FINRA warning, visit www.finra.org/Investors/ProtectYourself/InvestorAlerts/Mutual Funds/P119778.

## WHERE TO PURCHASE ETFs

You can open a brokerage account with any discount broker to buy and sell ETFs or any other vehicles of your choice. The commission varies from $1.00 to $9.95 per trade depending on whom you choose. During the 2009–2010 period, four firms began offering free ETF trades on a select ETF universe of their choosing. None of the firms has placed leverage or inverse ETFs in its program. The firms offering free trades include Fidelity Investments (25 ETFs; see Table 6-7 for a listing), TD Ameritrade (100 ETFs, which must be held 30 days or $19.95 commission is charged), Vanguard (62 Vanguard ETFs), and Charles Schwab (11 Schwab ETFs). Full information is provided on their Web sites.

If you buy and sell the same Vanguard ETF in a Vanguard brokerage account more than 25 times in a 12-month period, you may be restricted from purchasing that Vanguard ETF through your Vanguard brokerage account for 60 days.

## MARKET TIMING WITH ETFs

The many advantages of ETFs over index and active mutual funds make them much more attractive for a market timing approach. With the availability of inverse ETFs, there is no need to use margin and pay margin interest. Moreover, with the wide choices of leveraged ETFs, investors can get a bigger bang for their buck.

The most popular ETFs to use for market timing are those with huge volume (millions of shares a day), low bid-ask spreads ($0.02 or less), and have a big following, such as QQQQ, SPY, DIA, IWM, and leveraged ETFs such as QLD, QID, SDS, FAS, and many others. You can select your ETF portfolio after reviewing the market situation based on a consensus of the indicators in Chapter 4. Make sure that the trend is positive before going long or negative

**TABLE 6-7**

Fidelity Commission-Free ETFs

| | Value | Blend | Growth |
|---|---|---|---|
| **U.S. Equity Index Funds** | | | |
| Large cap | IVE S&P 500 Value | IVV S&P 500 | IVW S&P 500 Growth |
| | IWD Russell 1000 Value | IWB Russell 1000 | IWF Russell 1000 Growth |
| | | IWV Russell 3000 | |
| Midcap | IJJ S&P Mid Cap 400 Value | IJH S&P Mid Cap 400 | IJK S&P Mid Cap 400 Growth |
| Small cap | IJS S&P Small Cap 600 Value | IJR S&P Small Cap 600 | IJT S&P Small Cap 600 Growth |
| | IWN Russell 2000 Value | IWM Russell 2000 | IWO Russell 2000 Growth |
| **International Equity Index Funds** | | | |
| ACWI | MSCI ACW1 | | |
| EFA | MSCI EAFE | | |
| SCZ | MSCI EAFE Small Cap | | |
| EEM | MSCI Emerging Markets | | |
| **Fixed-Income Funds** | | | |
| AGG | Barclays Aggregate Bond | | |
| TIP | Barclays TIPS | | |
| LQD | iBoxx $ Investment Grade Corporate | | |
| EMB | JP Morgan USD Emerging Markets | | |
| MUB | S&P National AM-Free Municipal | | |

*Source:* Fidelity Investments

if you are going short with inverse ETFs. Alternatively, you can invest in ETFs with one or more of the strategies in Chapters 7 to 11. In all cases, make sure that you have the proper stop-limit orders in place to protect your capital, and use trailing stop-limits to protect your profits. To eliminate the cost of your ETF brokerage commissions, consider using one of the previously mentioned firms, after determining which firm offers the most suitable ETF choices.

## CONCLUSIONS

The current array of ETFs offers outstanding flexibility and wide-ranging investment options. Market timing strategies can be easily implemented with these vehicles. Best of all, ETFs can be bought and sold any time throughout the day, and they can be easily shorted using the inverse funds without the need for a margin account. ETFs have greatly expanded the universe of investment choices for market-timers, who should take advantage of this opportunity, but only after examining the details of each ETF available and all the risks involved, especially with commodity and leveraged ETFs. Never invest in any ETF that you don't fully understand. The Bibliography at the end of this book provides recommended ETF books, Web sites, and other resources. Make sure to check them out because they will speed your learning process and provide useful information on ETFs.

# PART 2

# Market Timing Strategies and Resources

## CHAPTER 7

# Calendar-Based Investing: The Best Six Months Strategy

*The only thing that works is to let the market indices tell you the time to enter and exit. Never fight the market—it's bigger than you are.*
—William J. O'Neil, *How to Make Money in Stocks* (McGraw-Hill, 2002)

## BACKGROUND

Investing based on the calendar has intrigued investors, market technicians, and other investment professionals for years. For the most part, the broadcast media have mentioned seasonal investing strategies more frequently in the past few years, but they have not given them the full attention they deserve. Therefore, most investors probably have heard about such strategies but have not taken them seriously or done any homework to determine their value. As it turns out, this lack of initiative on the part of most investors probably is a huge mistake because careful analysis of seasonal investing strategies reveals their superiority to the buy-and-hold strategy over a long time period. Many academic studies have been performed on the seasonal influences on stock market returns. This chapter will present two profitable strategies that have worked not only in the past but also in the present, although not perfectly.

Investing during specific months each year is an example of a seasonality pattern that will be covered in detail in this chapter. According to the *Wall Street Journal*, Ned Davis Research found that since 1950, on average, stocks have gone up 8 percent from the beginning of October through the end of April but have increased only 1 percent from the beginning of May through the end of September.[1]

That firm also found that from the years 1950 to 2000, investing $10,000 from the fourth trading day in May to the last trading day in September of the following year (or a continuous period of about six months) resulted in a miniscule total gain of $2,977 for that entire period. However, entering the market every October 1 and exiting the following May 3 resulted in a total gain of $585,909.[2]

More recent data compiled by Standard & Poor's (S&P) indicate that the best-performing months since January 1970 through September 2010 were March, April, November, and December (see Table 7-1). Therefore, the months of November through January continue to provide above-average performance. The average for all months was 0.64 percent.

Table 7-2 provides additional insight into the best-performing consecutive three-month periods. Note that the period November through January again offers the highest return compared with any of the other periods shown.

A research paper entitled, "The Halloween Indicator, Sell in May and Go Away: Another Puzzle" (September 1999), by Sven Bouman, ING Investment Management, Netherlands, and Ben Jacobsen, Faculty of Economics and Econometrics, University of Amsterdam, also weighed in on the best and worst months. Is the presence of the November–April period of stock market strength simply a manifestation of the U.S. economy, banking system, and markets? Not at all. Bouman and Jacobsen discovered that stock prices rose more sharply in the November–April time period than in the corresponding May–October period in 36 of 37 countries. This effect has occurred in the U.K. stock market since 1694. The authors found no evidence that this phenomenon can be explained

---

[1] E.S. Browning, "Danger to the Economy—Yes: Rally for Stocks Now," *Wall Street Journal*, November 4, 2002.

[2] Jonathan R. Laing, "Merry Month," *Barron's*, May 7, 2001.

**TABLE 7-1**

S&P 500 Average Monthly Performance*: January 1970 to September 2010

| Month | Performance Percentage |
|---|:---:|
| January | 1.00 |
| February | −0.08 |
| March | 1.11 |
| April | 1.30 |
| May | 0.72 |
| June | 0.15 |
| July | 0.44 |
| August | 0.23 |
| September | −0.65 |
| October | 0.44 |
| November | 1.30 |
| December | 1.69 |

*Price appreciation only.

*Source:* Standard & Poor's, Inc., January 1970 to February 2010.

**TABLE 7-2**

Best Consecutive Three-Month Periods for S&P 500 Index*

| Period | % Change |
|---|:---:|
| November, December, January | 4.1 |
| October, November, December | 3.6 |
| March, April, May | 3.2 |
| December, January, February | 2.5 |
| Average three months | 2.0 |

*Average cumulative change, October 1945–2010.

*Source:* Standard & Poor's, Inc., "Global Equity Strategy," October 29, 2010.

by the January effect, the stock market crash of 1987, dividend payment seasonality, or time-varying risk parameters. The main reason turns out to be the extent and timing of vacations. For example, summer vacations in Europe have a strong seasonal effect on financial markets.

A more recent paper entitled, "Are Monthly Seasonals Real? A Three Century Perspective" (October 25, 2010), which was authored by Ben Jacobsen (also coauthor of the study mentioned in the preceding paragraph) and Cherry Yi Zhang, both of Massey University's Department of Economics and Finance in New Zealand, examined seasonal patterns over 300 years in the United Kingdom using monthly stock price data. They found that the "Sell in May and go away" (the *Halloween strategy*) wisdom that originated in the United Kingdom had a persistence of positive returns in all their 100- and 50-year subsamples and in 24 of 32 of the 10-year subsamples.

More than 80 percent of the time horizons over five years and more than 90 percent of the horizons over 10 years had *returns that were, on average, three times higher than the market*. The authors found that the average returns for the six-month period (called the *winter period*) are positive and higher than the summer returns for all sample periods. They found that the Halloween strategy consistently beat buy-and-hold over the entire sample period and in all 100-year and 50-year subsamples. Its only underperformance was in the 1941–1970 subsample period (30 years). Figure 7-1 shows the returns in the winter and summer months with the significant outperformance of the winter months. Figure 7-2 shows the trend and performance since 1693 compared with buy-and-hold that clearly demonstrates the consistency of investing in the winter period.

## TESTS ON U.S. DATA

Let's take a look at the individual monthly performance of the S&P 500 Index over 50 years. Mark Vakkur, M.D, a psychiatrist by training, as well as a stock and options trader, analyzed the historical data.[3] His findings are shown in Table 7-3. This table provides the monthly performance of the S&P 500 Index (excluding reinvested dividends) from 1950 through March 2002 divided into two time frames. Clearly, there are specific strong and weak months. January, April, July, November, and December have been the best-performing months from 1950 through 1995. Excluding July, *the*

---

[3] Mark Vakkur, M.D., "Mark Your Calendars: Stock Market Seasonality," *Active Trader*, September 2002, pp. 96–97.

## FIGURE 7-1

Winter versus summer month returns.

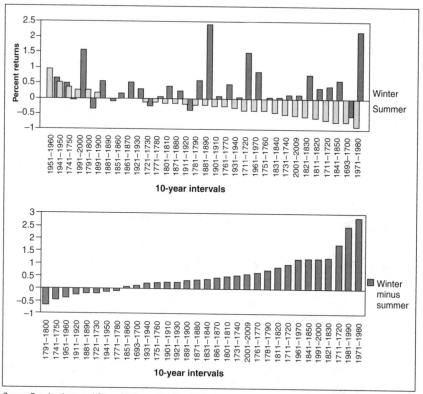

Source: Ben Jacobson and Cherry Yi Zhang, "Are Monthly Seasonals Real? A Three Century Perspective." *Social Science Research Network*, October 25, 2010.

*continuous months of November through January are the best performing,* with an average gain of 1.58 percent per month. By including February, March, and April, the performance falls to 1.19 percent, but it is still positive.

Now let's look at the period from 1996 to March 2002 in the same table. The best-performing months were January, March, April, June, October, November, and December. March, June, and October have now emerged as strong months. Five months— March, April, June, October, and November—have provided higher performance in the most recent six-year period compared with the prior period. Except for June, these are all months in the October–April time frame.

## FIGURE 7-2

Halloween indicator versus buy-and-hold.

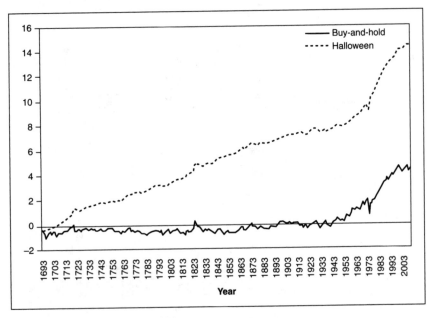

*Source:* Jacobson and Zhang, October 25, 2010.

The August 21, 2001, issue of the *Formula Research* newsletter, which is edited and published by Nelson Freeburg, a long-time trading systems developer who uses rigorous statistical testing on timing models, noted:

> Since 1950 there have been 34 declines of at least 10 percent in the Dow Jones Industrials. In 31 of these cases, key portions of the pull-back—often the brunt of the sell-off—occurred during the May–October period. Twelve declines took place entirely within the bearish period. The record since 1900 shows more "crashes," "massacres," and "panics" in October than in any other month. Of the 34 corrections cited above, fully 12 ended in October.

Freeburg goes on to say, "Over 90 percent of the net gain in the Dow since 1950 came in just 40 months, a mere 8 percent of the time span." Furthermore, he continues, "To a remarkable extent, almost all the stock market's advance since World War II came at a specific, recurring time of the year."

**TABLE 7-3**

Monthly Performance of the S&P 500: January 1950 to March 2002*

| Month | Average % Monthly Gain | | |
| --- | --- | --- | --- |
| | 1950–1995 | 1996–March 2002 | Difference |
| January | 1.55 | 1.31 | −0.24 |
| February | 0.37 | −0.87 | −1.24 |
| March | 0.76 | 1.76 | 1.00 |
| April | 1.23 | 2.75 | 1.51 |
| May | 0.16 | 0.35 | 0.19 |
| June | 0.08 | 2.31 | 2.22 |
| July | 1.29 | −0.63 | −1.92 |
| August | 0.39 | −3.24 | −3.63 |
| September | −0.60 | −0.15 | 0.45 |
| October | 0.45 | 2.64 | 2.19 |
| November | 1.43 | 3.50 | 2.07 |
| December | 1.77 | 1.77 | 0.00 |
| Average | 0.74 | 0.95 | 0.21 |
| November–January only | 1.58 | 2.14 | 0.56 |
| November–April only | 1.19 | 1.63 | 0.44 |
| May–October only | 0.29 | 0.21 | −0.08 |

*Bold numbers are the best-performing months.

Source: Mark Vakkur, M.D., "Mark Your Calendars: Stock Market Seasonality," *Active Trader,* September 2002, pp. 96–97. © *Active Trader Magazine.* All Rights Reserved.

History indicates that there is a consistent nonrandom period of strong and weak months. The risk-averse investor can take advantage of this strategy, especially in retirement accounts, where there are no capital gains implications for selling. As we'll see throughout this chapter, specific strategies will be provided to capitalize on these strong and weak monthly patterns.

# BEST SIX MONTHS STRATEGY

Astute investors should consider the preceding seasonal patterns because they have stood the test of time. The only seasonal strategy that I will cover in this chapter—the *best six months strategy*—has the following characteristics:

- There are only two signals a year—one buy and one sell.
- The buy signal is near November 1, and the sell signal is near April 30 (the beginning of the worst six months).
- The annual rate of return for the best six-month period beginning about November 1 each year exceeded the buy-and-hold return of the same period. One reason for the strategy's overall positive performance is that market crashes or corrections have tended to occur in the worst six-month period (e.g., September or October in 1929, 1974, 1987, 2001, 2002, and 2008).
- The strategy misses the brunt of bear markets because it is not invested in the weakest consecutive months of the year but instead is invested in the strongest consecutive months of the year.
- The strategy provides 50 percent less risk than buy-and-hold because it is invested only half of the year, and the proceeds can be placed in a money-market fund during the other half.
- The time required to implement the strategy is minimal (about 10 minutes a year).

These attributes should whet most investors' appetites because all the research data over six decades in the United States and over hundreds of years in the United Kingdom support it. The findings of well-respected researchers who have rigorously evaluated the U.S. stock market data are presented for your review. So let's begin the journey of understanding how successful the best six months investing strategy has been and why you definitely should consider it for investing your hard-earned cash.

Very few simple timing strategies have such a long-term track record as this strategy, developed in 1986 by Yale Hirsch. (I'll refer to it as the *best six months strategy* or the *BSM strategy*.) It was first published in the Hirsch Organization's 1987 edition of its *Stock Trader's Almanac*. It has been tweaked a bit over the years by Yale Hirsch's son Jeffrey and is updated annually in each year's edition of the almanac. Moreover, the BSM's current buy and sell signals are provided in real time to subscribers of the monthly "*Stock Trader's Almanac* blog," as well as via automatic Internet updates.

The BSM strategy's original buy and sell rules are simple: Invest in the stock market (e.g., an S&P 500 Index fund) on November 1 of each year, and then sell on April 30 of the following year (and go into cash equivalents—a money-market fund or T-bills) until November 1 of that year, when the next investment is made.

According to the *Stock Trader's Almanac 2011* (p. 48), from 1950 through 2009, an initial investment of $10,000 produced a total loss of $474.00 or a 0.4 percent average annual loss for all the May–October time periods.[4] Compare this with a *gain* of $527,388 or 7.4 percent average annual gain during the November–April time periods. The strategy assumed that the funds were invested in the Dow Jones Industrial Average (DJIA).[5] Without a doubt, the months selected for investing play a significant role in the total return over that extensive time period. On page 50 of the almanac, the same strategy is tested, but in conjunction with a technical indicator known as the *moving-average convergence-divergence* (MACD), developed by Gerald Appel based on the analysis of Sy Harding. This indicator was used to better identify the entry and exit dates in each of the periods. Using Hirsch's enhanced MACD's buy signal near November and sell signal near April, there was a gain of $1,472,790 or an average gain of 9.2 percent a year for the DJIA from November through May in the same period from 1950–2009, whereas the May through November period showed a loss of $6,542 or –1.2 percent a year. Clearly, this strategy almost tripled the previous strategy's return. Sy Harding's contribution to this strategy is covered in detail in the next section.

Keep in mind that for an investor who had been using the BSM strategy, the worst market meltdowns, as measured by the DJIA, all would have been avoided:

- The October 28 and 29, 1929, crash, in which the DJIA dropped 25.2 percent

---

[4] *Stock Trader's Almanac 2011* (Hoboken, NJ: Wiley, 2011).

[5] Since investing in the DJIA as an index back in the 1950s was not possible (e.g., Diamonds ETF, traded on the American Stock Exchange, did not exist then), the results presented are theoretical in nature, based on back-testing the data. Also, the almanac does not mention whether or not reinvested dividends have been included in the performance numbers.

- The October 19, 1987, stock market crash, in which the DJIA plunged over 508 points, dropping 22.6 percent
- The 555-point drop on October 27, 1997 (–7.2 percent)
- The 513-point drop on August 31, 1998 (–6.4 percent)
- The 357-point drop on August 27, 1998 (–4.2 percent)
- The 1,370-point drop the week of September 21, 2001 (–14.3 percent), after the terrorist attack on the World Trade Center and Washington, DC.
- The 1,651-point decline during the third-quarter 2002 (–17.9 percent)
- The 733.08-point drop on October 15, 2008 (–7.9 percent), the 678.91-point drop on October 9, 2008 (–7.3 percent), and 777.68-point drop on September 29, 2008 (–7.0 percent)
- The 1,874.19-point drop the week of October 10, 2008 (–18.2 percent)

Jeffrey Hirsch used a different monthly strategy employing the Nasdaq Composite Index instead of the DJIA to see how that index performed. In this case, he used the best eight months (November 1–June 30) and the worst four months (July 1–October 31) in conjunction with the MACD signal to identify the optimal dates. Since that index began in 1971, Hirsch ran the numbers from 1971 through 2009. He found that a $10,000 initial investment in 1971 mushroomed to $874,360 if invested during the best eight-month period compared with a *loss* of $7,461 if it was invested during the other four months.[6] Clearly, there is seasonality in the stock market, and it worked on this index as well, which further adds to the validity of the concept.

### Sy Harding's Street Smart Report's Seasonal Timing Strategy

Sy Harding, founder and president of Asset Management Research Corporation, publishes the *Sy Harding's Street Smart Report* newsletter on his Web site, www.StreetSmartReport.com. Harding is also the author of *Riding the BEAR: How to Prosper in the Coming*

---

[6] *Stock Trader's Almanac 2011*, p. 58.

*Bear Market* (Adams Media, 1999), a paperback book that predicted the 2000–2002 bear market.[7]

Harding was searching for a strategy that would allow an investor to make money in the bear market that he anticipated was about to occur. His research eventually led him to evaluating seasonality. Building on the pioneering work on seasonality of Yale Hirsch, Ned Davis, and Norman Fosback, Harding recognized that the market does indeed have a favorable season and an unfavorable season, but his additional research convinced him that the beginning of those seasons varies quite widely from year to year. Rather than being an even-keeled six-months-in, six-months-out situation, he found that the market's favorable season can vary from as few as four months to as many as eight months.

His initial research first led him to use the next-to-last trading day of October as a strictly calendar-based entry and the fourth trading day of May as the optimal calendar-based exit. But his research also led him to believe that the calendar alone could not produce optimal results.

His *seasonal timing strategy* (STS) incorporates the MACD, a short-term momentum-reversal indicator, to better pinpoint the entries and exits. The indicator is used to determine if a rally has begun prior to the arrival of the calendar-based entry date. If so, the buy signal of the MACD indicator is used to provide an early entry rather than waiting for the actual calendar date. However, if the MACD indicator remains on a sell signal when the calendar-based entry date arrives, the rule is to delay the entry until the MACD indicator does trigger a buy signal.

If the MACD indicator triggers a sell signal prior to the arrival of the calendar date in the market's favorable season, that signal is used as the exit signal rather than waiting for the calendar date. However, if the MACD is still on a buy signal when the calendar date arrives, the investor simply waits until it does trigger a sell signal before exiting.

Figure 7-3 shows Harding's STS applied to the DJIA from 2000 through 2010, a period that encompassed very different market conditions—a strong bull market and two devastating bear markets.

---

[7] Sy Harding, *Riding the BEAR: How to Prosper in the Coming Bear Market* (Holbrook, MA: Adams Media Corporation, 1999).

**FIGURE 7-3**

STS from 2000 through mid-2010 with MACD signals.

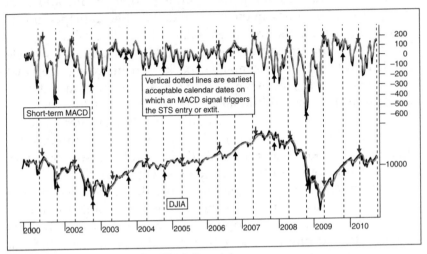

Source: Asset Management Resource Corp. Printed with permission.

The dotted vertical lines in the chart represent the typical calendar-based entries and exits. The arrows show the actual entries and exits of the strategy (as triggered by the MACD). Harding points out that the many short-term signals of the MACD throughout the year are ignored until within a week or two of the approaching calendar date. This means that the investor buys on the first MACD buy signal that takes place (or is already in place) on or after October 16 and exits on the first MACD sell signal that takes place (or is already in place) on or after April 20.

For comparisons of returns on an annual basis, Table 7-4 shows the conversion of the STS signals shown in Figure 7-3 to end-of-year numbers. Harding notes that the performance shown for the years 1999 forward is the actual performance of the actual *Street Smart Report* newsletter STS portfolio, which used various index funds in the favorable seasons. According to Harding, "There have been only seven years since 1970 in which the strategy was down for the year. The worst of those declines was the 3.6 percent decline in 2008, in the midst of one of the worst bear market years since the 1929 crash, and the 4.2 percent decline last year (2009). Prior to that, the worst decline for a year was 2.5 percent in 1977."

**TABLE 7-4**

Sy Harding's Seasonal Timing Strategy: 1999–2010*

| Year | Nasdaq | S&P 500 | DJIA | STS Using DJIA Index Fund |
|------|--------|---------|------|---------------------------|
| 1999 (bull market) | +85.6% | +20.1% | +26.8% | +35.1% |
| 2000 (bear market) | −39.3% | −9.1% | −4.6% | +2.1% |
| 2001 (bear market) | −21.1% | −11.9% | −5.3% | +11.1% |
| 2002 (bear market) | −31.5% | −22.1% | −14.7% | +3.1% |
| 2003 (bull market) | +50.0% | +28.7% | +27.6% | +11.2% |
| 2004 (bull market) | +8.6% | +10.9% | +5.5% | +8.1% |
| 2005 (bull market) | +1.4% | +4.8% | +1.6% | +0.6% |
| 2006 (bull market) | +9.5% | +15.4% | +18.5% | +14.2% |
| 2007 (bull market) | +9.8% | +5.4% | +8.6% | +11.2% |
| 2008 (bear market) | −40.5% | −36.1% | −31.3% | −3.6% |
| 2009 (bull market) | +43.8% | +22.4% | +18.8% | −4.2% |
| 2010 (to June 30) | −7.1% | −7.6% | −6.3% | +6.7% |
| 1-year return | +43.8% | +22.4% | +18.8% | −4.2% |
| 2-year return | −14.4% | −21.8% | −18.1% | −7.6% |
| 3-year return | −6.1% | −17.6% | −11.1% | +2.7% |
| 5-year return | +4.3% | −0.3% | +7.0% | +18.0% |
| 10-year return | −44.3% | −11.2% | +11.0% | +65.9% |
| 11-year return | +3.5% | +6.6% | +40.8% | +124.1% |

*Data include dividends and interest on cash.

Source: StreetSmart Report.com. Printed with permission.

Harding's STS resulted in good performance during bull market years but, more important, not losing in the 2000–2002 period, and losing only 3.6 percent in the crushing year of 2008, but unfortunately, underperforming badly in the 2009 recovery year. Thus, as you can see, STS underperformed in the bull markets of 2003, 2005, 2006, and 2009, yet overall returns were better than buy-and-hold with 50 percent less risk—certainly a commendable live performance.

As Table 7-4 indicates, over the 11-year period the STS using the DJIA Index produced a return of 124.1 percent compared with 40.8 percent for the same index using the buy-and-hold approach. The Nasdaq Composite and S&P 500 indexes were able to produce only single-digit gains. The STS wins hands down during bear market years. For example, during the 2000–2002 bear market, where the averages sustained large losses, STS actually gained a cumulative 16.3 percent and did not have a losing year. Again, in the brutal 2008 bear market, where the major averages lost between 31.3 and 40.5 percent, STS lost a meager 3.6 percent. In the first half of 2010, the STS was up 6.7 percent, whereas the three major averages were down about the same amount. The key point is that bear markets devastate portfolios. Therefore, any strategy that can consistently avoid bear markets is welcome.

## MARK VAKKUR'S CONTRIBUTION TO SEASONAL INVESTING

Mark Vakkur, M.D., mentioned in the beginning of this chapter, expanded on Hirsch's BSM strategy. Vakkur compared six strategies with buy-and-hold and cash for the 1950–1995 period. His work was published in the June 1996 issue of the *Technical Analysis of Stocks & Commodities* magazine.[8] Vakkur did *not* include reinvested dividends, which would have bolstered the buy-and-hold results.

Vakkur tested a number of different strategies, including:

1. Avoid September entirely. Liquidate investments on the last trading day of August, and buy back on the first trading day in October. Then, don't sell again until the last trading day of August of the next year. Do the same for all subsequent years.
2. Invest using Hirsch's BSM strategy using November entry and April exit dates.
3. Invest during Hirsch's worst months using a May entry and an October exit date.
4. Adopt a switching strategy: Be 100 percent invested in the best six months of November, December, January, March, April, and July. Be 50 percent invested and have 50 percent in cash (T-bills) in the next best three months of February, August, and October. And be 100 percent in cash for the worst three months of May, June, and September.

[8] Mark Vakkur, M.D., "Seasonality and the S&P 500," *Technical Analysis of Stocks & Commodities* 14(6), June 1996.

5. Have a 2:1 leverage, where 50 percent is invested with margin (2:1 leverage) for the best six months. As defined in strategy number 4, 100 percent is invested in the next best three months, and 100 percent is in cash for the worst three months.

6. Invest in all months of the year with 2:1 leverage.

## Results of Vakkur's Analysis

Table 7-5 shows the performance results of Vakkur's strategies. During this 45-year period, simply buying and holding the S&P 500 Index with a $10,000 stake in 1950 resulted in a total ending principal in 1995 of $372,388, which is equivalent to an average annual return of 8.4 percent. Investing solely in cash (T-bills) for the

**TABLE 7-5**

Vakkur's Seasonal Strategies Using the S&P 500 Index: January 1950 to December 1995*

| Strategy Used | Value of $10,000 | Average Annual Return | Standard Deviation | Risk-Adjusted Annual Return | Maximum Annual Gain | Maximum Annual Loss |
|---|---|---|---|---|---|---|
| Buy-and-hold | $372,388 | 8.40% | 14.40% | 7.30% | 57.00% | −41.30% |
| Ignore September | $624,135 | 9.60% | 13.90% | 8.70% | 56.80% | −33.50% |
| Nov.–April/T-bills† | $703,935 | 9.90% | 9.60% | 9.50% | 34.40% | −16.60% |
| May–Oct. | $58,670 | 4.00% | 8.60% | 3.60% | 32.90% | −26.90% |
| 100% Cash | $110,905 | 5.50% | 2.80% | 5.50% | 14.40% | N.A. |
| Switching‡ | $997,620 | 10.80% | 10.40% | 10.20% | 40.20% | −24.70% |
| 2:1 Leverage** | $1,839,958 | 12.30% | 21.50% | 10.00% | 79.10% | −49.60% |
| Jan.–Dec. 2:1 leverage†† | $54,903 | 3.90% | 28.50% | −0.20% | 119.40% | −70.60% |

N.A. = Not applicable.

\* Dividends were not included in this analysis.

† Invested in T-bills for the remaining months.

‡ Fully invested during the best six months, 50 percent invested and 50 percent in T-bills for the next-best three months, and 100 percent in T-bills for the worst three months, which are May, June, and September.

** Fifty percent margin invested for the best six months, 100 percent invested (no margin) for the next-best three months, and 100 percent in T-bills for the worst three months.

†† Always using 50 percent margin in all months. This is equivalent to 2:1 leverage.

Source: Mark Vakkur, M.D., "Seasonality and the S&P 500," *Technical Analysis of Stocks & Commodities* 14(6):38–47, June 1996. ©Technical Analysis, Inc. Used with permission.

entire 45 years rather than in the S&P 500 Index resulted in a total ending principal of $110,905. This provided a 5.5 percent annual return, with $261,483 less than buy-and-hold. Cash is not a viable investment, especially when adjusted for inflation.

Now let's review the results of not investing during September. By eliminating this one month each year, the total proceeds were $624,135, or an annual average return of 9.6 percent, which is $251,747 better than buy-and-hold. Moreover, the standard deviation (measure of volatility) and maximum 12-month loss encountered were lower than buy-and-hold. This means that an investor was getting a higher return with less risk. This is the smart way to invest.

According to the *Formula Research* newsletter (August 21, 2001), September has been the worst month over the past 25, 50, and 100 years: "In a study of 20 global markets from 1970 to 1992, September was the only month with negative returns in all 20 cases." The Hirsch BSM strategy of being invested from November to April did even better, totaling $703,935, or a 9.9 percent average annual return. This performance was $331,546 better than buy-and-hold. This strategy also had a much lower standard deviation and lower maximum 12-month loss than buy-and-hold. The opposite strategy of buying and remaining invested during the six unfavorable months of May through October resulted in an ending value of only $58,670, or 4 percent annualized with a lower standard deviation and lower maximum 12-month loss than buy-and-hold. Clearly, the worst six months are consistently poor in all respects.

A switching strategy also was tested, where a 100 percent invested position was taken during the best six months (as mentioned previously). Additionally, a 50 percent invested position and 50 percent cash position were taken for the next-best three months, respectively, and a 100 percent cash position (T-bills) was taken for the worst three months. This strategy resulted in an ending value of $997,620, with a 10.8 percent annual return, translating into $625,232 more than buy-and-hold. In essence, although the switching strategy is less risky than buy-and-hold, it returned 2.7 times the principal of buy-and-hold. This is an outstanding compromise of risk versus return.

The next strategy tested used margin for more leverage. The strategy of 2:1 leveraging consisted of using 50 percent margin during the best six months, 100 percent invested with no margin for the next-best three months, and going into cash during the worst three months. This strategy had an ending value of $1,839,958 and provided a 12.3 percent annual return. This translates into $1,467,570 more than buy-and-hold, an astounding difference. Of course, this strategy was more risky than buy-and-hold because of the leverage, and it had a higher standard deviation and larger yearly maximum gains and losses. Remember, though, that risk and reward usually go hand in hand. In this case, the higher risk turned into an exceptionally high reward, with a 394 percent increase in value. With the advent of leveraged mutual funds and leveraged exchange-traded funds (ETFs), this type of strategy now can be used without the need for the cost of margin.

## Performance from January 1996 to March 2002

Vakkur updated his 1996 data by publishing an article in the September 2002 issue of *Active Trader* magazine.[9] He did not provide the risk-adjusted return and 12-month maximum gain for this period, as he had in the previous article, nor did he include reinvested dividends in his calculations. And he didn't include the more aggressive strategies in his latest analysis. Table 7-6 provides the data for this latest time period.

**TABLE 7-6**

Vakkur's 1996–2001 Study Results: January 1996 to December 2001

| Strategy Used | Value of $10,000 | Average Annual Return | Standard Deviation | Maximum Annual Loss |
|---|---|---|---|---|
| Buy-and-hold | $18,629 | 10.93% | 19.03% | −14.90% |
| Ignore September | $19,411 | 11.69% | 14.87% | −9.40% |
| November–April/T-bills* | $20,834 | 13.00% | 12.60% | −10.00% |
| May–October | $11,984 | 3.06% | 10.36% | −12.80% |

*Invested in T-bills for the remaining months.

*Source:* Mark Vakkur, M.D., "Mark Your Calendar," *Active Trader*, September 2002, pp. 96–99. ©Active Trader Magazine. All rights reserved.

---

[9] Vakkur, "Mark Your Calendar," *Active Trader*, pp. 96–99.

Again, buy-and-hold is beaten by both the November–April strategy and by the September-avoidance strategy. In both instances, the annual returns were greater than buy-and-hold; the standard deviations and the maximum 12-month losses were lower as well. As expected, 100 percent cash fared poorly but better than investing during the weak monthly period of May to October. Moreover, the opposite strategy of buying in the weak period again showed the worst results. Thus, even during the last six years, the seasonal strategies continue to work as expected. This is consistent with Vakkur's prior (1996) work. Since that study was published, Vakkur has not updated it or it would have been included here.

## Additional Testing of September Avoidance Strategy

*Formula Research* (August 21, 2001) also tested Vakkur's September-avoidance strategy from 1950 through 2001.[10] With an initial $10,000 stake, this strategy would have returned an annualized total return of 13.4 percent, worth $5.6 million. During this same period, buy-and-hold would have generated a return of 12.5 percent and earned $3.9 million, whereas the Hirsch BSM strategy would have returned 12.1 percent a year, totaling $3.3 million. Clearly, the September-avoidance strategy has significantly outpaced the other two strategies. And remember that in the month of September in the years 2000, 2001, 2002, and 2008, the Nasdaq dropped –12.7, –17.0, –10.9, and –11.6 percent, respectively. Another four recent years of bad Septembers—the worst on record for the Nasdaq Composite.

Robert W. Colby also tested the September-avoidance strategy using the DJIA over a 101-year period from 1900 through 2000. In addition, instead of going to all-cash in September, Colby sold short on the last trading day in August and covered the short on the last trading day in September. Starting with $100 in 1900, this strategy would have resulted in a profit of $164,048, which was 644 percent greater than buy-and-hold (ending balance of $22,055).

Colby also tested a slight variation of this strategy—buying on October 27 (or the next closest trading day if the market was closed

---

[10] *Formula Research* (Vol. 6, No. 11), August 21, 2001.

on that day) while selling on the next September 5 (or the next closest trading day if the market was closed on that day). The same short strategy was used on September 5 and covered on October 27. This slight adjustment to the original test provided a substantial increase in profits to $644,467 compared with $20,699 for buy-and-hold. Thus this strategy beat buy-and-hold by 3,014 percent!

Of course, this strategy is not perfect. Not investing in September 2008 was an unexpected gift because the financial crisis was crushing Wall Street with a Nasadaq Composite loss of 11.6 percent. However, if you decided to sit out September 2010, you made a very big mistake because all the major averages had one of their best Septembers in decades, with the Nasdaq Composite up 12 percent, followed by the S&P 500 up 7.7 percent, and the DJIA up 6.7 percent.

## CONCLUSIONS

Now that you are thoroughly enlightened by the extensive research about the BSM strategy and the month of September, you're probably wondering how to go about using it to your advantage. You should consider the following alternatives:

- *Use the MACD indicator with the BSM strategy.* Use a free charting Web site such as www.bigcharts.com or www.StockCharts.com, or chart the index you are tracking (e.g., the DJIA or the S&P 500) for the past year using daily prices. Place the MACD indicator with settings of 12, 26, and 9 on the bottom of the chart. In the mid-April to May time frame, look for a MACD crossover sell signal to the downside (from above the 0 line). Likewise, in the mid-October to November time frame, look for a MACD crossover buy signal to the upside (from below its 0 line).
- *Avoid the stock market* entirely *each September.* If you're not using the BSM strategy, then you can avoid the stock market in September. Simply sell on the last day of August and buy on the first day of October. For the more venturesome investor, follow Colby's September strategy of shorting (using inverse mutual funds or ETFs) during September and covering and going long in October. And

you may want to consider using his other strategy of shorting (using inverse mutual funds or ETFs) on September 5 and covering the short on October 27 and then going long.

- *Subscribe to* Sy Harding's Street Smart Report *monthly newsletter for his STS signals for $275 a year.* Harding provides his newly revised methodology for the MACD-based signals via his hotline and on his Web site. This seasonal strategy is only one feature of this newsletter and hotline service. See Chapter 12 for complete information on this newsletter.

- *Subscribe to the monthly* Stock Trader's Almanac *for $295 a year.* Hirsch tracks the BSM strategy and provides his MACD buy and sell signals when they occur via Web and phone access. This is only one feature of the many features of this newsletter. Be aware, however, that Harding and Hirsch use a slightly different methodology for obtaining their MACD signals, so you have to decide which one has the best track record. In 2003, for example, Hirsch's MACD sell signal was triggered on April 10, whereas Harding's was hit on May 19. Harding's signal captured a higher return than Hirsch's signal.

It's your choice which alternative BSM to use based on your ability to work with the MACD and the charting software and on your understanding of the strategy. As far as actually using the September-avoidance strategy or the strategies with leverage illustrated by Vakkur, that choice is solely up to you based on your level of knowledge and comfort with the risks these strategies entail. As far as which investment vehicles to use, you can select from any of those mentioned in previous chapters, such as index funds, sector funds, leveraged funds, and the many ETFs. Be sure to use stop-limit orders on ETFs in case the buy strategy does not work in certain years, which is always a possibility. You would reenter the market on the next year's buy signal.

Finally, to visually observe the BSM (without using the MACD) performance over 60 years, look at Figure 7-4, which compares the BSM with the worst six months and the S&P 500 Index from 1950 to 2010 October. Clearly, with 50 percent less risk than

**FIGURE  7-4**

Best six-months' performance, 1950–2010.

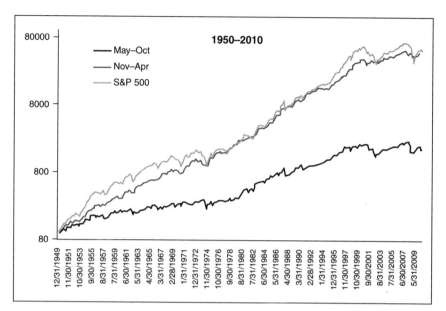

*Source:* www.mebanefaber.com. October 30, 2010 blog. Printed with permission of Mebane Faber.

buy-and-hold, a higher average annualized return, and the simplic-
ity of executing this strategy, it is definitely one to consider.

# Combining Presidential Cycle Years with Seasonality

*Bulls and bears aren't responsible for as many stock losses as bum steers.*

—Olin Miller

## PRESIDENTIAL CYCLE INVESTING

After spending time going through the monthly seasonality strategies presented in the last chapter, you probably thought that's about all you can squeeze out of the calendar. Guess again. There are even more profitable strategies in this chapter. If you are interested in pursuing seasonal strategies as a trader or investor, be sure to get a copy of *Stock Trader's Almanac 2011* (Wiley, 2011) at Amazon.com or your local book store. This book is updated yearly, so make sure to buy the latest edition.

### Vakkur Tests Optimal Months Combined with Optimal Presidential Cycle Years

Mark Vakkur made another significant research contribution by publishing another seminal article in the October 1996 issue of *Technical Analysis of Stocks & Commodities.*[1] In this nine-page article,

---

[1] Mark Vakkur, M.D., "Seasonality and the Presidential Election Cycle," *Technical Analysis of Stocks & Commodities* (Vol. 14, No. 10), October 1996.

Vakkur combined the optimal months with the optimal presidential cycle years. The results were outstanding, so let's get right to them. The election cycle years are:

- *Pre-election year.* The year before the election year (e.g., 1987, 1991, 1995, 1999, 2003, 2007, and 2011).
- *Election year.* The year of the election (e.g., 1988, 1992, 1996, 2000, 2004, 2008, and 2012).
- *Post-election year.* The year after the election year (e.g., 1989, 1993, 1997, 2001, 2005, 2009, and 2013).
- *Midterm election year.* Two years after the last election year and also prior to the next election year (e.g., 1990, 1994, 1998, 2002, 2006, 2010, and 2014).

Historically, there is a four-year cycle in the stock market encompassing the presidential election years. Usually, the market rises more in the pre-election year than in the election year itself. The election year is the second best of those four years. And in the two years after the election, the market usually does not make much progress. Table 8-1 contains the data from 1950 through 1995 delineating the average monthly returns of the Standard & Poor's (S&P) 500 Index in each of the four years of the presidential election cycle as compiled by Vakkur.

**TABLE 8-1**

Average Monthly Return of the S&P 500 (Dividends Excluded), 1950–1995

| | Average Monthly Return of S&P 500 | % Plus or Minus to All Years | % of Months Market Rose | % Annual Return | Percentage of Years Market Rose |
|---|---|---|---|---|---|
| All years | 0.74% | NA | 57% | 9.00% | 71% |
| Post-election | 0.12% | −0.62% | 49% | 2.00% | 45% |
| Midterm | 0.46% | −0.28% | 57% | 4.63% | 55% |
| Pre-election | 1.50% | 0.76% | 66% | 18.72% | 100% |
| Election | 0.84% | 0.10% | 62% | 10.08% | 91% |

*Source:* Vakkur, Mark, M.D., "Seasonality and the Presidential Election Cycle," *Technical Analysis of Stocks & Commodities* 14(10):22, October 1996. © 1996 Technical Analysis, Inc. Used with permission.

As the table indicates, the pre-election years' stock market returns are by far superior to any of the other three years of the presidential election cycle. The average annual return since 1950 was 18.72 percent, and the market rose every pre-election year. The next-best-performing year was the election year, with an average annual return of 10.08 percent and a 91 percent success ratio.

Conversely, the worst-performing presidential cycle year was the post-election year, with an average annual return of only 2 percent and with the markets rising only 45 percent of the time in those years. Next-worst performance was the midterm year, which sported an average annual return of a meager 4.63 percent, with a positive market in 55 percent of the years.

## Freeburg Tests Presidential Cycle Back to 1886

Nelson Freeburg tested the quadrennial presidential cycle back to 1886 through 2001 to double-check and expand on the data tested by Vakkur. In the May 31, 2002, issue of *Formula Research*, Freeburg provided the statistics for the Dow Jones Industrial Average (DJIA; see Table 8-2).[2] Keep in mind that Vakkur used the S&P 500 Index (without dividends) in calculating his numbers (nominal return), whereas Freeburg used the DJIA (without dividends) because that index had a much longer price history available. Clearly, there has been a definite bias toward higher stock market returns in the pre-

**TABLE 8-2**

DJIA Annual Gain by Year in Electoral Cycle, 1886–2001

| Year | Annual Gain | Percentage Years Up |
|------|-------------|---------------------|
| All years | 7.60% | 64% |
| Pre-election | 11.10% | 79% |
| Election | 8.40% | 69% |
| Midterm | 4.00% | 55% |
| Post-election | 5.00% | 52% |

*Source: Formula Research, May 31, 2002.*

[2] *Formula Research* (Vol. 6, No. 12), May 31, 2002.

election and election years during the 45 years observed in Vakkur's analysis, as well as in Freeburg's more up-to-date and comprehensive analysis.

How did the electoral cycle work out in recent years? Actually, it was a mixed bag. The election cycle performance was as follows:

- 2002, 2006, and 2010 (midterm): –16.8%, +16.3%, +6.8% (October 22, 2010 price)
- 2003 and 2007 (pre-election): +25.3%, +6.4%
- 2004 and 2008 (election): +3.1%, –33.8%
- 2005 and 2009 (post-election): +3.1%, +18.8%

## Vakkur's Leveraged Strategies Earn Millions

Table 8-3 shows how an investor fared by taking advantage of Vakkur's several strategies from 1950 to 1995.[3] First, let's get the lowdown on the returns from buy-and-hold. This often-touted simple, no-decision strategy had an average annual return of 8.4 percent that turned a $10,000 initial investment into $372,388 with a 12-month maximum drawdown (or maximum loss) of 41.3 percent during the test period. This means that the buy-and-hold investor sat through this loss without flinching. In reality, the average investor would have a hard time doing this.

Now compare those results with the simple strategy of investing only during the best-performing two presidential cycle years—the pre-election and election years—and remaining in cash for the other two years. This strategy has an average annual return of 10.0 percent, which is 1.6 percentage points a year better than buy-and-hold. However, over 45 years, that incremental difference resulted in growth of the $10,000 investment to $733,605 compared with $372,388 for buy-and-hold. This translates into a 97 percent improvement over buy-and-hold, with a standard deviation of only 8.3 percent versus 14 percent for buy-and-hold, and a maximum 12-month drawdown of only 18.7 percent. Thus, on all counts, this presidential cycle strategy provided superior results with 50 percent less risk because the investor was invested for only two years out of four. Higher return with less risk is always a win-win strategy.

---

[3] Vakkur, "Seasonality and the Presidential Election Cycle."

**TABLE 8-3**

Comparison of the Buy-and-Hold Scenario with Presidential Election Cycle Scenario, January 1950 to December 1995

| Strategy Used | Value of $10,000 | Average Annual Return | Standard Deviation | Risk-Adjusted Annual Return | Maximum Annual Gain | Maximum Annual Loss |
|---|---|---|---|---|---|---|
| Buy-and-hold | $372,388 | 8.40% | 14.40% | 7.30% | 57.00% | −41.30% |
| 100% cash | $110,905 | 5.50% | 2.80% | 5.50% | 14.40% | 0.90% |
| Pre-election and election years | $733,605 | 10.00% | 8.30% | 9.70% | 43.40% | −18.70% |
| Post-election and midterm years | $56,297 | 3.90% | 11.80% | 3.20% | 38.90% | −41.30% |
| 2:1 Leverage* | $1,272,369 | 11.40% | 14.80% | 10.03% | 86.30% | −46.00% |
| Leverage best months† | $2,183,257 | 12.70% | 15.20% | 11.60% | 64.20% | −21.20% |
| Optimal months‡ | $5,189,384 | 14.90% | 15.50% | 13.70% | 60.10% | −21.00% |

*2:1 leverage (50 percent margin) in pre-election year and 100 percent invested in election year.

†Leveraged 2:1 (November–April) in the pre-election and election years, 100 percent invested during these same months in the post-election and midterm election years, and 100 percent invested during the May–October period during the same two years. The only time there would be a 100 percent cash allocation would be in the May–October post-election and midterm election years.

‡Optimal months: 2:1 leverage in pre-election and election years in the following months in those years: January to April, July, November, and December; 100 percent cash in May and September of all four years and June and August of the post-election and midterm election years; and 100 percent invested in all the other months not mentioned—January to April, July, and October to December—in the post-election/midterm years and June and August in the pre-election years.

Source: Mark, Vakkur, M.D., "Seasonality and the Presidential Election Cycle," *Technical Analysis of Stocks & Commodities* (Vol. 14, No. 10), October 1996. Copyright 1996 © Technical Analysis, Inc. Used with permission.

You may be curious to see the results of investing only in the worst two performing presidential cycle years—the post-election and midterm election years. As expected, the performance results were much worse than buy-and-hold, with only a 3.9 percent average annual return and the same annual maximum drawdown of −41.3 percent. Even the lowly 100 percent cash portfolio (not investing at all) beat these two years' performance by generating an average annual return of 5.5 percent with no negative drawdown. When cash is able to beat buy-and-hold (for the worst two presidential cycle years), you know that you should avoid investing at all. Vakkur tested a number of different strategies to determine their profitability. The first strategy used was with 2:1 leveraging. This strategy used 50 percent margin in the pre-election year, invested funds with no margin in the election year, and was 100 percent in cash for the other two years. As expected, this strategy increased the return by 3.41 percent over buy-and-hold.

With an average annual return of 11.4 percent and an ending balance of $1,272,369, this leveraged strategy provided an additional return of $538,764 over the nonleveraged pre-election and election year strategy. Using this more aggressive strategy also resulted in more than doubling the maximum annual drawdown (largest loss incurred) to –46 percent from –18.7 percent in the prior strategy. Also, the maximum annual gain jumped about 100 percent, to 86.3 percent from 43.4 percent. And the standard deviation (variability around the 11.4 percent return) rose to 14.8 percent from 8.3 percent.

As Milton Friedman, the Noble Laureate economist, said, "There is no such thing as a free lunch." And, as the saying goes, "No pain, no gain." As mentioned earlier, risk and reward go hand in hand. Investors who have a higher risk tolerance may want to consider using this leveraged strategy. However, they should use a stop-loss limit order to minimize the risk of a large intrayear drawdown and avoid getting clobbered when the market goes against them. And leveraged exchanged-traded funds (ETFs) can be used instead of using margin and paying for margin interest.

Vakkur tested another leveraged strategy called the *leveraged best months* (LBM) *strategy*. Here, the best-performing months (November to April) of the year were leveraged 2 to 1 (50 percent margin) in the pre-election and election years, 100 percent was invested during these same months in the post-election and midterm election years, and 100 percent was invested during the May–October period during the same two years. The only time that there would be a 100 percent cash allocation would be in the May–October post-election and midterm election years.

This strategy really hit pay dirt, with an annual return of 12.7 percent and total ending principal of $2,183,257. Moreover, both the maximum drawdown and the maximum yearly gain were reduced. And the standard deviation moved up only slightly to 15.2 percent from that of the previously reviewed 2:1 leveraged strategy of 14.8 percent. On a risk-adjusted basis, the LBM strategy is the best tested so far. This strategy was less risky than the 2:1 leveraged strategy while providing an additional $910,888, quite an astounding difference in the bottom line.

Before reviewing another highly profitable leveraged strategy that more than doubled the LBM returns, let's look at Table 8-4 showing the monthly returns over 45 years in each of the four election cycle years. The best seven months in the pre-election and election years were January, February, March, April, July, November, and December. The worst months in all the four election cycle years were May and September. Two more worst months occurred in June and August of the post-election and midterm election years.

## TABLE 8-4

Monthly Results During Quadrennial Presidential Election Year Cycle, January 1950 to December 1995

| Month | Post-election Average S&P 500 Return (%) | Midterm Average S&P 500 Return (%) | Pre-election Average S&P 500 Return (%) | Election Average S&P 500 Return (%) |
|---|---|---|---|---|
| All | 0.12 | 0.46 | 1.50 | 0.84 |
| January | 0.71 | −0.90 | 5.38 | 0.87 |
| February | −1.17 | 0.97 | 1.44 | 0.08 |
| March | 0.90 | −0.36 | 2.29 | 0.19 |
| April | 0.24 | 0.39 | 3.27 | 0.93 |
| May | 1.00 | −0.20 | −0.14 | 0.01 |
| June | −1.07 | −2.12 | 1.59 | 2.00 |
| July | 1.10 | 1.27 | 1.65 | 1.10 |
| August | −1.03 | 0.49 | 1.56 | 0.43 |
| September | −1.28 | −0.98 | −0.40 | 0.27 |
| October | 1.45 | 2.51 | −2.54 | 0.44 |
| November | 0.35 | 2.46 | 0.58 | 2.32 |
| December | 0.18 | 1.97 | 3.35 | 1.43 |
| Nov.–Jan. | 0.41 | 1.18 | 3.10 | 1.54 |
| Nov.–Apr. | 0.20 | 0.76 | 2.72 | 0.97 |
| May–Oct. | 0.03 | 0.16 | 0.29 | 0.71 |

*Source:* Mark, Vakkur, M.D., "Seasonality and the Presidential Election Cycle," *Technical Analysis of Stocks & Commodities* (Vol. 14, No. 10), page 30, October 1996. Copyright © 1996 Technical Analysis, Inc. Used with permission.

All the other months not mentioned—January, February, March, April, July, October, November, and December in the post-election/midterm years and June and August in the pre-election years—were considered average months.

Using this information, Vakkur formulated another highly profitable strategy that he referred to as the *optimal months strategy*. Look at the footnotes in Table 8-3, which provide the exact optimal months strategy used. That strategy produced an annual return of 14.9 percent, or an astonishing $5,189,384, over the 45 years tested. With only a slightly higher 0.3 percent standard deviation than the LBM strategy and virtually equivalent drawdowns, this strategy added another $3 million to the bottom line. Also, on a risk-adjusted basis, this strategy had the highest annual return of all the strategies illustrated, at 13.7 percent.

Freeburg also tested the strategy of investing in the market (using the DJIA) only in the pre-election and election years from 1886 to 2001 and going into cash in the other two years.[4] He found that this strategy resulted in an annual return of 5.9 percent compared with 5.2 percent for buy-and-hold. This 70-basis-point difference on a $10,000 initial investment was valued at $8.4 million at the end of the test period compared with $3.7 million for buy-and-hold. The opposite strategy of investing in the two weakest performing years and going to cash during the two strong years since 1886 has returned 3.6 percent per year, worth $607,000. This is 93 percent less than the optimal strategy.

Freeburg ran additional leveraged tests of the data using the strongest months in the strongest years, and they confirmed Vakkur's results. Since Vakkur analyzed the data through 1995, the question is how has the four-year presidential cycle performed since then (in particular, using the strongest months in the strongest years)? Freeburg, who updated the data from 1995 through April 2002, found that using Vakkur's methodology produced an annual gain of 17.4 percent per year compared with 10.7 percent for buy-and-hold with the S&P 500 Index. Even since 1886, use of the same methodology has given an annual return of 8.3 percent compared with 5.2 percent for the DJIA.

---

4 *Formula Research* (Vol. 6, No. 12), page 8, May 31, 2002.

In conclusion, *focusing on the optimal months in the presidential election cycle years really brings home the bacon.* This strategy is far superior to just investing during the entire pre-election and election years with outstanding return and risk parameters.

## MIDTERM TO ELECTION YEAR PHENOMENA

Over the years, a number of analysts have scrutinized the presidential cycle years to look for patterns. One very consistent pattern that has been uncovered occurs from the lows of the midterm election cycle year to the highs of the following election year. These results are shown in Table 8-5, which was prepared by the Hays Advisory Group.[5] Of the 23 midterm years until the election years, 22 have produced gains. Although the S&P 500 Index gains have ranged from 18.4 to 121.9 percent, the average gain has been 55 percent. Excluding the only loss of 43.6 percent from 1930 to 1932, the average gain for the period has been 59.44 percent.

Table 8-6, also provided by the Hays Advisory Group, provides the S&P 500 Index data not only for the midterm year but also for the other surrounding years.[6] Just examining the midterm year November to April performance since 1950, we see that in every instance there was a positive return. The mean return was 16.4 percent, with the lowest return being 3.52 percent in 2002 and the highest being 24.86 percent in 1970. The next-best year was the pre-election year, with a mean return of 5.1 percent, with three years of small negative returns.

The election year November–April period returned an average 2.8 percent with four negative years. Lastly, the post-election year performance was the third best, with a mean return of 3.7 percent with seven down periods.

## MINTON'S PRESIDENTIAL CYCLE STRATEGY

Dr. Jerry Minton is president of Alpha Investment Management, a money management firm using asset-allocation strategies that are

---

[5] Don Hays, "Morning Market Comments," September 16, 2002. Reprinted with permission of the Hays Advisory Group. Updated in 2010.
[6] Ibid.

**TABLE 8-5**

Presidential Election Cycle, Low to High

| Midyear | Midyear Low | Election Year | Election Year High | % Gain or (Loss) |
|---|---|---|---|---|
| 1918 | 73.38 | 1920 | 109.88 | 49.70% |
| 1922 | 78.59 | 1924 | 120.51 | 53.30% |
| 1926 | 135.2 | 1928 | 300 | 121.90% |
| 1930 | 157.51 | 1932 | 88.78 | −43.60% |
| 1934 | 85.51 | 1396 | 184.9 | 116.20% |
| 1938 | 98.95 | 1940 | 152.8 | 54.40% |
| 1942 | 92.92 | 1944 | 152.53 | 64.20% |
| 1946 | 163.12 | 1948 | 193.16 | 18.40% |
| 1950 | 196.81 | 1952 | 292 | 48.40% |
| 1954 | 279.87 | 1956 | 521.05 | 86.20% |
| 1958 | 436.89 | 1960 | 685.47 | 56.90% |
| 1962 | 535.76 | 1964 | 891.71 | 66.40% |
| 1966 | 744.32 | 1968 | 985.21 | 32.40% |
| 1970 | 631.16 | 1972 | 1036.27 | 64.20% |
| 1974 | 577.6 | 1976 | 1014.79 | 75.70% |
| 1978 | 742.12 | 1980 | 1000.17 | 34.80% |
| 1982 | 776.92 | 1984 | 1286.64 | 65.60% |
| 1986 | 1502.29 | 1988 | 2183.5 | 45.30% |
| 1990 | 2365.1 | 1992 | 3413.21 | 44.30% |
| 1994 | 3593.25 | 1996 | 6560.91 | 82.60% |
| 1998 | 7539.07 | 2000 | 11722.98 | 55.50% |
| 2002 | 7286.24 | 2004 | 10854.54 | 48.97% |
| 2006 | 10667.39 | 2008 | 13058.2 | 22.41% |
| 2010 | 9686.48 | 2012 | | |
| Average of all years | | | | 54.96% |
| Average of all up years | | | | 59.44% |

*Note:* The DJIA is used as the index in these comparisons.

*Source:* "Morning Market Comments by Don Hays," September 16, 2002. Updated by Mark Dodson through 2010. Reprinted with permission of the Hays Advisory Group.

based on long-term seasonal factors. The research in this section was published under the title, "The Election Cycle: How to Use the Political Class for Investment Gains." The complete research paper can be found on his Web site www.alphaim.net (select the "Alpha Research" tab, then click on "Recent Articles").

**TABLE 8-6**

Election Cycle and November–April Returns*

| Nov.–Apr. | Midterm | Pre-election | Election | Post-election |
|---|---|---|---|---|
| 1950 | 14.85% | 1.66% | 0.41% | 12.66% |
| 1954 | 19.82% | 14.27% | 0.35% | 15.16% |
| 1958 | 12.20% | –5.48% | 22.33% | 5.80% |
| 1962 | 23.50% | 7.36% | 5.01% | –4.93% |
| 1966 | 17.22% | 4.46% | 0.27% | –1.47% |
| 1970 | 24.86% | 14.26% | –4.13% | –16.06% |
| 1974 | 18.13% | 14.15% | –4.33% | –16.60% |
| 1978 | 9.24% | 4.39% | 4.24% | 4.86% |
| 1982 | 22.97% | –2.15% | 8.27% | –4.47% |
| 1986 | 18.19% | 3.79% | 10.99% | 24.08% |
| 1990 | 23.47% | 5.73% | 5.14% | –2.81% |
| 1994 | 8.97% | 12.50% | 13.62% | –3.60% |
| 1998 | 21.53% | 6.57% | –12.59% | 21.55% |
| 2002 | 3.52% | 5.38% | 2.36% | 1.61% |
| 2006 | 7.58% | –10.57% | –9.90% | 8.58% |
| 2010 | | | | 14.52% |
| Mean | 16.4% | 5.1% | 2.8% | 3.7% |
| Median | 18.1% | 5.4% | 2.4% | 3.2% |
| Standard deviation | 6.7% | 7.3% | 9.0% | 12.0% |

*The data in this table represent percentage changes for the S&P 500 Index.

Source: Mark Dodson and the Hays Advisory Group, "Morning Market Comments," September 26, 2002. Updated 2010 by Mark Dodson. Reprinted with permission.

Since 1933, the DJIA (with dividends) has advanced an average of 17.1 percent during every pre-election year (year three of the presidential term), about triple the average return of the other three years. Every bear market with the exception of the 1987 collapse has occurred outside the pre-election year over this 78-year period. As you can see in Table 8-7, the best quarters of the presidential election cycle years are the fourth quarter of the midterm year and all the quarters of the pre-election year.

Table 8-8 provides the percentage return during this consecutive 15-month cycle period (dubbed the "power zone" by Minton) since 1934, showing an average return of 25.6 percent, which is an annualized return of 19.9 percent without dividends.

**TABLE 8-7**

Four-Year Presidential Election Cycle: Quarterly % Changes

| | Dow Jones Industrials (1933–2009) | | | | |
|---|---|---|---|---|---|
| | Q1 | Q2 | Q3 | Q4 | Year |
| Post-election | −0.4% | 4.7% | −0.6% | 1.3% | 5.0% |
| Midterm | 0.4% | 0.9% | −1.4% | 7.2% | 6.7% |
| Pre-election | 5.8% | 5.5% | 3.3% | 1.6% | 17.1% |
| Election | 0.6% | 0.8% | 1.1% | 2.2% | 4.8% |

*Source:* Dr. Jerry Minton.

**TABLE 8-8**

Dow Appreciation During the 15-Month Favorable Period of the Election Cycle*

| Start Date | Start Year | End Date | End Year | Percentage (±) |
|---|---|---|---|---|
| Sept. 30 | 1934 | Dec. 31 | 1935 | 55.6 |
| Sept. 30 | 1938 | Dec. 31 | 1939 | 3.2 |
| Sept. 30 | 1942 | Dec. 31 | 1943 | 24.5 |
| Sept. 30 | 1946 | Dec. 31 | 1947 | 5.1 |
| Sept. 30 | 1950 | Dec. 31 | 1951 | 18.9 |
| Sept. 30 | 1954 | Dec. 31 | 1955 | 35.5 |
| Sept. 30 | 1958 | Dec. 31 | 1959 | 27.7 |
| Sept. 30 | 1962 | Dec. 31 | 1963 | 31.8 |
| Sept. 30 | 1966 | Dec. 31 | 1967 | 16.9 |
| Sept. 30 | 1970 | Dec. 31 | 1971 | 17.0 |
| Sept. 30 | 1974 | Dec. 31 | 1975 | 40.2 |
| Sept. 30 | 1978 | Dec. 31 | 1979 | (3.1) |
| Sept. 30 | 1982 | Dec. 31 | 1983 | 40.4 |
| Sept. 30 | 1986 | Dec. 31 | 1987 | 9.7 |
| Sept. 30 | 1990 | Dec. 31 | 1991 | 29.1 |
| Sept. 30 | 1994 | Dec. 31 | 1995 | 33.1 |
| Sept. 30 | 1998 | Dec. 31 | 1999 | 46.6 |
| Sept. 30 | 2002 | Dec. 31 | 2003 | 37.7 |
| Sept. 30 | 2006 | Dec. 31 | 2007 | 13.6 |
| Average | | | | 25.6 |

*Dividends not included.
*Source:* Jay Kaeppel, *Seasonal Stock Market Trends* (Hoboken, NJ: Wiley, 2008).

Over the past 50 years (Table 8-9), the performance of the S&P 500 over the power-zone periods has averaged 30.3 percent.

In comparison, Table 8-10 shows the Nasdaq's remarkable performance of the power-zone periods since 1962. Clearly, the

## TABLE 8-9

Performance of Power-Zone Periods (S&P 500 without Dividends)

| | |
|---|---|
| 1954–1955 | 40.8% |
| 1958–1959 | 19.7% |
| 1962–1963 | 18.9% |
| 1966–1967 | 26.0% |
| 1970–1971 | 21.2% |
| 1974–1975 | 50.1% |
| 1978–1979 | 12.8% |
| 1982–1983 | 44.9% |
| 1986–1987 | 11.1% |
| 1990–1991 | 42.2% |
| 1994–1995 | 37.6% |
| 1998–1999 | 46.8% |
| 2002–2003 | 39.5% |
| 2006–2007 | 12.6% |
| **Average** | **30.3%** |

Source: Dr. Jerry Minton.

## TABLE 8-10

Nasdaq 15-Month Cycle Performance (without Dividends)

| | |
|---|---|
| 1962–1963 | 26.0% |
| 1966–1967 | 67.9% |
| 1970–1971 | 37.2% |
| 1974–1975 | 39.5% |
| 1978–1979 | 13.7% |
| 1982–1983 | 48.5% |
| 1986–1987 | –5.9% |
| 1990–1991 | 70.1% |
| 1994–1995 | 37.8% |
| 1998–1999 | 140.8% |
| 2002–2003 | 71.1% |
| 2006–2007 | 17.8% |
| **Average** | **47.0%** |

Source: Dr. Jerry Minton.

average performance of 47 percent is substantial by any measure. Moreover, there was only one losing period of –5.9 percent in 1986–1987.

## Minton's Strategy Description

The strategy is to invest in the stock market only during every power-zone period, as described previously, with the portfolio split evenly between the S&P 500 Index and the Nasdaq 100 Composite. This portfolio contains large-cap stocks with an overweight to growth and technology companies. During the remaining periods, the funds are invested in the Barclay's Capital 1–3 Year Treasury Index.

Figure 8-1 shows the performance of this approach. Since 1989, $1 invested in the five power-zone periods grew to $19.50. The same dollar, invested continuously in the S&P 500, with dividends, grew to $4.20. Invested just 30 percent of the time in equities, this simple election cycle strategy produced a 20-year average return of 16.1 percent, with no down years. The S&P 500, over the same period, returned 7.43 percent, with dividends, with multiple down years and more volatility.

**FIGURE 8-1**

50% S&P 500/50% Nasdaq 100 invested during power zones and Barclays Capital 1- to 3-Year Treasury Index invested in all other periods.

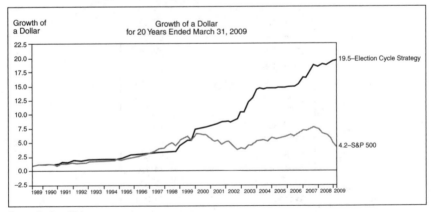

*Source:* Dr. Jerry Minton.

Over the past decade, the stock market has destroyed capital and reduced purchasing power at an alarming rate. For the 10-year period ending March 31, 2009, the total return of the S&P 500 Index was –26.3 percent. In real, inflation-adjusted terms, the total return was –65.3 percent, a real loss of 6.35 percent per year. To recover this loss will require about a 200 percent real increase. Minton indicated that he has no doubt that the recovery period will exceed 10 years, which means at least a 20-year dead zone for the market. Pity the poor indexer who staked it all on the market in the late 1990s.

If the past decade has taught us anything, it is that the doctrine of being continuously invested in the market is bankrupt. Any investment strategy that results in a 65 percent real loss over a decade cannot be a sound choice for serious investors. It certainly cannot be a strategy for retirees who are drawing down their savings constantly.

The simple election cycle strategy described in this section is a good alternative to the conventional buy-and-hold doctrine. By accepting market risk only during the power-zone period, the entire political establishment is on our side. This is a powerful form of portfolio insurance. It shows up in the real-return comparisons for the past decade. Look at Figure 8-2 to see the exceptional return of this strategy compared with buy-and-hold with the S&P 500 Index.

## FIGURE 8-2

Cumulative real return for 10 years, ending March 31, 2009.

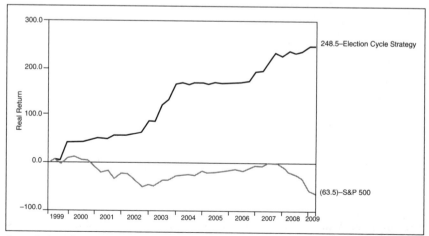

*Source:* Dr. Jerry Minton.

## CONCLUSIONS

Based on the research by Freeburg, Vakkur, the Hays Advisory Group, and Dr. Jerry Minton,[7] the intelligent investor should carefully consider the potential financial benefits of combining the strongest seasonal monthly and presidential cycle years.

With seasonality investing, there is always something happening, either on the long or the short side of the market, and you can invest on either side of the market if you know what you are doing. Buy-and-hold is certainly not a recommended strategy in any circumstance, especially in light of the ability to use calendar-based investing strategies to limit losses during the weak presidential cycle years. The recommended investment vehicles to use for both the seasonal and presidential cycle strategies are either index funds or regular ETFs (such as the SPY and QQQQs), as well as leveraged ETFs (such as QLD and QID). Of course, you will be paying capital gains taxes if you are investing in nonretirement funds, and you won't be if you are investing your retirement funds. Therefore, these strategies are particularly attractive for your retirement accounts, where your profits compound year over year tax-free.

---

[7] Arthur Jerry Minton, "The Election Cycle: How to Use Political Class for Investment Gain" (New York: Alpha Investment Management, 2009).

## CHAPTER 9

# Using Simple Moving Averages to Time the Market

*There is only one side of the market and it is not the bull side or the bear side, but the right side.*

—Jesse Livermore

**U**sing a moving average on a price chart of an index or exchange-traded fund (ETF) indicates to an investor which side of the market to be on. This approach will enable an investor to capture approximately 75 percent of the move in each direction. Expect to miss the first part of a trend change because the moving-average line lags the market, being based on historical data. When a new moving-average signal is given, the odds are in your favor that you will make money if you invest with the new trend.

## SIMPLE MOVING-AVERAGE BASICS

A simple moving average is calculated each day by adding the last day's closing price to the total of all closing prices over the time period chosen and then subtracting the first day's closing price. However, you need not calculate it because all the Internet charting Web sites automatically do it for you once you indicate the time frame you wish to graph.

Securities prices, market indexes, and mutual-fund prices vacillate up and down from day to day, week to week, and month to month. It is often difficult to discern which way the prices are actually moving. The moving average is used to smooth the data so that the trend can be easily detected. A rising moving-average line indicates that prices are trending up, whereas a declining line indicates the opposite. A flat line indicates a market stuck in a trading range that can't seem to make up its mind where it is going. Frequently, the market is in a fixed trading range bouncing between the upper and lower limits (price levels) for an extended period of time. The smart investor waits for this trading range to be pierced either up or down before making a move in the direction of the breakout.

You can create a moving average of any length (e.g., 9-, 25-, 65-, or 100-day moving average) and for any time period (minutes, hours, days, weeks, or months) depending on what you are trying to achieve, for example, for trading for day trading (minute charts) or for intermediate investing (daily and weekly charts) and for long-term investing (weekly and monthly charts).

Basically, when timing the market, you want to be long (invested) the market at the instant when the price of the stock or index crosses above the moving-average line and out-of-the-market (in cash) or short the market when the price of the stock or index crosses below its moving-average line. The major market indexes, such as the Dow Jones Industrial Average (DJIA), the Nasdaq Composite, the Standard & Poor's (S&P) 500 Index, or the Wilshire 500 Index, can be used to determine the market trend using the moving-average approach.

## 50-Day Moving Average (dma)

Figure 9-1 (which shows both the 50- and 200-dmas for comparative purposes) shows that when S&P 500 Index's price crossed below the 50-day moving average (line closest to index price) in June and September 2008, you would have exited the market, missing the bulk of the devastation from September 2008 through March 2009. And at the end of March 2009, the index crossed the 50-dma to the upside, indicating a buy signal on the market. However, as you can see, there were whipsaws above and below this moving-average line in June, July, and November 2009, followed by more whipsaws in 2010. This would have resulted in numerous buy and sell signals, resulting in commission costs and some small losses because the

**FIGURE 9-1**

S&P 500 index with 50-dma and 200-dma.

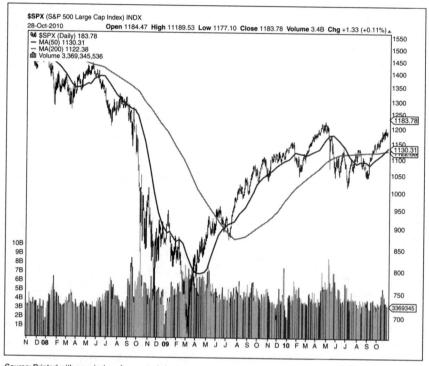

Source: Printed with permission of www.stockcharts.com

trend was up during this period. Whipsaws are a common feature of moving averages, but such is the price you pay to stay on the right side of the market. Once the clear trend is established, it will continue until a trend reversal occurs.

## 200-Day Moving Average

The 200-dma is most indicative of the long-term trend because it covers 40 weeks. Viewing the same chart in Figure 9-1 but now looking at the 200-dma, you can see that the index was below this moving average at the beginning of 2008. The index actually crossed it in December 2007, but it was blocked by the description in the left corner of the chart. Thus you would have had a market sell signal in December 2007, missing the entire brutal 2008 bear market. The first buy signal occurred in early June 2009, then two minor whipsaws occurred, then another buy signal occurred in early July, and then other whipsaws occurred in May through September. Thus even the longer 200-dma has whipsaws as the market rests before making its next move.

Unfortunately, no one can predict whether that move will be up or down, so just pay attention to what the charts are saying, and follow the indicator if you are using it in your arsenal of tools. Some of the more popular moving-average periods used by market professionals are the 20-dma, the 50-dma, and the 200-dma.

## Using the Single Moving Average as an Investing Trigger

If you are using the S&P 500 Index with a single moving average, then you could invest in an ETF of your choice (such as SPY or DIA) when the index price rises above the moving-average line (e.g., 50- or 200-dma). Likewise, you would sell the ETF when the index price declines below its moving-average line. When you sell, you can either place the proceeds into a money-market fund or, if you are an aggressive investor, go short using a no-load bear (inverse) mutual fund offered by Rydex or ProFunds or using the inverse ETFs from RydexShares™ or ProShares. This is the way you would handle any investment vehicle, whether it is a stock, an index fund, a sector fund, or an ETF. Whenever the price crosses above or below the moving-average line, you act on that signal.

## Dual Moving Averages

One interesting variation of the moving-average approach is to use a combination of two different moving-average time periods. This is often referred to as a *dual-moving-average crossover system*. One of the most well-known and widely followed combinations is the 50/200-dma. In this case, a buy signal is given when the 50-dma crosses over the 200-dma (known as the *golden cross*), and a sell signal is given when the 50-dma falls below the 200-dma (known as the *death cross*). The difference between the single-moving-average system and the dual-moving-average system is that in the single system the trading signals are given when the price crosses the moving-average line, whereas in the dual system the signal is given when the faster moving-average line (50-dma) crosses the slower moving-average line (200-dma). Also, dual-moving-average signals tend to be slower than single-moving-average signals.

In Figure 9-1 both the golden cross and the death cross are illustrated, which is quite rare in such a short time period. Note the golden cross buy signal in late June 2009 and the death cross sell signal in early July 2010 and finally the golden cross buy signal again in late October, all the way on the right side of the chart. The research on the performance of the stock market three months, six months, and twelve months after each type of cross is mixed. During the July to October 2010 period, there were numerous articles appearing in the press and on the Internet written about the significance of these crossovers, but most of the well-known researchers are not that impressed with the track record of crossovers in forecasting future stock market performance.

## RESEARCHERS' MOVING-AVERAGE TESTS

Over the years, a number of researchers have tested various moving-average lengths. This section focuses on the work of Robert W. Colby, Michael McDonald, Paul Merriman, John J. Murphy, and Mark Courter.

### Robert W. Colby's Moving-Average DJIA Tests

Robert W. Colby is the author of The Encyclopedia of Technical Market Indicators (McGraw-Hill, 2003). This 820-page book covers hundreds of technical market indicators that Colby backtested against a buy-and-hold strategy. As you may recall from previous chapters, backtesting involves using historical data to determine how an index of stocks would have performed in the past using a particular strategy. The results do not mean that anyone could have achieved the results shown. Basically, backtesting is used to test specific strategies to determine their validity on a theoretical basis. If the results are valid over long time frames, then they may work as well in the future.

Colby tested many simple moving-average lengths using DJIA daily closing prices from 1900 through 2001. His assumptions in testing the data were that all profits were reinvested but that dividends, transaction costs, and taxes were excluded from the calculations. A buy signal was generated when the DJIA price pierced the moving average (being tested) to the upside, and a sell signal was generated when the DJIA price declined below the moving average to the downside. All sell signals were used to short the market. Surprisingly, Colby found that all the simple moving averages between 1 and 385 days beat buy-and-hold. In particular, he discovered that all the moving averages between 1 and 100 days beat buy-and-hold by more than a ratio of 7:1.

Colby's best results were with the shortest lengths, the 1-, 4-, and 5-dmas, which produced outstanding results with net profits in the billions of dollars. For the intermediate-term lengths, the 66-dma was 31 times better than buy-and-hold over the 102-year test period. The price crossovers of the 66-day simple moving average generated a net profit of $639,933 on a $100 initial one-time investment compared with $20,105 profit for buy-and-hold. Testing the popular 200-dma, Colby determined that the net profit was only $121,257, about 19 percent of the 66-dma's profit but still six times better than buy-and-hold.

*Of the long-term period lengths, Colby determined that the 126-dma was the most profitable strategy,* with a net profit of $426,746. This was 2,022.54 percent more profitable than buy-and-hold. Colby also noted that since the crash of 1987, the short-selling strategy on the sell signals has not been profitable. Interestingly, only 185 of 886 trades (21 percent) were profitable over this 102-year time frame. But the average winning trade amount of $6,886.30 compares very well with the average trade loss of approximately $1,238.08. This is why, overall, this strategy is profitable. The average number of days for each trade's length is 42.

You may be wondering why Colby's test results for the short-term moving averages had much higher returns than those for the intermediate- and longer-term moving averages. Clearly, the faster moving averages (fewer days) react more quickly to changes in direction than longer-term moving averages; therefore, overall, the profits keep mounting and the losses are cut short more quickly. One downside of using short-term moving averages is the large number of trades during the year. For the average investor, an intermediate- to long-term moving-average approach is much easier to implement and track and much less expensive in commission brokerage charges.

## Michael McDonald's Moving-Average S&P 500 Index Tests

Michael McDonald, in his book, *Predict Market Swings with Technical Analysis* (Wiley, 2002), backtested numerous moving-average lengths to determine which ones provided the best performance compared with buy-and-hold on the S&P 500 Index, including reinvested dividends. He found that superior results were obtained using the 72- and 132-dmas. Remember that Colby, who did his backtesting with the DJIA, found that the 66- and 126-dmas were high-profitability strategies. Results this similar on two different indexes for different time periods provide confirmation that these moving-average lengths are valid timing tools.

In 1983, McDonald backtested all daily moving averages using the S&P 500 Index between 5 and 200 days in 1-day increments to determine the most profitable time frame. McDonald used the next day's closing price, after the signal was given, as the buy or sell price. This approach is a more conservative one than using the same-day price when the moving average crossovers occurred because acting on the same-day price usually provided increased profits for the investor. McDonald replicated his research in 1992 and in 1999 to confirm the results of his original study. To do this, he divided the data into four distinct periods: the Great Depression, the 20-year post–World War II bull market, the 1966–1982 sideways market, and the 1982–1999 bull market. According to McDonald, the original results were confirmed by the later studies.

Over the 71-year total test period, the buy-and-hold strategy produced an average return of 10.3 percent a year, including reinvested dividends, whereas the shorter moving averages of 50 days or less produced average returns of 9.5 percent a year, not keeping up with buy-and-hold. One of the best returns was obtained with the 130-dma, which provided an annual return of 12.5 percent. Remember that Colby's short-term moving-average results did not include reinvested dividends and used the DJIA instead of the S&P 500 Index; therefore, his results were different.

## Paul Merriman's 100-Day Moving-Average Nasdaq 100 Index Tests

Paul Merriman, president of Merriman, Inc., is a well-known investment advisor and educator who has conducted extensive backtesting on market timing and diversification strategies. Merriman wrote an article on April 20, 2001, entitled, "All About Market Timing," that focused on the 100-dma to make buy and sell decisions. You can read it on his Web site at www.fundadvice.com/fehtml/mtstrategies/0104.html.

Merriman tested what would have happened if you had invested $1,000 at the beginning of 1942 and left the money untouched through year end 2001 compared with using a 100-day simple moving average to move in and out of the market. The simple 100-dma system was used to generate buy and sell signals on the S&P 500 Total Return Index (dividends reinvested) and on the Nasdaq 100 Index. The signals were initiated when the index prices crossed their respective moving averages to the upside (a buy signal) and the downside (a sell signal).

Merriman compared the results with a buy-and-hold strategy and a 50 percent (equivalent to a beta of 1.5) and 100 percent leveraged position (a beta of 2.0). On all sell signals, the proceeds were invested into a money-market account. Merriman did not go short on the sell signals. The data in these original studies ended at year end 2000, but Merriman was kind enough to provide me with the updated data through year end 2001 (more up-to-date data through 2009 will be available on the Web site by the time this book is published). The results of the Nasdaq Index testing are presented here.

Merriman tested the 100-dma using the Nasdaq 100 Index over a 30-year period from 1972 to 2001 with and without leverage. From 1972 through 1999, this timing approach had only one loss in 1993 of –1.7 percent, this compared with five years of losses (1973, 1974, 1981, 1984, and 1990) for buy-and-hold. Moreover, even though 2000 was a big down year for buy-and-hold at –36.8 percent, the moving-average timing lost merely –19 percent. In 2000, buy-and-hold lost –32.7 percent, whereas the 100-dma was up 1.7 percent. This is quite an accomplishment.

The buy-and-hold strategy for the Nasdaq 100 Index from 1972 through 2001 yielded an annualized return of 11.8 percent compared with 18.9 percent for the 100-dma approach. Thus the 100-dma approach beats buy-and-hold with a lower standard deviation: 19.3 versus 28.0 percent. This was coupled with less than half the drawdown levels (maximum loss) experienced by buy-and-hold during the worst months. Since 1972, a $1,000 investment in the Nasdaq 100 Index would have accumulated to $28,396 with the buy-and-hold scenario compared with $180,476 for the 100-dma approach without using leverage. Therefore, the 100-dma results were 534 percent better than buy-and-hold with less risk—a great combination.

Using 50 percent leverage on the Nasdaq 100 Index with the 100-dma approach increased the annual return to 23.2 percent, with an ending value of $522,782. For the 100 percent leveraged case (a beta of 2.0 and similar to investing in ProShares leveraged ETFs), the annualized return was 26.9 percent, with an ending value of $1,270,131. In both leveraged cases, the standard deviations were higher than buy-and-hold, but both leveraged strategies had better drawdown numbers—certainly a desirable situation. Again, be aware that investing in instruments with higher betas entails much more risk and that moves in either direction are much deeper and much faster.

Looking at the numbers on a risk-versus-reward basis, the 100-dma timing approach with the Nasdaq Composite Index is superior to buy-and-hold with regard to total return, being out-of-the-market for 36.4 percent of the time, and with regard to minimizing the losses the bear market slaughters. Also, more aggressive investors may want to use the ProShares leveraged ETFs as their investing vehicle to replicate a leveraged strategy.

In his November 2002 article, Merriman summed up what was learned about using the moving-average approach:

> Contrary to [what] many of the critics of timing [say], a timing system can be "wrong" more than 60 percent of the time and still produce a phenomenal increase in return. . . . [T]iming is more effective when it is applied to more volatile assets instead of less volatile ones. . . . [T]iming is even more effective using leverage. And we saw that it always reduces risk by taking investors out of the market at least some of the time.

## John Murphy's 50-dma Nasdaq Composite Index Test

According to John J. Murphy, chief technical analyst at StockCharts.com:

> In the 30 years from 1972 to 2002 a "buy-and-hold" strategy reaped a gain of 1,105 percent in the NASDAQ. A simple timing strategy of selling whenever the NASDAQ fell under its 50-dma (and reentering when it rose back above it) reaped a profit of 13,794 percent. In the 10 years from 1993 to 2002, a "buy-and-hold" strategy yielded a NASDAQ profit of 93 percent. By utilizing the "sell discipline" of the 50-day average, that NASDAQ profit jumped to 280 percent.[1]

## Mark Courter Backtests 50-, 200-, and 50/200-dma with the S&P 500 Index for Market Buy and Sell Signals

Mark Courter analyzed the performance of using the 200-, 50-, and dual combination 50/200-dma crossovers in comparison with buy-and-hold from 1971 through 2009 for market buy and sell signals using a backtesting approach.[2] These are exactly the same moving-average lengths that were described at the beginning of this chapter, except that Courter exclusively used exponential moving averages instead of the simple moving average. This latter average is more sensitive to current data than the simple moving average, which is the reason Courter decided to use it.

In running the analysis, Courter used intraday highs and lows as crossover points above and below the moving-average line for his buy and sell signals because he wanted to avoid whipsaws. Most studies use the end-of-day close or the open on the next trading day for the price component of the backtest. When a sell signal was given, the proceeds were not invested until the next buy signal was generated.

The difficulty with buy-and-hold is the large drawdowns that occur in big bears; for example, the losses in three bear markets—

---

[1] Steve Halpern, *The Money Show Digest*, February 21, 2003 (www.moneyshow digest.com). Comments by John Murphy.

[2] Mark Courter, "Moving Averages: Are They Effective?" *Journal of Indexes*, July–August 2010, pp. 24–27, 63.

1973–1974 of 48.2 percent, 2000–2002 of 49.15 percent, and 2008 of 56.78 percent—were hard to sit through not knowing when and how long the market needed to recover to the prior highs. Interestingly, the 200-dma strategy lost much less in these three bears, declining 10.4, 11.3, and 15.6 percent, respectively. The 50-dma had worse performance in 2000–2002, losing 31.8 percent, but better performance than the 200-dma in 1973–1974, declining only 7 percent, and in 2008, declining only 15.2 percent.

In conclusion, Courter found the 50/200-dma to be the superior strategy of the three, as Table 9-1 reveals with the best annual return, the lowest standard deviation and the highest ending balance, the second lowest number of trades, and the second highest percent of profitable trades. These results indicate that using the 50/200-dma strategy with different equity investments in conjunction with portfolio diversification can lower an investor's risk while providing comparable market returns.

## TradeStation Nasdaq Moving-Average Tests

In the first edition of this book, I tested the moving-average timing strategy using the Nasdaq Composite Index, first on a weekly basis by using the 25-week moving average (wma) from 1971 through 2002. This is a strategy that an investor with limited time can use. Since Merriman's research had shown excellent performance using

**TABLE 9-1**

Courter's S&P 500 Moving-Average Test Results: 1971–2009

|  | 39-Year Annual Returns | 39-Year Standard Deviation of Annual Returns | Growth of $100,000 | No. of Trades | Percentage of Profitable Trades |
|---|---|---|---|---|---|
| Buy-and-hold | 6.62% | 17.72% | $1,219,355 | 2 | 100 |
| 200-dma | 6.68 | 13.02 | 1,243,706 | 174 | 41 |
| 50-dma | 5.39 | 14.65 | 775,953 | 436 | 30 |
| 50/200-dma | 7.02 | 11.82 | 1,408,397 | 34 | 76 |

*Source: Journal of Indexes, July–August 2010.*

the Nasdaq Composite Index with the 100-dma, I used the 25-wma, which is equivalent to a 125-dma, which is also very close to McDonald's 132-dma. I used the TradeStation software to backtest this 25-wma on the Nasdaq Composite Index from February 5, 1971, through December 27, 2002, in the book's first edition.

### Nasdaq Composite Index 25-wma 1971–2002 Test

TradeStation is a powerful trading platform with an extensive back-testing capability. It provides extensive performance reports and charts detailing all aspects of each strategy. The reports show all the pertinent statistics on the test period, including the following:

- Every buy and sell signal delineated with dates and profits or losses
- Daily, weekly, and monthly performance in detail
- Annual net profits by year
- Win/loss ratio statistics
- Graphs of the equity curve
- Monthly net profit, average profit by month, and monthly rolling net profit

The buy and sell rules are shown in the box below. An initial $100,000 was invested at the first signal, and no additional funds were invested. All investments were made on the same day the moving-average crossover signal was given. Dividends, taxes, and margin interest were not included in this analysis.

### Nasdaq Composite 25-wma Strategy

**Buy signal.** When the closing weekly price of the Nasdaq Composite Index pierces the 25-wma from below, a buy signal is given.

**Sell signal.** When the closing weekly price of the Nasdaq Composite Index drops below the 25-wma, a sell signal is given and a short position is taken.

Table 9-2 shows the key statistics of this simple strategy. Over the total 31-year time frame, buy-and-hold had a return of 968 per-

## TABLE 9-2

### TradeStation Strategy Performance Report 25-wma Nasdaq Composite Weekly: February 5, 1971 to December 27, 2002

**Strategy Analysis**

| | | | |
|---|---|---|---|
| Net profit | $4,274,869.56 | Open position | $43,668.18 |
| Gross profit | $6,439,144.31 | Interest earned | $9,958.90 |
| Gross loss | ($2,164,274.74) | Commission paid | $0.00 |
| Percent profitable | 42.27% | Profit factor | 2.98 |
| Ratio average win/ average loss | 4.06 | Adjusted profit factor | 2.21 |
| Annual rate of return | 13.52% | Sharpe ratio | 0.79 |
| Return on initial capital | 4,274.87% | Return retracement ratio | 1.30 |
| Return on maximum drawdown | 155.52% | K-ratio | 1.66 |
| Buy/hold return | 968.40% | RINA index | 16.96 |
| Cumulative return | 4,274.87% | Percent in the market | 93.76% |
| Adjusted net profit | $2,980,030.80 | Select net profit | $488,376.36 |
| Adjusted gross profit | $5,433,518.92 | Select gross profit | $2,652,651.10 |
| Adjusted gross loss | ($2,453,488.12) | Select gross loss | ($2,164,274.74) |

**Total Trade Analysis**

| | | | |
|---|---|---|---|
| Number of total trades | 97 | | |
| Average trade | $44,070.82 | Average trade ± 1 SD | $288,308.04/ ($200,166.40) |
| 1 Standard deviation (SD) | $244,237.22 | Coefficient of variation | 554.19% |

**Run-Up**

| | | | |
|---|---|---|---|
| Maximum run-up | $3,425,832.55 | Maximum run-up date | 3/10/2000 |
| Average run-up | $145,966.63 | Average trade ± 1 SD | $561,284.22/ $0.00 |
| 1 SD | $415,317.60 | Coefficient of variation | 284.53% |

**Drawdown**

| | | | |
|---|---|---|---|
| Maximum drawdown | ($556,526.87) | Maximum drawdown date | 7/14/2000 |
| Average drawdown | ($30,712.31) | Average trade ± 1 SD | $0.00/($100,744.32) |
| 1 SD | $70,032.01 | Coefficient of variation | 228.03% |
| Reward/risk ratio | | | |
| Net profit/largest loss | 7.75 | Net profit/maximum drawdown | 7.68 |
| Adjusted net profit/ largest loss | 5.40 | Adjusted net profit/ maximum drawdown | 5.35 |

**Outlier Trades** — **Total trades/profit(loss)**

| | |
|---|---|
| Positive outliers | 3/$3,786,493.21 |
| Negative outliers | 0/$0.00 |
| Total outliers | 3/$3,786,493.21 |

*Source:* Created with TradeStation. Printed with permission.

cent. This did not even come close to the performance of the 25-wma strategy, which returned 4,275 percent. In total dollars, the original $100,000 investment returned a profit of $4,274,870 compared with a profit of $968,400 for buy-and-hold. The annual rate of return for the 25-wma strategy was 13.52 percent.

The ratio of average winning dollars per trade compared with average losing dollars per trade was 4:1, where the average winning trade amount was $157,052 and the average losing trade was $38,648. Only 42 percent of all trades were profitable; however, the profit factor was 2.98. Thus, here again is a case where less than 50 percent of trades were profitable but buy-and-hold was still demolished.

In total, there were 97 trades over the 31 years, averaging just over 3 trades a year, certainly a reasonable number. Twenty-four years had profits and five years had losses. The worst years were 2000 and 1994, with similar losses—of about 16 percent. Two years with back-to-back losses were 1987 and 1988, with about a 7.5 percent average loss per year. And 1977 had a minor loss of 1.4 percent.

### Nasdaq Composite Index 25-wma 1971–2010 Test

This original backtest was updated through 2010 in this second edition of this book. Over the nearly 40-year time frame, buy-and-hold returned 1,830 percent, but the 25-wma returned 45,065 percent, more than 25 times more. In total dollars, the strategy had a profit of $4,506,537 compared with $1,830,090 for buy-and-hold. Compared with the prior test period ending in 2002, this strategy has not made much progress from the $4,274,870 gain from eight years ago, whereas buy-and-hold has doubled its return. Table 9-3 provides the complete statistics.

Table 9-4 lists annual returns for this test for 1973–2010, and it shows that the strategy encountered losses in 2004, 2005, 2007, and 2010. These losses held back the progress of this strategy, whereas buy-and-hold did much better, except for the 2008 crash. However, the strategy did have a 17 percent positive return in the big bear market year of 2008. The equity curve (Figure 9-2) for this strategy in the past few years has not been a pretty picture and illustrates the volatility of this strategy.

**TABLE 9-3**

TradeStation Performance Summary Nasdaq Composite
25-wma 1971–2010

|  | All Trades | Long Trades | Short Trades |
|---|---|---|---|
| Total net profit | $4,506,537.34 | $4,674,143.07 | ($167,605.73) |
| Gross profit | $11,407,707.21 | $7,452,723.20 | ($3,954,984.01) |
| Gross loss | ($6,901,169.87) | ($2,778,580.13) | ($4,122,589.74) |
| Profit factor | 1.65 | 2.68 | 0.96 |
| Rollover credit | $0.00 | $0.00 | $0.00 |
| Open position profit/loss (P/L) | $326,333.56 | $326,333.56 | $0.00 |
| Select total net profit | $3,575,768.11 | $3,191,580.78 | $384,187.33 |
| Select gross profit | $9,925,144.92 | $5,970,160.91 | $3,954984.01 |
| Select gross loss | ($6,349,376.81) | ($2,778,580.13) | ($3,570,796.68) |
| Select profit factor | 1.56 | 2.15 | 1.11 |
| Adjusted total net profit | $2,232,655.23 | $2,951,306.24 | ($1,623,667.37) |
| Adjusted gross profit | $9,869,492.28 | $6,192,983.06 | $3,070,622.70 |
| Adjusted profit factor | 1.29 | 1.91 | 0.65 |
| Total number of trades | 143 | 71 | 72 |
| Percent profitable | 38.46% | 49.30% | 27.78% |
| Winning trades | 55 | 35 | 20 |
| Losing trades | 88 | 36 | 52 |
| Even trades | 0 | 0 | 0 |
| Average trade net profit | $31,514.25 | $65,833.00 | ($2,327.86) |
| Average winning trade | $207,412.86 | $212,934.95 | $197,749.20 |
| Average losing trade | ($78,422.38) | ($77,182.78) | ($79,280.57) |
| Ratio average win/average loss | 2.64 | 2.76 | 2.49 |
| Largest winning trade | $1,482,562.29 | $1,482,562.29 | $1,346,378.85) |
| Largest losing trade | ($551,793.06) | ($320,380.08) | ($551,793.06) |
| Largest winner as % of gross profit | 13.00% | 19.89% | 34.04% |
| Largest loser as % of gross loss | 8.00% | 11.53% | 13.38% |
| Net profit as % of largest loss | 816.71% | 1458.94% | (30.37%) |
| Select net profit as % of largest loss | 648.03% | 996.19% | 69.63% |
| Adjusted net profit as % of largest loss | 404.62% | 921.19% | (294.25%) |
| Maximum consecutive winning trades | 4 | 6 | 4 |
| Maximum consecutive losing trades | 7 | 7 | 13 |
| Average bars in total trades | 14.73 | 18.30 | 11.22 |
| Average bars in winning trades | 28.35 | 30.66 | 24.30 |
| Average bars in losing trades | 6.23 | 6.28 | 6.19 |
| Average bars in even trades | 0.00 | 0.00 | 0.00 |
| Maximum shares/contracts held | 331,200,000 | 318,600,000 | 331,200,000 |
| Total shares/contracts held | 245,814 | 126,000 | 119,814 |
| Account size required | $1,791,874.50 | $803,215.97 | $1,903,758.79 |

*(continued on next page)*

**TABLE 9-3**

TradeStation Performance Summary Nasdaq Composite
25-wma 1971–2010 (continued)

|  | All Trades | Long Trades | Short Trades |
|---|---|---|---|
| Total slippage | $0.00 | $0.00 | $0.00 |
| Total commission | $0.00 | $0.00 | $0.00 |
| Return on initial capital | 45,065.37% | | |
| Annual rate of return | 16.17% | | |
| Buy/hold return | 1830.09% | | |
| Return on account | 251.50% | | |
| Average monthly return | $20,418.45 | | |
| SD of monthly return | $252,207.65 | | |
| Return retracement ratio | 0.18 | | |
| RINA index | 47.99 | | |
| Sharpe ratio | 0.22 | | |
| K-ratio | 2.31 | | |
| Trading period | 37 years, 8 months, 16 days | | |
| % of time in the market | 99.80% | | |
| Longest flat period | n/a | | |
| Date of maximum equity run-up | n/a | | |
| Maximum equity run-up as % of initial capital | n/a | | |

**Maximum Drawdown (Intraday Peak to Valley)**

|  | All Trades | Long Trades | Short Trades |
|---|---|---|---|
| Value | ($2,748,670.71) | ($2,817,638.55) | ($2,388,206.67) |
| Date | n/a | | |
| As % of initial capital | n/a | n/a | n/a |
| Net profit as % of drawdown | 163.95% | 165.89% | (7.02%) |
| Select net profit as % of drawdown | 130.09% | 113.27% | 16.09% |
| Adjusted net profit as % of drawdown | 81.23% | 104.74% | (67.99%) |

**Maximum Drawdown (Trade Close to Trade Close)**

|  | All Trades | Long Trades | Short Trades |
|---|---|---|---|
| Value | ($1,791,670.71) | ($803,215.97) | ($1,903,758.79) |
| Date | 9/5/2008 | | |
| As % of initial capital | 17,918.75% | 8032.16% | 19,037.59% |
| Net profit as % of drawdown | 251.50% | 581.93% | (8.80%) |
| Select net profit as % of drawdown | 199.55% | 397.35% | 20.18% |
| Adjusted net profit as % of drawdown | 124.60% | 367.44% | (85.29%) |
| Maximum trade drawdown | ($556,526.88) | ($453,239.52) | ($556,526.88) |

*Source:* Created with TradeStation, used with permission.

**TABLE 9-4**

Nasdaq Composite 25-wma TradeStation Periodical Returns: Annual 1973–2010

| Period | Net Profit | % Gain | Profit Factor | No. of Trades | % Profitable |
|---|---|---|---|---|---|
| Last 12 months | ($497,537.79) | (9.32%) | 0.61 | 9 | 33.33% |
| 1/1/2010 | ($750,677.75) | (13.42%) | 0.51 | 9 | 33.33% |
| 1/1/2009 | $1,527,402.85 | 37.56% | 100.00 | 2 | 100.00% |
| 1/1/2008 | $584,567.17 | 16.79% | 1.99 | 6 | 33.33% |
| 1/1/2007 | ($762,960.52) | (17.98%) | 0.16 | 13 | 15.38% |
| 1/1/2006 | $384,585.03 | 9.96% | 100.00 | 3 | 100.00% |
| 1/1/2005 | ($266,249.50) | (6.45%) | 0.36 | 5 | 40.00% |
| 1/1/2004 | ($724,547.20) | (14.94%) | 0.41 | 9 | 22.22% |
| 1/1/2003 | $582,951.22 | 13.66% | 1.70 | 7 | 14.29% |
| 1/1/2002 | $367,429.48 | 9.42% | 1.62 | 5 | 20.00% |
| 1/1/2001 | $491,295.70 | 14.41% | 100.00 | 2 | 100.00% |
| 1/1/2000 | ($653,125.77) | (16.08%) | 0.60 | 6 | 33.33% |
| 1/1/1999 | $1,950,124.44 | 92.33% | 100.00 | 1 | 100.00% |
| 1/1/1998 | $421,319.82 | 24.92% | 4.38 | 4 | 75.00% |
| 1/1/1997 | $266,451.52 | 18.71% | 11.06 | 4 | 50.00% |
| 1/1/1996 | $2,631.82 | 0.19% | 1.01 | 5 | 40.00% |
| 1/1/1995 | $402,834.85 | 39.54% | 21.48 | 4 | 50.00% |
| 1/1/1994 | ($207,520.99) | (16.92%) | 0.01 | 6 | 16.67% |
| 1/1/1993 | $126,869.20 | 11.54% | 4.48 | 3 | 33.33% |
| 1/1/1992 | $7,992.94 | 0.73% | 1.04 | 7 | 42.86% |
| 1/1/1991 | $343,346.65 | 45.89% | 24.95 | 2 | 50.00% |
| 1/1/1990 | $126,297.10 | 20.31% | 35.64 | 3 | 66.67% |
| 1/1/1989 | $113,673.63 | 22.37% | 25.75 | 3 | 66.67% |
| 1/1/1988 | ($52,541.91) | (9.37%) | 0.21 | 5 | 60.00% |
| 1/1/1987 | ($49,378.47) | (8.09%) | 0.47 | 3 | 33.33% |
| 1/1/1986 | $128,448.64 | 26.67% | 100.00 | 2 | 100.00% |
| 1/1/1985 | $71,339.68 | 17.39% | 2.82 | 6 | 33.33% |
| 1/1/1984 | $17,422.65 | 4.43% | 1.66 | 3 | 33.33% |
| 1/1/1983 | $113,324.99 | 40.54% | 11.20 | 4 | 75.00% |
| 1/1/1982 | $97,830.15 | 53.83% | 12.55 | 4 | 75.00% |
| 1/1/1981 | $4,631.48 | 2.62% | 1.23 | 6 | 33.33% |
| 1/1/1980 | $51,011.56 | 40.46% | 3.63 | 3 | 33.33% |
| 1/1/1979 | $2,794.39 | 2.27% | 1.10 | 6 | 33.33% |
| 1/1/1978 | $24,203.97 | 24.43% | 2.54 | 4 | 50.00% |
| 1/1/1977 | ($2,734.39) | (2.69%) | 0.83 | 7 | 28.57% |
| 1/1/1976 | $6,743.33 | 7.09% | 1.23 | 10 | 20.00% |
| 1/1/1975 | $26,972.45 | 39.60% | 6.47 | 3 | 66.67% |
| 1/1/1974 | $35,311.68 | 107.66% | 100.00 | 1 | 100.00% |
| 1/1/1973 | $22,799.01 | 227.99% | 3.62 | 5 | 60.00% |

**FIGURE 9-2**

Equity curve line—Nasdaq Composite 25-wma (02/05/71 to 10/22/10).

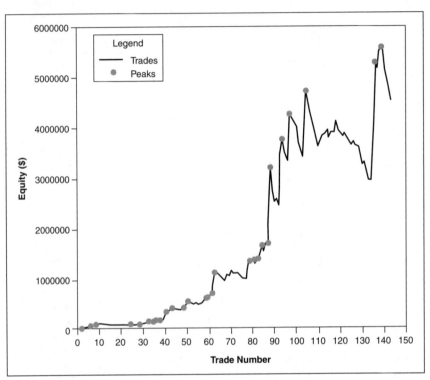

*Source:* Created with TradeStation. Printed with permission.

### Nasdaq Composite Index 20-dma 1971–2002 Test

The second backtest in the first edition of this book of the Nasdaq Composite Index used a 20-dma with the same $100,000 starting capital. This is a much faster moving average than the 25-wma and a popular moving average among traders. Using the exact same 31-year test period from February 7, 1971, through December 27, 2002, and the same assumptions and buy and sell rules (except now the 20-dma is substituted for the 25-wma), the results are hard to believe.

The simple 20-dma Nasdaq Composite Index strategy produced a total profit of $46,563,046, which is over 10 times greater than the $4,274,870 realized from the original 25-wma strategy (see Table 9-5). The buy-and-hold strategy for the 20-dma resulted in

**TABLE 9-5**

Nasdaq Composite 20-dma, February 25, 1971 to December 27, 2002, TradeStation Strategy Performance Report.

| Strategy Analysis | | | |
|---|---|---|---|
| Net profit | $46,563,045.76 | Open position | $920,062.48 |
| Gross profit | $119,057,567.11 | Interest earned | $3,136.99 |
| Gross loss | ($72,494,521.35) | Commission paid | $0.00 |
| Percent profitable | 38.25% | Profit factor | 1.64 |
| Ratio average win/average loss | 2.65 | Adjusted profit factor | 1.47 |
| Annual rate of return | 21.74% | Sharpe ratio | 1.19 |
| Return on initial capital | 46563.05% | Return retracement ratio | 3.07 |
| Return on maximum drawdown | 364.07% | K-ratio | 1.30 |
| Buy/hold return | 1139.26% | RINA index | (123.20) |
| Cumulative return | 46563.05% | Percent in the market | 98.03% |
| Adjusted net profit | $35,512,460.38 | Select net profit | ($19,312,535.48) |
| Adjusted gross profit | $111,587,230.95 | Select gross profit | $53,181,985.87 |
| Adjusted gross loss | ($76,074,770.57) | Select gross loss | ($72,494,521.35) |
| **Total Trade Analysis** | | | |
| Number of total trades | 664 | | |
| Average trade | $70,125.07 | Average trade ± 1 SD | $908,816.90/ ($768,566.76) |
| 1 SD | $838,691.83 | Coefficient of variation | 1195.99% |
| **Run-Up** | | | |
| Maximum run-up | $11,251,371.85 | Maximum run-up date | 4/4/2001 |
| Average run-up | $436,199.97 | Average trade ± 1 SD | $1,705,601.80/ $0.00 |
| 1 SD | $838,691.83 | Coefficient of variation | 291.01% |
| **Drawdown** | | | |
| Maximum drawdown | ($2,355,552.45) | Maximum drawdown date | 8/15/2002 |
| Average drawdown | ($159,903.98) | Average trade ± 1 SD | $0.00/ ($497,609.31) |
| 1 SD | $337,705.33 | Coefficient of variation | 211.19% |
| **Reward/Risk Ratio** | | | |
| Net profit/largest loss | 19.77 | Net profit/maximum drawdown | 19.77 |
| Adjusted net profit/largest loss | 15.08 | Adjusted net profit/ maximum drawdown | 15.08 |
| **Outlier Trades** | **Total Trades/Profit (Loss)** | | |
| Positive outliers | 14/$65,875,581.24 | | |
| Negative outliers | 0 $0.00 | | |
| Total outliers | 14/$65,875,581.24 | | |

*Source:* Created with TradeStation. Printed with permission.

total returns of $1,139,260. Thus the 20-dma strategy beat buy-and-hold by a ratio of 46:1. The percent of winning trades was only 38 percent. There were 664 trades during the test period, or about 21 per year, compared with only 97 trades, or 3 per year, for the 25-wma strategy. Thus this strategy had 567 more trades than the weekly strategy, resulting in much higher commission costs.

Now look at the equity curve in Figure 9-3 on page 180. The equity curve is a line graph that plots the continuous profit and loss of each trade. The graph indicates a slow but solid start; then, around trade 190, a rise to a peak at trade 350; then a flat period until trade 500; and then an upward surge punctuated by huge downswings after trade 600. Although this equity curve was not a smooth, upward-sloping curve, which would be the ideal scenario, at least it held its own during high-volatility periods and the 2000–2002 bear market, and it ended at its high for the period.

Overall, the 20-dma strategy had only three negative years (–7 percent in 1977, –11 percent in 1993, and –1 percent in 1994) in its 31-year history. In the terrible bear market years of 1973 and 1974, this strategy had a 49 percent and a 4 percent back-to-back *positive* return. In the 1987 bear market, it *gained* 46 percent. And in the 2000–2002 bear market years, it gained 4, 32, and 16 percent, respectively.

### Nasdaq Composite Index 20-dma 1971–2010 Test

The most recent backtest of the entire period 1971–2010 had a total profit of $45, 814,597 (see Table 9-6). This was actually less than the profit for the strategy ending in 2002. The return on capital was 458,146 percent compared with only 2,179 percent for buy-and-hold, a 210-fold increase. There were negative annual returns in 2003 (–15.7 percent), 2006 (–1.42 percent), 2007 (–16.56 percent), and 2009 (–12.11 percent). Interestingly, in the 2008 big bear market, there was a gain of 26.21 percent. All the annual returns are shown in Table 9-7.

**TABLE 9-6**

Nasdaq Composite 20-dma 1971–2010 TradeStation
Performance Summary

|  | All Trades | Long Trades | Short Trades |
|---|---|---|---|
| Total net profit | $45,814,597.21 | $41,213,257.28 | $4,601,339.93 |
| Gross profit | $217,543,743.86 | $122,878.045.26 | $94,665698.60 |
| Gross loss | ($171,729,146.65) | ($81,664,787,98) | |
| ($90,064,358.67) | | | |
| Profit factor | 1.27 | 1.50 | 1.05 |
| Rollover credit | $0.00 | $0.00 | $0.00 |
| Open position P/L | $5,402,224.98 | $5,402,224.98 | $0.00 |
| Select total net profit | $6,035,828.70 | $20,183,069.20 | ($14,147,240.50) |
| Select gross profit | $157,055,044.30 | $94,126,414.40 | $62,928,629.90 |
| Select gross loss | ($151,019,215.60) | ($73,943,345.20) | ($77,075,870.40) |
| Select profit factor | 1.04 | 1.27 | 0.82 |
| Adjusted total net profit | $26,547,963.96 | $27,171,894.30 | ($8,590,728.48) |
| Adjusted gross profit | $205,401.636.12 | $113,843,871.70 | $86,548,181.91 |
| Adjusted profit factor | 1.15 | 1.31 | 0.91 |
| Total number of trades | 904 | 452 | 452 |
| Percent profitable | 35.51% | 40.93% | 30.09% |
| Winning trades | 321 | 185 | 136 |
| Losing trades | 581 | 266 | 315 |
| Even trades | 2 | 1 | 1 |
| Average trade net profit | $50,679.86 | $91,179.77 | $10,179.96 |
| Average winning trade | $677,706.37 | $664,205.65 | $696,071.31 |
| Average losing trade | ($295,575.12) | ($307,010.48) | ($285,918.60) |
| Ratio average win/average loss | 2.29 | 2.16 | 2.43 |
| Largest winning trade | $10,779,089.12 | $7,323,975.88 | $10,779,089.12 |
| Largest losing trade | ($2.101,120.00) | ($2,066,298.16) | ($2,101,120.00) |
| Largest winner as % of gross profit | 4.95% | 5.96% | 11.39% |
| Largest loser as % of gross profit | 1.22% | 2.53% | 2.33% |
| Net profit as % of largest loss | 2180.48% | 1994.55% | 218.99% |
| Select net profit as % of largest loss | 287.27% | 976.77% | (673.32%) |
| Adjusted net profit as % of largest loss | 1263.51% | 1315.00% | (408.86%) |
| Maximum consecutive winning trades | 6 | 6 | 8 |
| Maximum consecutive losing trades | 11 | 8 | 18 |
| Average bars in total trades | 11.93 | 13.89 | 9.98 |
| Average bars in winning trades | 22.91 | 25.18 | 19.82 |

*(continued on next page)*

**TABLE 9-6**

Nasdaq Composite 20-dma 1971–2010 TradeStation
Performance Summary (continued)

|  | All Trades | Long Trades | Short Trades |
|---|---|---|---|
| Average bars in losing trades | 5.88 | 6.03 | 5.75 |
| Average bars in losing trades | 10.00 | 17.00 | 3.00 |
| Maximum shares/contracts held | 3,200,000,000 | 3,200,000,000 | 3,200,000,000 |
| Total shares/contracts held | 10,562,271 | 5,310,397 | 5,251,874 |
| Account size required | $11,808,910.65 | $10,934,933.19 | $18,811,430.18 |
| Total slippage | $0.00 | $0.00 | $0.00 |
| Total commission | $0.00 | $0.00 | $0.00 |
| Return on initial capital | 458145.97% | | |
| Annual rate of return | 21.44% | | |
| Buy/hold return | 2179.48% | | |
| Return on account | 387.97% | | |
| Average monthly return | $306,910.87 | | |
| SD of monthly return | $2,438,808.54 | | |
| Return retracement ratio | 0.24 | | |
| RINA index | (54.75) | | |
| Sharpe ratio | 0.29 | | |
| K-ratio | 1.96 | | |
| Trading period | 39 years, 3 months, 21 days | | |
| Percent of time in market | 99.99% | | |
| Time in the market | 39 years, 3 months, 19 days | | |
| Longest flat period | n/a | | |
| Maximum equity run-up | $56,270,379.19 | | |
| Date and time of maximum equity run-up | 11/21/08, 16:00 | | |
| Maximum equity run-up as % of initial capital | 562,703.79% | | |

*Source:* Created with TradeStation. Printed with permission.

**TABLE 9-7**

Nasdaq Composite 20-dma TradeStation Periodical Annual
Returns: 1971–2010

| Period | Net Profit | % Gain | Profit Factor | No. of Trades | % Profitable |
|---|---|---|---|---|---|
| Last 12 months | $8,345,296.20 | 19.46% | 1.91 | 19 | 36.84% |
| 1/1/2010 | $8,905,551.53 | 21.04% | 2.35 | 15 | 46.67% |
| 1/1/2009 | ($5,828,878.17) | (12.11%) | 0.73 | 27 | 22.22% |
| 1/1/2008 | $10,118,530.79 | 26.61% | 1.78 | 29 | 34.48% |
| 1/1/2007 | ($7,548,628.61) | (16.56%) | 0.50 | 38 | 21.05% |
| 1/1/2006 | ($658,039.46) | (1.42%) | 0.94 | 37 | 37.84% |
| 1/1/2005 | $2,268,466.04 | 5.16% | 1.25 | 36 | 30.56% |
| 1/1/2004 | $5,425,906.02 | 14.08% | 1.68 | 25 | 44.00% |
| 1/1/2003 | ($7,172,478.73) | (15.69%) | 0.66 | 38 | 26.32% |
| 1/1/2002 | $6,827,760.93 | 17.56% | 1.41 | 30 | 36.67% |
| 1/1/2001 | $9,413,798.70 | 31.94% | 1.69 | 24 | 29.17% |
| 1/1/2000 | $1,103,647.94 | 3.89% | 1.06 | 30 | 36.67% |
| 1/1/1999 | $8,915,804.80 | 45.83% | 2.47 | 29 | 41.38% |
| 1/1/1998 | $7,878,573.17 | 68.05% | 3.98 | 25 | 44.00% |
| 1/1/1997 | $1,339,378.31 | 13.08% | 1.35 | 26 | 34.62% |
| 1/1/1996 | $2,089,858.72 | 25.65% | 2.68 | 23 | 34.78% |
| 1/1/1995 | $779,153.85 | 10.57% | 1.48 | 26 | 30.77% |
| 1/1/1994 | ($106,611.87) | (1.43%) | 0.92 | 31 | 29.03% |
| 1/1/1993 | ($971,674.05) | (11.50%) | 0.55 | 33 | 27.27% |
| 1/1/1992 | $74,294.87 | 0.89% | 1.03 | 29 | 24.14% |
| 1/1/1991 | $1,681,939.94 | 25.14% | 2.15 | 23 | 39.13% |
| 1/1/1990 | $1,578,420.60 | 30.88% | 2.56 | 21 | 38.10% |
| 1/1/1989 | $467,136.95 | 10.06% | 1.79 | 15 | 33.33% |
| 1/1/1988 | $613,618.86 | 15.22% | 2.54 | 17 | 47.06% |
| 1/1/1987 | $1,299,602.67 | 47.58% | 3.21 | 24 | 41.67% |
| 1/1/1986 | $467,089.86 | 20.63% | 2.39 | 24 | 41.67% |
| 1/1/1985 | $553,963.15 | 32.38% | 3.53 | 19 | 47.37% |
| 1/1/1984 | $150,107.34 | 9.62% | 1.62 | 28 | 42.86% |
| 1/1/1983 | $363,677.52 | 30.39% | 3.31 | 15 | 53.33% |
| 1/1/1982 | $439,671.85 | 58.07% | 6.52 | 13 | 61.54% |
| 1/1/1981 | $131,375.78 | 20.99% | 2.46 | 14 | 50.00% |
| 1/1/1980 | $203,412.89 | 48.16% | 2.57 | 13 | 38.46% |
| 1/1/1979 | $92,927.90 | 28.21% | 2.63 | 17 | 52.94% |
| 1/1/1978 | $92,060.61 | 38.78% | 2.51 | 17 | 41.18% |

*(continued on next page)*

## TABLE 9-7

Nasdaq Composite 20-dma TradeStation Periodical Annual Returns: 1971–2010 (continued)

| Period | Net Profit | % Gain | Profit Factor | No. of Trades | % Profitable |
|---|---|---|---|---|---|
| 1/1/1977 | ($24,351.37) | (9.30%) | 0.56 | 29 | 20.69% |
| 1/1/1976 | $30,706.82 | 13.29% | 1.43 | 27 | 33.33% |
| 1/1/1975 | $62,554.50 | 37.13% | 1.95 | 24 | 45.83% |
| 1/1/1974 | $78,918.33 | 88.10% | 7.29 | 10 | 80.00% |
| 1/1/1973 | $59,438.51 | 197.24% | 5.98 | 14 | 64.29% |
| 1/1/1972 | $10,618.36 | 54.41% | 1.94 | 22 | 40.91% |
| 1/1/1971 | $9,516.34 | 95.16% | 4.72 | 7 | 28.57% |

*Source:* Created with TradeStation. Printed with permission.

Figure 9-4 on page 182 shows the equity curve for this strategy, and you can see the choppy performance during the past few years.

### Other Nasdaq Composite Daily Moving-Average Backtests
In this book's first edition, I also ran a TradeStation optimization analysis of the daily Nasdaq Composite Index moving averages

## FIGURE 9-3

Equity curve Nasdaq composite 20-dma: 1971–2002.

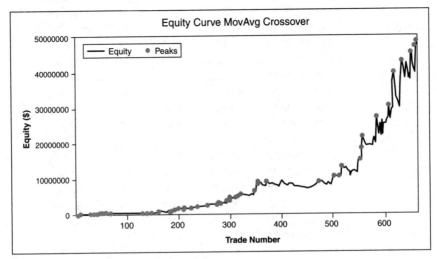

*Source:* Created with TradeStation. Printed with permission.

between 15 and 125 days to determine their profitability. The exact same test period as the other backtests was used: the 31-year period from February 7, 1971, through December 27, 2002, along with the same assumptions. Using an 18- to 22-dma, I found the total returns for the period to be in the $37 million to $56 million range. The 23- to 50-dmas produced returns in the $19 million to $28 million range. By contrast, 100- and 125-dmas had total returns of about $6 million. Thus my testing confirms Colby's findings that shorter moving averages have higher returns than intermediate- and long-term moving averages.

The highest returns for the Nasdaq Composite Index were clearly in the 18- to 22-dma range. The optimal strategy turned out to be the 18-dma, with a total return of $56.02 million and an annualized return of 22.47 percent. This return was almost $10 million better than the 20-dma strategy, which had a 21.74 percent annualized return. Thus, as you can see, the selected Nasdaq Composite Index moving averages provided outstanding returns.

## Current Daily Moving-Average Optimization Backtests of the Nasdaq Composite

For this second edition of this book, I also ran another optimization backtest analysis of the daily Nasdaq Composite Index with moving averages in the range of 20 to 30 days. Table 9-8 provides comparative results for 20 to 26 days. Note that the same daily moving average was used for both the buy and sell criteria unless otherwise noted (last two examples in Table 9-8).

Clearly, moving-average lengths greater than 22 days had inferior results to the ones that were shorter in length. Interestingly, dramatically improved results would have been attained using a combination of 21 for the moving average for the buy signal and 22 for the moving average for the sell signal. This combination had a total profit of $65.42 million. However, this observation is known only in hindsight and by using an optimization program, so these optimal moving averages may not be optimal going forward. Nevertheless, both the 21- and 22-dmas are so close to the 20-dma that using the 21/22-dma or even the 20/22-dma combination could be the more profitable approach going forward.

**FIGURE 9-4**

Equity curve Nasdaq Composite 20-dma, 1971–2010.

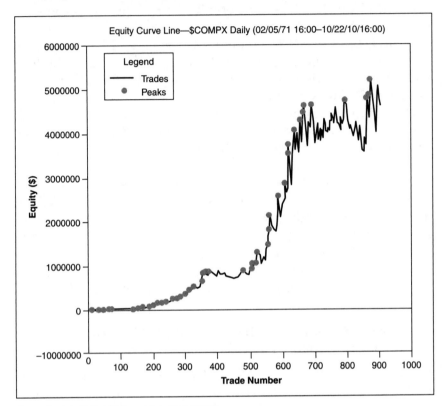

Equity Curve Line—$COMPX Daily (02/05/71 16:00–10/22/10/16:00)

*Source:* Created with TradeStation. printed with permission.

**TABLE 9-8**

Nasdaq Moving Average Optimization Results

| Daily Moving Average Length (Days) | Total Profit (Millions of $) |
| --- | --- |
| 20 | 45.81 |
| 21 | 46.61 |
| 22 | 33.44 |
| 23 | 15.22 |
| 24 | 23.21 |
| 25 | 26.24 |
| 26 | 24.80 |
| 21 buy and 22 sell | 65.42 |
| 20 buy and 22 sell | 62.31 |

*Source:* Created with TradeStation. Printed with permission.

## MARKET TIMING USING MOVING AVERAGES

Using moving averages as a market timing strategy is quite simple to execute but often difficult to sit through because the price volatility from year to year can be quite high and unnerving. As the research on moving averages indicates, there are profitable strategies whether you selected the Nasdaq Composite 20/22-dma, the 25-wma, or the combination 50/200-dma. So it is your choice to determine if any of these strategies best fits your risk profile.

Keep in mind that when using shorter-term daily moving averages, you will have many more trades than using longer-term daily or weekly moving averages. This will result in a greater frequency of smaller gains and losses than using longer-term moving averages. Moreover, be careful to assess your risk when using intermediate- and long-term moving averages. With these strategies, you should carefully consider implementing a stop-loss rule to protect your profits so that the investment does not go too far against you when the trend changes. For example, if you are making a profit of 30 percent on your investment, you don't want to give it all back when the market reverses direction and goes all the way down, crossing the moving average. Thus consider using an 8 to 10 percent trailing stop-limit order to protect those profits. If you wait until the actual moving-average sell signal occurs, then you could be giving back most of your profits. Use common sense in protecting your capital when the market goes against you.

If you decide to use a moving-average strategy, you can go online to any of the charting Web sites mentioned previously and bring up a multiyear chart of the index you select with a selected moving average. For example, let's say that you choose the Nasdaq Composite Index's 25-wma strategy. Each Friday afternoon before the market closes or on the weekend, you would bring up the weekly chart to determine if the moving average crossed over or under the index's price. When a buy crossover occurs, you could purchase the QQQQs (Nasdaq 100) or a bullish Nasdaq fund such as Fidelity's ONEQ ETF. Then you would wait for the index's price to decline below the moving average or hit it's stop-limit order (whichever occurs first) to either sell your position by going into cash or going short the QQQQs or an inverse Nasdaq 100 fund such as a ProShares Short QQQQ (ticker: PSQ).

## CONCLUSIONS

Moving averages, as a timing tool, have been used for decades by savvy investors. Overall, they perform better than buy-and-hold in bear markets but sometimes worse in bull markets (owing to whipsaws that reduce overall profits), but overall they are a viable strategy. Nevertheless, with a portion of an investor's money, for example, 20 percent, the moving-average approach, such as the 50/200-dma crossover strategy, certainly has performed well with less risk than buy-and-hold. The more aggressive Nasdaq 25-wma and 20/22-dma are more suited for aggressive investors who want the opportunity for higher returns with more risk.

## CHAPTER 10

# The Value Line 4 Percent Strategy versus the Value Line 3 Percent Strategy

*The safest way to double your money is to fold it over once and put it in your pocket.*

—Frank McKinney Hubbard

**A**nother simple market timing strategy is presented in this chapter that signals when to buy to take advantage of market uptrends and then signals when to sell to retain your profits. All the so-called experts on Wall Street will tell you that no strategy can do this consistently. Remember that in the last chapter we reviewed some simple moving-average strategies that do just that.

By using the *Value Line 4 percent strategy* (hereafter abbreviated VL4%), developed over 30 years ago, or better yet the *Value Line 3 percent* (VL3%) *strategy*, you can achieve positive returns. Moreover, both these strategies reduce your overall risk and beat buy-and-hold. The VL4% and VL3% strategies presented in this chapter are for conservative investors with a low risk tolerance. Because the VL4% strategy was thoroughly reviewed in the first edition of this book, along with its long-term track record, this chapter first will focus extensively on the prior and more recent backtests before presenting the better-performing VL3%, so please bear with me as I cover the VL4% first.

## BRIEF HISTORY OF VL4% STRATEGY

On June 30, 1961, the *Value Line Investment Survey* instituted the Value Line Composite Index (VLCI). It represents a weighted index of about 1,700 stocks in 90 industries and thus provides the *median* performance of all the stocks tracked. The VLCI includes blue-chip, midcap, and small-cap issues. About 80 percent of the stocks are traded on the New York Stock Exchange (NYSE), and 20 percent are traded on the Nasdaq.

This index has a different weighting scheme than the Dow Jones Industrial Average (DJIA) and the Standard & Poor's (S&P) 500 Index. The DJIA is price-weighted by each of the 30 components (the highest-priced stocks have the most impact on the average), and the S&P 500 Index is market-capitalization-weighted (the number of common shares outstanding multiplied by the stock's price). In the latter case, the big-cap stocks exert a larger influence on the index. I originally came across the VL4% strategy in *Martin Zweig's Winning on Wall Street* (Warner Books, 1986). According to Zweig, Ned Davis of Ned Davis Research developed the "4 percent model" using the VLCI. The model's goal was to help investors stick with the existing market trend and not get shaken out of the market by small, random day-to-day fluctuations.

## HOW THE VL4% WEEKLY STRATEGY WORKS

The VL4% strategy is very simple: If the VLCI rises 4 percent from its last market low (e.g., if it rises from 100.00 to 104.00 or higher), based solely on its weekly Friday closing price, this is a market buy signal, and an investment is made in an appropriate index fund, sector fund, or exchange-traded fund (ETF) of your choice.

If the VLCI declines 4 percent from its last market top (e.g., if it drops from 120.00 to 115.20 or lower), based on a weekly Friday closing price, this is a market sell signal. The proceeds of the sale then can be placed into a money-market account. Alternatively, a more aggressive investor may short the market by using a bear (inverse) ETF. Note that ETFs cannot be shorted in retirement accounts, but you can buy inverse funds in retirement accounts.

Keep in mind that you cannot buy or sell the actual VLCI because it is just an index. The VLCI is tradable as futures or options contracts on the Kansas City Board of Trade (KCBT), but trading in these vehicles is for the more experienced and knowledgeable investor.

The remainder of this chapter focuses on multiple historical tests of the VL4% strategy by different researchers, as well as the latest analysis through October 2010. The earlier backtesting is presented first. If you are interested only in the latest backtests, then skip to page 192 and beyond.

## VL4% Weekly Backtest from 1966 to 1988

The VL4% backtested results in this chapter are only theoretical in nature because the trades identified are not executable by an investor owing to the fact that a trading vehicle mirroring the index does not exist. However, backtesting of data against past years is a common and accepted practice used by researchers to determine the viability of specific trading strategies. Of course, backtesting does not guarantee that the same performance that occurred in the past will occur in the future. However, if the same strategy that was tested and worked well in past years still works well today, then that performance says something about the strategy's longevity and validity. The VL4% fits this paradigm, although it has had its losing periods.

According to Zweig's book, Ned Davis backtested the VL4% strategy from May 6, 1966, through December 27, 1988. Davis went long on the buy signal and short on the sell signal. His option was to go into cash and wait for the next buy signal, but he decided instead to go short. This decision, as we'll see, paid off with higher returns. Davis's results were published in the first (1986) and second (1990) editions of Zweig's book. The data presented below are from the later edition.

In the 22.7 years of the time period studied by Davis, a one-time initial investment of $10,000 had an ending value for the hypothetical investments made with the VL4% strategy of $233,981, which meant that the investment provided a 14.9 percent annualized return. Buy-and-hold produced a meager return of $17,242, or 2.4 percent annualized. Neither dividends nor transaction costs were factored into this analysis in either case.

The breakdown on the long and short sides of the signals is as follows:

- *Longs (buys)*. Fifty trades were made, averaging 97 days each and producing an annual profit of 16.6 percent. Twenty-six of these trades produced losses averaging –3.9 percent, whereas 24 trades produced gains averaging 14.6 percent.
- *Shorts (sells)*. Fifty-one trades were made, averaging 67 days each and producing an annual profit of 12.5 percent. Twenty-seven of these trades produced losses averaging –3.5 percent, whereas 24 trades produced gains of 9.3 percent.
- *Total trades*. One hundred and one trades were made, averaging 82 days and producing an annual profit of 14.9 percent. Fifty-three trades showed losses averaging –3.7 percent, whereas 48 trades showed gains averaging 11.9 percent. The ratio of percentage profits to losses was better than 3:1. This is a great example of cutting losses and letting profits run.

In summary, the VL4% strategy, tested by Davis, was a simple timing system that worked well during the 1966 to 1988 time frame. Even though 52 percent of the trades were unprofitable, the average loss of –3.7 percent was far less than the 48 percent of profitable trades, where the average gain was 11.9 percent, a win-to-loss percentage ratio of 3.22, which is excellent.

### VL4% Weekly Backtest from 1961 to 1992

Nelson Freeburg published an updated analysis of VL4% in his November 30, 1992, newsletter *Formula Research*. Freeburg back-tested the period April 19, 1985, through November 6, 1992, a full four years beyond Davis's test period.

Freeburg found that the VL4% strategy gained 168 Value Line points over that extended seven-year time frame, whereas the index itself gained only 57 points under a buy-and-hold scenario. On an annualized basis, excluding dividends, the VL4% strategy returned 8.5 percent compared with 3.5 percent for buy-and-hold.

Freeburg even tested the period prior to Davis's research, going back to July 1961 and testing through mid-1966. During this five-year mostly bullish period, VL4% provided an annual return of 10.7 percent compared with 5.5 percent for buy-and-hold. Thus the VL4% strategy performed well in three different time frames, confirming its consistency and usefulness as a profitable strategy.

Over the entire expanded period from 1961 through 1992, VL4% rose an annualized 13.6 percent compared with about 3 percent for buy-and-hold. This accomplishment is impressive—doubly so because 60 of the 127 buy and sell signals were profitable only 47 percent of the time.

Not satisfied with testing only a fixed 4 percent up or down move on the VLCI, Freeburg tested every percentage point swing from 1 to 8 percent for both the long and short trades to determine if the strategy still would be profitable. After testing 64 parameter sets over 31 years, Freeburg found that all the parameter sets tested exceeded buy-and-hold results by a minimum ratio of 2:1.

The greatest gain in Value Line points occurred with a buy signal set at 4 percent and a sell signal set at 2 percent, that is, a buy if the VLCI rises 4 percent from a bottom and a sell if the VLCI drops 2 percent from a top. This produced 645 Value Line points compared with 149 points for buy-and-hold. Other top combinations were +2 percent and –2 percent, producing 588 points, and the standard strategy of +4 percent and –4 percent, producing 584 points. The worst strategy tested produced 313 points, which still was better than double the buy-and-hold approach. According to Freeburg, this consistent performance over many different percentage point parameters indicates the strength and soundness of the VL4% strategy.

David Penn, a staff writer for *Technical Analysis of Stocks & Commodities* magazine, wrote an article in the May 2002 issue entitled, "Trends and the 4% Solution." He reviewed the VL4% weekly strategy from 1985 to 2000. Penn tested the VL4% strategy using the Nasdaq Composite Index and the S&P 500 Index as the investment vehicles. He found, based on the VL4% buy and sell signals, that investing in the Nasdaq Composite Index produced triple the gain of an investment in the S&P 500 Index. Penn did not provide detailed data regarding his analysis in his article. Also, Penn did not provide any performance results or use of the actual VLCI as the index in which to invest. Therefore, his results cannot be compared with Freeburg's work, which measured only VLCI point changes.

## Backtesting Through 2002

I used TradeStation, a popular trading and backtesting platform, to bring the test period current through November 2002 for the first edition of this book. Neither dividends, taxes, nor margin interest were figured into any of the strategies tested with this software.

## VL4% Weekly Backtests from 1992 to 2002

I updated the VL4% strategy from December 25, 1992, through November 29, 2002—a period containing both bull and bear markets. The strategy was set up with $100,000 of initial capital. It went long on a VLCI weekly buy signal, and it went short on a weekly sell signal. The funds were never placed in cash because they were always invested long or short the market. During this 10-year time frame, the strategy produced a net profit of $81,998 (see Table 10-1) and a cumulative return of 82 percent. This result compares favorably with a small loss of −1.32 percent for buy-and-hold.

The equity curve in Figure 10-1 shows the investment value after each trade was made. As you can see, there was a big drop after the twenty-first trade, and the fall continued through trade 36. Of these 15 trades, 14 were losers from January 28, 2000, through January 12, 2001. If you looked at a chart of the VLCI during this time frame, then you would see that the VLCI was in a trading range of 980 to 1,180 with numerous up and down moves in price. And each of those trades resulted in a loss. Shortly after you went long on a buy signal, the market reversed down, and a sell-short signal occurred at a lower price, resulting in a loss. Similarly, right after you went short, the market reversed up, and that was offset by a buy signal at a higher price, resulting in a loss. All these whip-saws in price resulted in losses that overcame all the profits built up over the previous years. Actually, the total capital did drop below the original $100,000 investment during this period. From the twenty-first to forty-fifth trades, the VL4% strategy made no progress, as the equity curve shows. This was a disturbing and costly problem. On the positive side, substantial positive annual

**TABLE 10-1**

## TradeStation Strategy Performance Report: 4% Model
## Weekly: December 25, 1992 to November 29, 2002

| Strategy Analysis | | | |
|---|---|---|---|
| Net profit | $81,998.28 | Open position | $21,772.92 |
| Gross profit | $213,665.24 | Interest earned | $6,315.07 |
| Gross loss | ($131,666.96) | Commission paid | $0.00 |
| Percent profitable | 42.22% | Profit factor | 1.62 |
| Ratio average win/average loss | 2.22 | Adjusted profit factor | 1.05 |
| Annual rate of return | 7.25% | Sharpe ratio | 0.58 |
| Return on initial capital | | Return retracement ratio | 0.29 |
| Return on maximum drawdown | 90.38% | K-ratio | 0.62 |
| Buy/hold return | −1.32% | RINA index | 24.42 |
| Cumulative return | 82.00% | Percent in the market | 87.29% |
| Adjusted net profit | $7,158.10 | Select net profit | $81,998.28 |
| Adjusted gross profit | $164,647.07 | Select gross profit | $213,665.24 |
| Adjusted gross loss | ($157,488.97) | Select gross loss | ($131,666.96) |

| Total Trade Analysis | | | |
|---|---|---|---|
| Total number of trades | 45 | | |
| Average trade | $1,822.18 | Average trade ± 1 SD | $11,864.82/ ($8,220.45) |
| 1 Standard deviation (SD) | $10,042.63 | Coefficient of variation | 551.13% |
| Run-up | $42,640.00 | Maximum run-up date | 7/26/2002 |
| Maximum run-up | $10,669.97 | Average trade ± 1 SD | $21,353.21/ $0.00 |
| Average run-up 1 SD | $10,683.24 | Coefficient of variation | 100.12% |
| Drawdown | ($10,521.90) | Maximum drawdown date | 4/28/2000 |
| Maximum drawdown | ($3,847.26) | Average trade ± 1 SD | ($691,82)/ ($7,002.69) |
| Average drawdown 1 SD | $3,155.43 | Coefficient of variation | 82.02% |
| Reward/risk ratios | | | |
| Net profit/largest loss | 8.12 | Net profit/maximum drawdown | 7.79 |
| Adjusted net profit/largest loss | 0.71 | Adjusted net profit/ maximum drawdown | 0.68 |
| Outlier trades | Total trades | Profit/Loss | |
| Positive outliers | 0 | $0.00 | |
| Negative outliers | 0 | $0.00 | |
| Total outliers | 0 | $0.00 | |

*Source:* Created with TradeStation. Printed with permission.

**FIGURE 10-1**

Equity curve for the VL4% weekly strategy, 1992–2002.

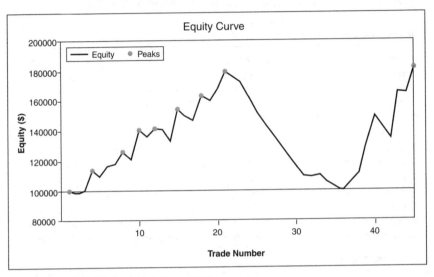

returns of 32 percent a year for 2001 and 2002 were impressive because these were down years for the market. And by the end of 2002, the equity curve was at an all-time high.

However, despite this large loss and recovery, the VL4% strategy continued to beat the buy-and-hold benchmark in all the time frames tested by Davis, Freeburg, and me. The cumulative returns for the period 1993 through 2002 may appear to be very low, but remember that we are measuring only the performance of the VLCI itself during this period. If you would have used the VL4% buy and sell signals to trade index funds that tracked the Nasdaq Composite Index, your results would have been better. Recall David Penn's study earlier, where he tested the Nasdaq Composite Index using the VL4% signals and produced excellent results.

## LATEST VL4% WEEKLY BACKTEST 1992–2010

TradeStation was used to evaluate the VL4% weekly strategy from 1992 through 2010, thereby including a portion of the time from the last test ending in 2002 (see Table 10-2). The net profit for the 1992 to 2010 time frame on the original $100,000 investment was $168,958, or an annual rate of return of 18.93 percent. The return on capital was 1,690 percent compared with 382 percent for buy-and-hold. The profit factor on each trade was 1.28, just a bit better than breakeven. This test resulted in an 11 percentage point increase in the annual rate of return compared with the prior period ending in 2002. The equity curve (Figure 10-2) had some severe drawdowns during 2000 and during 2010. Table 10-3 provides the annual performance data. Interestingly, the strategy performed very well during the bear market years of 2002 and 2008 but got hit hard in 1995 and especially 2000 (–75 percent drop), the beginning of that three-year bear market. Thus, overall, this strategy has had mediocre results during the most recent period, taking into account the large drawdowns, but it still outpaced buy-and-hold.

## TABLE 10-2

TradeStation Performance Summary VL4% Weekly 1992 to 2010

| | All Trades | Long Trades | Short Trades |
|---|---|---|---|
| Total net profit | $168,958.45 | $280,573.37 | ($111,614.92) |
| Gross profit | $770,571.44 | $548,214.49 | $222,356.95 |
| Gross loss | ($601,612.99) | ($267,641.12) | ($333,971.87) |
| Profit factor | 1.28 | 2.05 | 0.67 |
| Rollover credit | $0.00 | $0.00 | $0.00 |
| Open position profit/loss (P/L) | $24,564.06 | $24,564.06 | $0.00 |
| Select total net profit | $93,461.04 | $170,129.09 | ($76,668.05) |
| Select gross profit | $660,127.16 | $437,770.21 | $222,356.95 |
| Select gross loss | ($566,666.12) | ($267,641.12) | ($299,025.00) |
| Select profit factor | 1.16 | 1.64 | 0.74 |
| Adjusted total net profit | ($36,718.37) | ($112,862.52) | ($229,737.19) |
| Adjusted gross profit | $643,890.28 | $436,310.68 | $160,686.23 |
| Adjusted gross loss | ($680,608.65) | ($323,448.15) | ($390,423.42) |
| Adjusted profit factor | 0.95 | 1.35 | 0.41 |
| Total number of trades | 95 | 47 | 48 |
| Percent profitable | 38.95% | 51.06% | 27.08% |
| Winning trades | 37 | 24 | 13 |
| Losing trades | 58 | 23 | 35 |

*(continued on next page)*

**TABLE 10-2**

TradeStation Performance Summary VL4% Weekly 1992 to 2010 (continued)

|  | All Trades | Long Trades | Short Trades |
|---|---|---|---|
| Even trades | 0 | 0 | 0 |
| Average trade net profit | $1,778.51 | $5,969.65 | ($2,325.31) |
| Average winning trade | $20,826.26 | $22,842.27 | $17,104.38 |
| Average losing trade | ($10,372.64) | ($11,636.57) | ($9,542.05) |
| Ratio average win/average loss | 2.01 | 1.96 | 1.79 |
| Largest winning trade | $110,444,28 | $110,444.28 | $62,218.24 |
| Largest losing trade | ($34,946.87) | ($33,520.63) | ($34,946.87) |
| Largest winner as % of gross profit | 14.33% | 20.15% | 27.98% |
| Largest loser as % of gross loss | 5.81% | 12.52% | 10.46% |
| Net profit as % of largest loss | 483.47% | 837.02% | (319.38%) |
| Select net profit as % of largest loss | 267.44% | 507.54% | (219.38%) |
| Adjusted net profit as % of largest loss | (105.07%) | 336.70% | (657.39%) |
| Maximum consecutive winning trades | 5 | 4 | 3 |
| Maximum consecutive losing trades | 7 | 5 | 9 |
| Average bars in total trades | 9.16 | 12.13 | 6.25 |
| Average bars in winning trades | 14.95 | 18.04 | 9.23 |
| Average bars in losing trades | 5.47 | 5.96 | 5.14 |
| Average bars in even trades | 0.00 | 0.00 | 0.00 |
| Maximum shares/contracts held | 26,000,000 | 26,000,000 | 25,900,000 |
| Total shares/contracts held | 14,680 | 7,428 | 7,252 |
| Account size required | $171,559.95 | $57,916.14 | $166,370.66 |
| Total slippage | $0.00 | $0.00 | $0.00 |
| Total commission | $0.00 | $0.00 | $0.00 |
| Return on initial capital | 1,689.58% | | |
| Annual rate of return | 18.93% | | |
| Buy/hold return | 382.45% | | |
| Return on account | 98.48% | | |
| Average monthly return | $20.10 | | |
| SD of monthly return | $26,434.52 | | |
| Return retracement ratio | 0.20 | | |
| RINA index | 7.47 | | |
| Sharpe ratio | 0.18 | | |
| K-ratio | 2.19 | | |
| Trading period | 15 years, 2 months, 25 days | | |

**TABLE 10-2**

TradeStation Performance Summary VL4% Weekly 1992 to 2010 (continued)

|  | All Trades | Long Trades | Short Trades |
|---|---|---|---|
| Percent of time in the market | 98.36% | | |
| Time in the market | 14 years, 11 months, 25 days | | |
| Longest flat period | n/a | | |
| Maximum equity run-up | n/a | | |
| Date of maximum equity run-up | n/a | | |
| Maximum equity run-up as % of initial capital | n/a | | |
| **Maximum Drawdown (Intraday Peak to Valley)** | | | |
| Value | ($209,300.17) | ($114,158.900) | ($208,112.76) |
| Date | n/a | | |
| As % of initial capital | n/a | n/a | n/a |
| Net profit as % of drawdown | 80.73% | 245.77% | (53.63%) |
| Select net profit as % of drawdown | 44.65% | 149.03% | (36.84%) |
| Adjusted net profit as % of drawdown | (17.54%) | 98.86% | (110.39%) |
| **Maximum Drawdown (Trade Close to Trade Close)** | | | |
| Value | ($171,559.95) | ($57,916.14) | ($166,370.66) |
| Date | 9/3/2010 | | |
| As % of initial capital | 1715.60% | 579.16% | 1,663.71% |
| Net profit as % of drawdown | 98.48% | 484.45% | (67.09%) |
| Select net profit as % of drawdown | 54.48% | 293.75% | 46.08% |
| Adjusted net profit as % of drawdown | (21.40%) | 194.87% | (138.09%) |
| Maximum trade drawdown | ($37,839.23) | ($37,839.23) | ($37,492.84) |

Source: Created with TradeStation. Printed with permission.

# VL4% DAILY BACKTEST FROM 1992 TO 2002

All the published research performed on the VL4% by Davis, Freeburg, and Penn used weekly Value Line data. I have not come across any published findings of research in which daily Value Line data were used. Therefore, in the first edition of the book, I decided to test a VL4% daily strategy using TradeStation.

**TABLE 10-3**

VL4% Weekly 1992–2010 Annual Performance

| Period | Net Profit | % Gain | Profit Factor | No. of Trades | % Profitable |
|---|---|---|---|---|---|
| Last 12 months | ($123,619.91) | (37.79%) | 0.32 | 13 | 23.08% |
| 1/1/2010 | ($94,652.26) | (31.74%) | 0.29 | 11 | 18.18% |
| 1/1/2009 | $76,601.24 | 34.57% | 1.46 | 13 | 38.46% |
| 1/1/2008 | $48,146.64 | 27.76% | 1.87 | 11 | 45.45% |
| 1/1/2007 | ($24,134.56) | (12.22%) | 0.16 | 7 | 28.57% |
| 1/1/2006 | $45,090.04 | 29.57% | 100.00 | 3 | 100.00% |
| 1/1/2005 | ($37,729.33) | (19.84%) | 0.34 | 7 | 28.57% |
| 1/1/2004 | $19,324.17 | 11.31% | 1.55 | 7 | 42.86% |
| 1/1/2003 | $48,159.57 | 39.24% | 2.52 | 6 | 33.33% |
| 1/1/2002 | $36,107.24 | 41.69% | 2.48 | 8 | 50.00% |
| 1/1/2001 | $68,847.57 | 387.61% | 100.00 | 5 | 100.00% |
| 1/1/2000 | ($52,762.40) | (74.81%) | 0.03 | 11 | 18.18% |
| 1/1/1999 | $13,666.87 | 24.04% | 3.26 | 5 | 80.00% |
| 1/1/1998 | $19,409.31 | 51.83% | 1.64 | 8 | 37.50% |
| 1/1/1997 | $16,773.62 | 81.13% | 4.49 | 4 | 50.00% |
| 1/1/1996 | $14,509.66 | 235.35% | 7.44 | 3 | 66.67% |
| 1/1/1995 | ($3,834.87) | (38.35%) | | | |

With the use of daily data, I expected to find many more buy and sell signals with improved performance over the weekly data. This is so because daily data, in theory, should provide faster buy and sell signals and higher annualized returns than weekly data. I tested VL4% *daily* from December 4, 1992, through November 29, 2002, which resulted in a total profit of $111,234 (as opposed to $81,998 on the weekly test). The annual rate of return for the daily test was 8.14 percent compared with 7.25 percent for the weekly test. The cumulative daily return was 111.23 percent compared with a meager buy-and-hold return of 4.57 percent, so the daily strategy performed better than the weekly strategy by approximately $29,236 during the test period. Unfortunately, the equity curve (not shown) had a big drop in the 2000 time period, where 18 of 20 trades were losers. Thus, even the daily signals could not overcome the numerous whipsaws that produced multiple consecutive losses.

**FIGURE 10-2**

VL4% weekly 1992–2010 equity curve.

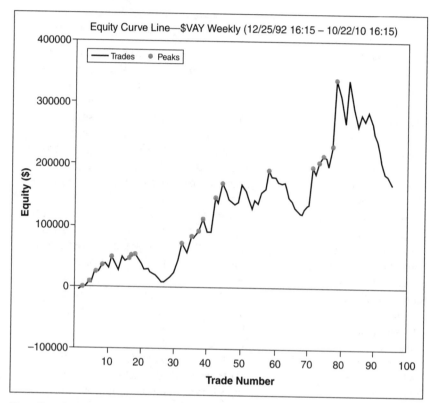

Source: Created with TradeStation. Printed with permission.

## LATEST VL4% DAILY BACKTEST FROM 1992 TO 2010

For the second edition of this book, I ran the same backtest parameters but analyzed the period from 1992 to 2010. This test produced a profit of $460,000, or an annual rate of return of 22.27 percent. This is a return of capital of 4,600 percent compared with 470.5 percent for buy-and-hold. There were 167 trades during this test period, of which 46 percent were profitable. For more details on this test, see Table 10-4.

The annual performance data are shown in Table 10-5. The biggest losses occurred in 1994 (–75.4 percent), 2000 (–48.2 per-

**TABLE 10-4**

## TradeStation Performance Summary VL4% Daily 1992–2010

|  | All Trades | Long Trades | Short Trades |
|---|---|---|---|
| Total net profit | $460,007.43 | $545,604.56 | ($85,597.13) |
| Gross profit | $1,887,598.09 | $1,140,058.94 | $747,539.15 |
| Gross loss | ($1,427,590.66) | ($594,454.38) | ($833,136.28) |
| Profit factor | 1.32 | 1.92 | 0.90 |
| Rollover credit | $0.00 | $0.00 | $0.00 |
| Open position P/L | $59,110.92 | $59,110.92 | $0.00 |
| Select total net profit | $306,553.61 | $383,350.45 | ($76,796.84) |
| Select gross profit | $1,554,277.65 | $919,842.85 | $634,434.80 |
| Select gross loss | ($1,247,724.04) | ($536,492.40) | ($711,231.64) |
| Select profit factor | 1.25 | 1.71 | 0.89 |
| Adjusted total net profit | ($94,414.40) | ($277,755.71) | ($331,622.30) |
| Adjusted gross profit | $1,672,486.32 | $966,201.58 | $619,337.24 |
| Adjusted gross loss | ($1,578,071.93) | ($688,445.87) | ($950,959.54) |
| Adjusted profit factor | 1.06 | 1.40 | 0.65 |
| Total number of trades | 167 | 83 | 84 |
| Percent profitable | 46.11% | 51.81% | 40.48% |
| Winning trades | 77 | 43 | 34 |
| Losing trades | 90 | 40 | 50 |
| Even trades | 0 | 0 | 0 |
| Average trade net profit | $2,754.54 | $6,573.55 | ($1,019.01) |
| Average winning trade | $24,514.26 | $26,513.00 | $21,986.45 |
| Average losing trade | ($15,862.12) | ($14,861.36) | ($16,662.73) |
| Ratio average win/average loss | 1.55 | 1.78 | 1.32 |
| Largest winning trade | $113,104.35 | $112,367.09 | $113,104.35 |
| Largest losing trade | ($61,295.28) | ($57,961.98) | ($61,295.28) |
| Largest winner as % of gross profit | 5.99% | 9.86% | 15.13% |
| Largest loser as % of gross loss | 4.29% | 9.75% | 7.36% |
| Net profit as % of largest loss | 750.48% | 941.31% | (139.65%) |
| Select net profit as % of largest loss | 500.13% | 661.38% | (125.29%) |
| Adjusted net profit as % of largest loss | 154.03% | 479.20% | (541.02%) |
| Maximum consecutive winning trades | 4 | 5 | 3 |
| Maximum consecutive losing trades | 7 | 5 | 11 |
| Average bars in total trades | 25.73 | 34.78 | 16.79 |
| Average. bars in winning trades | 41.73 | 55.49 | 24.32 |
| Average bars in losing trades | 12.04 | 12.53 | 11.664 |

**TABLE 10-4**

TradeStation Performance Summary VL4% Daily 1992–2010 (continued)

|  | All Trades | Long Trades | Short Trades |
|---|---|---|---|
| Average bars in even trades | 0.00 | 0.00 | 0.00 |
| Maximum shares/contracts held | 57,700,000 | 57,700,000 | 57,200,000 |
| Total shares/contracts held | 47,836 | 24,119 | 23,717 |
| Account size required | $250,410.98 | $148,442.07 | $305,911.62 |
| Total slippage | $0.00 | $0.00 | $0.00 |
| Total commission | $0.00 | $0.00 | $0.00 |
| Return on initial capital | 4600.07% | | |
| Annual rate of return | 22.27% | | |
| Buy/hold return | 470.49% | | |
| Return on account | 183.70% | | |
| Average monthly return | $1,021.92 | | |
| SD of monthly return | $60,658.01 | | |
| Return retracement ratio | 0.24 | | |
| RINA index | 11.36 | | |
| Sharpe ratio | 0.15 | | |
| K-ratio | 3.43 | | |
| Trading period | 17 years, 3 months, 13 days | | |
| Percent of time in the market | 95.82% | | |
| Time in the market | 16 years, 6 months, 24 days | | |
| Longest flat period | n/a | | |
| Maximum equity run-up equity run-up | $726,223.39 | | |
| Date and time of maximum | 03/26/09 16:15 | | |
| Maximum equity run-up as % of initial capital | 7,262.23% | | |

**Maximum Drawdown (Intraday Peak to Valley)**

|  | All Trades | Long Trades | Short Trades |
|---|---|---|---|
| Value | ($320,964.54) | ($192,221.02) | ($352,235.48) |
| Date and time | 11/30/09 16:15 | | |
| As % of initial capital | 3,209.65% | 1,922.21% | 3,522.35% |
| Net profit as % of drawdown | 143.32% | 283.84% | (24.30%) |
| Select net profit as % of drawdown | 95.51% | 199.43% | (21.80%) |
| Adjusted net profit as % of drawdown | (29.42%) | 144.50% | (94.15%) |

*(continued on next page)*

**TABLE 10-4**

TradeStation Performance Summary VL4% Daily 1992–2010 (continued)

| | All Trades | Long Trades | Short Trades |
|---|---|---|---|
| **Maximum Drawdown (Trade Close to Trade Close)** | | | |
| Value | ($250,410.98) | ($148,442.07) | ($305,911.62) |
| Date and time | 11/09/09 16:15 | | |
| As % of initial capital | 2,504.11% | 1,484.42%% | 3,059.12% |
| Net profit as % of drawdown | 183.70% | 367.55% | (27.98%) |
| Select net profit as % of drawdown | 122.42% | 258.25% | (25.10%) |
| Adjusted net profit as % of drawdown | (37.70%) | 187.11% | (108.40%) |
| Maximum trade drawdown | ($69,799.20) | ($58,011.93) | ($69,799.20) |

*Source:* Created with TradeStation. Printed with permission.

**TABLE 10-5**

TradeStation VL4% Daily Annual Returns 1992–2010

| Period | Net Profit | % Gain | Profit Factor | No. of Trades | % Profitable |
|---|---|---|---|---|---|
| Last 12 months | $95,957.54 | 22.15% | 2.04 | 15 | 46.67% |
| 1/1/2010 | $82,288.52 | 18.42% | 1.98 | 13 | 46.15% |
| 1/1/2009 | ($64,880.92) | (12.68%) | 0.86 | 29 | 37.93% |
| 1/1/2008 | $49,845.63 | 10.79% | 1.11 | 31 | 41.94% |
| 1/1/2007 | ($11,413.96) | (2.41%) | 0.81 | 9 | 55.56% |
| 1/1/2006 | $86,767.81 | 22.45% | 3.74 | 5 | 60.00% |
| 1/1/2005 | ($4,696.91) | (1.20%) | 0.91 | 7 | 42.86% |
| 1/1/2004 | ($6,738.29) | (1.69%) | 0.92 | 11 | 45.45% |
| 1/1/2003 | $115,303.54 | 40.79% | 2.87 | 8 | 37.50% |
| 1/1/2002 | $110,049.86 | 63.76% | 3.49 | 14 | 64.29% |
| 1/1/2001 | $92,196.69 | 114.68% | 4.16 | 9 | 55.56% |
| 1/1/2000 | ($74,856.66) | (48.22%) | 0.13 | 15 | 20.00% |
| 1/1/1999 | $44,973.32 | 40.78% | 13.31 | 5 | 60.00% |
| 1/1/1998 | $59,303.99 | 116.34% | 4.27 | 10 | 70.00% |
| 1/1/1997 | $5,326.98 | 11.67% | 1.28 | 6 | 33.33% |
| 1/1/1996 | $25,289.30 | 124.21% | 100.00 | 3 | 100.00% |
| 1/1/1995 | $17,903.86 | 729.11% | 7.59 | 3 | 66.67% |
| 1/1/1994 | ($7,544.41) | (75.44%) | 0.09 | 6 | 50.00% |

*Source:* Created with TradeStation. Printed with permission.

cent), and 2009 (–12.7 percent). However, in the bear market years of 2001 (+114.7 percent), 2002 (+63.7 percent), and 2008 (+10.8 percent), there were outstanding gains. Overall, this daily strategy produced 2.7 times the return on capital as the weekly strategy. Therefore, as was the case with the weekly strategy, the volatility and large losses may result in conservative investors not willing to take on the risk of the VL4% strategy altogether. The equity curve (Figure 10-3) illustrates the inconsistent returns over time.

**FIGURE 10-3**

Equity curve VL4% daily, 1992–2010.

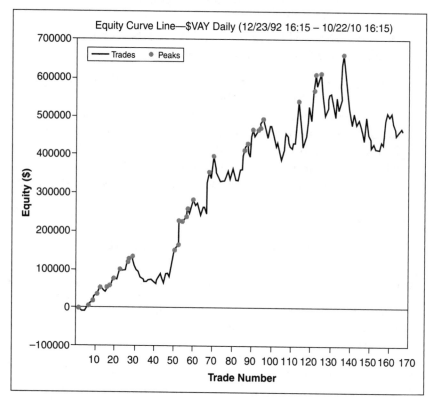

*Source:* Created with TradeStation. Printed with permission.

## WEEKLY VL3% BACKTEST 1992–2010 OUTPERFORMS VL4% WEEKLY AND DAILY

Based on the mediocre results of the VL4% weekly and daily strategies in more recent years, I decided to determine if a slight variation of the weekly strategy would produce more consistent results, fewer whipsaws, and higher profits. Using TradeStation, I ran an optimization of different values near the 4 percent weekly to see if the performance would be improved for the period 1992–2010. I discovered that simply using a 3 percent value instead of 4 percent resulted in superior results all around. For example, compare the VL4% and VL3% weekly in terms of net profits:

- VL3% $885,293 (long and short) versus VL4% $168,958 (long and short)
- VL3% $647,154 (long only and no shorts) versus VL4% $284,651 (long only and no shorts)

Clearly, using VL3% with long and short trades greatly improved the bottom-line profits compared with VL4%. Table 10-6 provides the details on the VL3% performance results. Table 10-7 provides the annual returns. As you can see, except for the horrific 59.32 percent loss in the brutal 2000 bear market, this strategy had only three other annual losses, all of which were less than 9 percent. And more important, this strategy had tremendous gains in three

**TABLE 10-6**

VL3% versus VL4% Weekly and Daily 1992–2010

| Metric | VL3% Weekly | VL4% Weekly | VL4% Daily |
|---|---|---|---|
| Total net profits | $885,293 | $168,958 | $460,007 |
| Profit factor | 2.06 | 1.28 | 1.32 |
| Total no. of trades | 111 | 95 | 167 |
| % profitable trades | 42.34% | 38.95% | 46.11% |
| Ratio average win/average loss | 2.81 | 2.01 | 1.55 |
| Return of initial capital | 8,852.9% | 1,689.6% | 4,600.1% |
| Annual rate of return | 29.50% | 18.93% | 22.27% |
| Buy/hold return | 382.4% | 382.4% | 470.05 |
| Sharpe ratio | 0.29 | 0.18 | 0.15 |

**TABLE 10-7**

VL3% Weekly Annual Returns 1992–2010

| Period | Net Profit | % Gain | Profit Factor | No. of Trades | % Profitable |
|---|---|---|---|---|---|
| Last 12 months | $461.71 | 0.05% | 1.00 | 13 | 38.46% |
| 1/1/2010 | $37,019.69 | 3.90% | 1.16 | 11 | 36.36% |
| 1/1/2009 | $360,566.51 | 61.36% | 2.44 | 13 | 46.15% |
| 1/1/2008 | $168,863.32 | 40.32% | 2.73 | 12 | 58.33% |
| 1/1/2007 | ($41,151.89) | (8.95%) | 0.19 | 8 | 37.50% |
| 1/1/2006 | $122,841.21 | 36.44% | 100.00 | 3 | 100.00% |
| 1/1/2005 | ($3,018.70) | (0.89%) | 0.93 | 7 | 28.57% |
| 1/1/2004 | $51,335.77 | 17.78% | 2.24 | 7 | 42.86% |
| 1/1/2003 | $83,582.80 | 40.74% | 3.59 | 6 | 33.33% |
| 1/1/2002 | $78,938.14 | 62.53% | 5.35 | 10 | 60.00% |
| 1/1/2001 | $77,855.73 | 160.89% | 9.92 | 7 | 71.43% |
| 1/1/2000 | ($70,553.71) | (59.32%) | 0.05 | 17 | 5.88% |
| 1/1/1999 | $50,040.77 | 72.63% | 100.00 | 5 | 100.00% |
| 1/1/1998 | $19,436.64 | 39.29% | 1.63 | 10 | 30.00% |
| 1/1/1997 | $15,317.40 | 44.86% | 2.30 | 6 | 50.00% |
| 1/1/1996 | $24,508.21 | 254.22% | 100.00 | 3 | 100.00% |
| 1/1/1995 | ($359.58) | (3.60%) | 0.88 | 2 | 50.00% |

Source: Created with TradeStation. Printed with permission.

bear market years: 2001: +160.89 percent; 2002: +62.53 percent; and 2008: +40.32 percent. Also, in the big bull market year of 2009, this strategy had a 61.36 percent return, beating all the major averages. Moreover, the equity curve (Figure 10-4) is much smoother and steeper than that for the VL4% strategy (refer back to Figure 10-2).

Let's compare the VL3% weekly (Table 10-8) and VL4% weekly and daily on key metrics that were obtained from the tables in this chapter.

By carefully examining the performance and annual return tables and equity curves for both the VL4% strategies and the VL3% weekly strategy, you can determine for yourself which strategy is superior. Based on my review, it is clear that the VL3% strategy wins hands down in all respects, except that there were 16 more trades for the VL3% weekly strategy compared with the VL4% weekly strategy over the backtest period. The number of

**FIGURE 10-4**

VL3% weekly equity curve, 1992–2010.

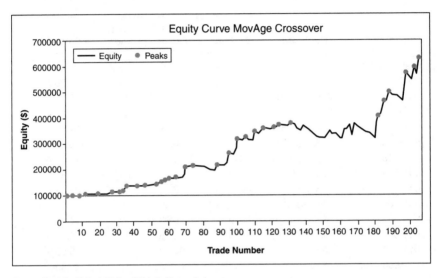

*Source:* Created with TradeStation. Printed with permission.

**TABLE 10-8**

TradeStation Performance Summary VL3% Weekly,
1992–2010

|  | All Trades | Long Trades | Short Trades |
|---|---|---|---|
| Total Net Profit | $885,292.87 | $792,822.56 | $92,470.31 |
| Gross Profit | $1,718,803.06 | $1,202,319.39 | $516,483.67 |
| Gross Loss | ($833,510.19) | ($409,496.83) | ($424,013.36) |
| Profit Factor | 2.06 | 2.94 | 1.22 |
| Roll Over Credit | $0.00 | $0.00 | $0.00 |
| Open Position P/L | $89,929.44 | $89,929.44 | $0.00 |
| Select Total Net Profit | $592,792.00 | $500,321.69 | $92,470.31 |
| Select Gross Profit | $1,286,893.77 | $770,410.10 | $516,483.67 |
| Select Gross Loss | ($694,101.77) | ($270,088.41) | ($424,013.36) |
| Select Profit Factor | 1.85 | 2.85 | 1.22 |
| Adjusted Total Net Profit | $530,390.90 | $489,248.52 | ($98,050.11) |
| Adjusted Gross Profit | $1,468,089.87 | $979,054.28 | $394,747.30 |
| Adjusted Gross Loss | ($937,698.96) | ($489,805.77) | ($492,797.41) |

**TABLE 10-8**

TradeStation Performance Summary VL3% Weekly, 1992–2010 (continued)

| | All Trades | Long Trades | Short Trades |
|---|---|---|---|
| Adjusted Profit Factor | 1.57 | 2.00 | 0.80 |
| Total Number of Trades | 111 | 55 | 56 |
| Percent Profitable | 42.34% | 52.73% | 32.14% |
| Winning Trades | 47 | 29 | 18 |
| Losing Trades | 64 | 26 | 38 |
| Even Trades | 0 | 0 | 0 |
| Avg. Trade Net Profit | $7,975.61 | $14,414.96 | $1,651.26 |
| Avg. Winning Trade | $36,570.28 | $41,459.29 | $28,693.54 |
| Avg. Losing Trade | ($13,023.60) | ($15,749.88) | ($11,158.25) |
| Ratio Avg. Win:Avg. Loss | 2.81 | 2.63 | 2.57 |
| Largest Winning Trade | $240,455.46 | $240,455.46 | $133,880.32 |
| Largest Losing Trade | ($77,635.00) | ($77,635.00) | ($46,443.60) |
| Largest Winner as % of Gross Profit | 13.99% | 20.00% | 25.92% |
| Largest Loser as % of Gross Loss | 9.31% | 18.96% | 10.95% |
| Net Profit as % of Largest Loss | 1140.33% | 1021.22% | 199.10% |
| Select Net Profit as % of Largest Loss | 763.56% | 644.45% | 199.10% |
| Adjusted Net Profit as % of Largest Loss | 683.19% | 630.19% | (211.12%) |
| Max. Consecutive Winning Trades | 5 | 3 | 3 |
| Max. Consecutive Losing Trades | 9 | 4 | 8 |
| Avg. Bars in Total Trades | 7.98 | 10.31 | 5.70 |
| Avg. Bars in Winning Trades | 12.89 | 15.83 | 8.17 |
| Avg. Bars in Losing Trades | 4.38 | 4.15 | 4.53 |
| Avg. Bars in Even Trades | 0.00 | 0.00 | 0.00 |
| Max. Shares/Contracts Held | 56,500,000 | 56,500,000 | 53,400,000 |
| Total Shares/Contracts Held | 28464 | 14541 | 13923 |
| Account Size Required | $176,819.71 | $111,883.15 | $183,172.10 |
| Total Slippage | $0.00 | $0.00 | $0.00 |
| Total Commission | $0.00 | $0.00 | $0.00 |
| Return on Initial Capital | 8852.93% | | |
| Annual Rate of Return | 29.50% | | |
| Buy & Hold Return | 382.45% | | |
| Return on Account | 500.68% | | |
| Avg. Monthly Return | $12,883.53 | | |
| Std. Deviation of Monthly Return | $50,675.02 | | |

*(continued on next page)*

**TABLE 10-8**

TradeStation Performance Summary VL3% Weekly,
1992–2010 (continued)

|  | All Trades | Long Trades | Short Trades |
|---|---|---|---|
| Return Retracement Ratio | 0.33 |  |  |
| RINA Index | 42.49 |  |  |
| Sharpe Ratio | 0.29 |  |  |
| K-Ratio | 2.05 |  |  |
| Trading Period | 15 Yrs, 2 Mths, 25 Dys |  |  |
| Percent of Time in the Market | 98.36% |  |  |
| Time in the Market | 14 Yrs, 11 Mths, 25 Dys |  |  |
| Longest Flat Period | n/a |  |  |
| Max. Equity Run-up | n/a |  |  |
| Date of Max. Equity Run-up | n/a |  |  |
| Max. Equity Run-up as % of Initial Capital | n/a |  |  |
| **Max. Drawdown (Intra-day Peak to Valley)** |  |  |  |
| Value | ($262,720.51) | ($178,392.12) | ($275,014.56) |
| Date | n/a |  |  |
| as % of Initial Capital | n/a | n/a | n/a |
| Net Profit as % of Drawdown | 336.97% | 444.43% | 33.62% |
| Select Net Profit as % of Drawdown | 225.64% | 280.46% | 33.62% |
| Adjusted Net Profit as % of Drawdown | 201.88% | 274.25% | (35.65%) |
| **Max. Drawdown (Trade Close to Trade Close)** |  |  |  |
| Value | ($176,819.71) | ($111,883.15) | ($183,172.10) |
| Date | 9/3/2010 |  |  |
| as % of Initial Capital | 1768.20% | 1118.83% | 1831.72% |
| Net Profit as % of Drawdown | 500.68% | 708.62% | 50.48% |
| Select Net Profit as % of Drawdown | 335.25% | 447.18% | 50.48% |
| Adjusted Net Profit as % of Drawdown | 299.96% | 437.29% | (53.53%) |
| Max. Trade Drawdown | ($94,290.00) | ($94,290.00) | ($53,085.27) |

additional trades certainly is manageable based on the low commissions offered by discount brokers and the huge quintuple difference in performance.

Even though the VL4% daily strategy is superior to the VL4% weekly strategy, the much larger number of trades, worse ratio of average wins to average losses, and comparable Sharpe ratio indicate that the daily strategy has some shortcomings. According to Wikipedia, "The Sharpe ratio is a measure of the excess return (or Risk Premium) per unit of risk in an investment asset or a trading strategy. The Sharpe ratio is used to characterize how well the return of an asset compensates the investor for the risk taken; the higher the Sharpe ratio number, the better."

## MTR STOCK-TIMING MODEL (MTR-TM) USES VL4% WEEKLY AS BASIS OF THE MODEL

Additional research on the VL4% weekly model has been conducted by the MTR Investors Group. MTR has worked with and tested the VL4% weekly model and has enhanced it based on additional backtesting. MTR calls its model the *MTR timing model* (MTR-TM), and it is a mechanical stock market timing model. MTR originally used the VL4% weekly model that issued buy and sell signals based on a Friday-to-Friday percentage change in the VLCI. For example, if the index was up 4 percent from any previous week, MTR went long the market. Likewise, if the index was down 4 percent from any previous week, MTR went short the market. The main issue encountered with this model was that it created too many false (inaccurate) or whipsaw signals. Interestingly, this is the same conclusion that I came to after extensive backtesting, as mentioned earlier in this chapter.

Accordingly, the MTR-TM was revised with additional parameters that are currently proprietary. This change resulted in better overall net risk-adjusted returns and a higher percentage of accurate trades. The MTR-TM was in testing for over a year until it produced better results for intermediate- and long-term stock market moves than the original unadjusted model. The system was backtested from January 1990 to December 2008. Signals after December 1, 2008, were "out of sample," and this reflects what would have happened if this model had been live on December 1, 2008. The MTR-TM went live in March of 2009. The model was run from January 1997 to March 2010 and produced 811 percent returns for 72 trades (long and short) compared with a buy-and-hold return of 74.49 percent. Table 10-9 provides the data on the backtest.

**TABLE 10-9**

MTR-TM January 1997 to March 2010

| Category | All Trades | Long Trades | Short Trades |
|---|---|---|---|
| Initial capital | 10,000.00 | 10,000.00 | 10,000.00 |
| Ending capital | 91,131.64 | 79,524.43 | 21,607.22 |
| Net profit | 81,131.64 | 69,524.43 | 11,607.22 |
| Net profit % | 811.32% | 695.24% | 116.07% |
| Exposure % | 98.07% | 66.90% | 31.17% |
| Net risk-adjusted return % | 827.26% | 1,039.27% | 372.33% |
| Annual return % | 18.23% | 17.01% | 6.01% |
| Risk-adjusted return % | 18.59% | 25.43% | 19.28% |
| All trades | 72 | 36 (50.00%) | 36 (50.00%) |
| Average P/L | 1,126.83 | 1,931.23 | 322.42 |
| Average P/L % | 3.55% | 5.82% | 1.27% |
| Average bars held | 46.22 | 62.69 | 29.75 |
| Winners | 40 (55.56%) | 24 (33.33%) | 16 (22.22%) |
| Total profit | 122,721.34 | 89,502.45 | 33,218.89 |
| Average profit | 3,068.03 | 3,729.27 | 2,076.18 |
| Average profit % | 9.50% | 11.03% | 7.21% |
| Average bars held | 64.95 | 78.42 | 44.75 |
| Maximum consecutive | 4 | 5 | 4 |
| Largest win | 25,187.84 | 25,187.84 | 10,425.57 |
| No. of bars in largest win | 67 | 67 | 40 |
| Losers | 32 (44.44%) | 12 (16.67%) | 20 (27.78%) |
| Total loss | −41,589.69 | −19,978.02 | −21,611.67 |
| Average loss | −1,299.68 | −1,664.84 | −1,080.58 |
| Average loss % | −3.89% | −4.59% | −3.48% |
| Average bars held | 22.81 | 31.25 | 17.75 |
| Maximum consecutive | 5 | 2 | 5 |
| Largest loss | −6,583.50 | −6,305.37 | −6,583.50 |
| No. of bars in largest loss | 7 | 7 | 7 |

*Source:* www.MTRIG.com

The vertical lines in Figure 10-5 indicate the buy and sell signal dates. As you can see, they have been accurate. Since it may be a bit difficult to read the exact signal dates, Table 10-10 provides them from January 4, 2008, through September 2, 2010. All of the dates and signals are provided on the MTR Web site (www.MTRIG.com).

**FIGURE 10-5**

MTR-TM signals.

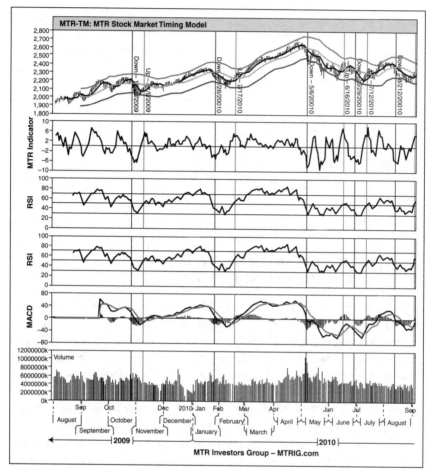

At the Web site, the market timing model chart and signals are shown daily, and you can sign up for a nightly e-mail so that you can view them. The signals are provided free of charge; therefore, you should bookmark this site and check it at least weekly for the latest signals if you don't sign up for the e-mail service. Also, you may want to check out other features of this Web site, including the blog.

**TABLE 10-10**

MTR-TM Buy and Sell Signal Dates

| Signal Date | Up or Down | Signal Date | Up or Down | Signal Date | Up or Down |
|---|---|---|---|---|---|
| 1/4/2008 | Down | 1/14/2009 | Down | 5/6/2010 | Down |
| 1/28/2008 | Up | 3/13/2009 | Up | 6/16/2010 | Up |
| 3/5/2008 | Down | 6/17/2009 | Down | 6/29/2010 | Down |
| 3/24/2008 | Up | 7/1/2009 | Up | 7/12/2010 | Up |
| 6/11/2008 | Down | 7/7/2009 | Down | 8/12/2010 | Down |
| 7/17/2008 | Up | 7/16/2009 | Up | 9/2/2010 | Up |
| 9/9/2008 | Down | 10/26/2009 | Down | | |
| 11/3/2008 | Up | 11/9/2009 | Up | | |
| 11/11/2008 | Down | 1/26/2010 | Down | | |
| 12/3/2008 | Up | 2/17/2010 | Up | | |

Source: www.MTRIG.com

# TIMING THE MARKET WITH THE VL3% WEEKLY STRATEGY

If you prefer to check on your investments once a week, then use the VL3% weekly strategy. With this approach, you can calculate the percentage change from the previous high or low, as the case may be, once a week (on Friday evening or over the weekend) and then make your investment on Monday if there is a signal change. If at all possible, try to make the investment on Friday afternoon, if you have access to the information, because that timing usually will produce better results than waiting until Monday.

If you are using this strategy for the first time and you are currently in cash, then look for a buy signal when the weekly price goes up by 3 percent from any previous weekly close. Alternatively, a sell signal is generated when the index closes down 3 percent from a prior high. At that point, you can go short or stay in cash if that is your preference.

Once a buy signal is given, you can go long the market with an index fund, an ETF (e.g., a DIA or QQQQ), or an investment vehicle of your choice, as discussed previously. When a sell signal occurs, then you go into cash or buy an inverse (bear) fund—e.g., the ProShares Short QQQQ (PSQ), depending on your risk tolerance. Remember, you cannot short an ETF in a retirement account, but you can buy a bear fund.

To prevent a potentially large loss, you always should use a stop-limit order about 8 to 10 percent below your purchase price depending on your risk tolerance. Of course, it is up to you to select the percentage loss that you are willing to tolerate. Be sure that you cut your losses quickly; otherwise, small losses can turn into big losses.

## CONCLUSIONS

The use of a mechanical trading strategy, such as VL3% weekly or the MTR-TM, hopefully will take the emotion and uncertainty out of the investing decision. All serious investors should use a systematic investing approach to improve their results. The VL3% weekly strategy requires minimal time to track the signals, provides less risk, and produces a much better return than buy-and-hold, but it had some losing years that may be difficult for some investors to stomach. Of course, one approach is to place a stop-limit order after a position is taken based on a VL3% buy signal and then wait for the next signal before taking a new position.

Although the VL4% weekly strategy has been popular over a number of decades, its poor performance during the 2001–2002 bear market and in more recent years has resulted in mediocre results, although it still beats buy-and-hold. Based on the backtested results of the VL3% weekly strategy, investors now have a much better performer to work with. Remember, though, that there is no guarantee that this strategy will continue to outperform going forward. However, the key is to put the odds in your favor. This is what market timing is all about—being on the right side of the market at the right time. Simple strategies do work. Investors who decide to use the VL3% weekly strategy going forward hopefully will perform better than 99 percent of the financial gurus and other investors who have no specific action plan with simple buy and sell rules.

## CHAPTER 11

# Nasdaq Composite
# 6 Percent Strategy

*Forecasting is very difficult, especially if it involves the future.*
—Casey Stengel, former manager, New York Yankees

**W**hat would happen if the logic behind the Value Line 4 percent (VL4%) or Value Line 3 percent (VL3%) strategy, as presented in Chapter 10, were applied to two Nasdaq indexes? Using TradeStation, I backtested a similar strategy using both the Nasdaq Composite Index (COMPX) and the Nasdaq 100 Index (NDX) with both weekly and daily prices. In the first edition of this book, I provided the results of these four tests through 2002. With this edition, I have updated the results through 2010.

## PART 1. ORIGINAL TESTS: RESULTS THROUGH 2002

Four original tests covering the period 1971–2002 are summarized herewith.

### Original Test 1: Weekly Nasdaq Composite Index 6 Percent Strategy (NC6%): 1971–2002

The Nasdaq Composite Index (COMPX) contains a much different mix of stocks than the Value Line Composite Index (VLCI). It contains about 2,000 companies compared with 1,626 in the VLCI. Also, the COMPX tends to be more volatile and has wider price swings than the VLCI.

Because of the higher volatility of the COMPX, I arbitrarily changed the filter percentage from 4 to 6 percent. Therefore, the first strategy tested set the weekly buy and sell signals at the 6 percent mark. This means that if the COMPX rises 6 percent from any previous weekly low, then a buy signal is generated on that Friday. Likewise, a 6 percent drop from any previous weekly high generates a sell signal on that Friday. On the sell signal, the strategy went *short* instead of going into cash. This is the same approach used for the VL4% and VL3% strategies.

The first test period tested the COMPX from its inception on February 5, 1971, through November 29, 2002. An initial investment of $100,000 was made on that beginning date, and no further funds were invested. After each trade, all the proceeds were reinvested in the next trade—either short or long. This strategy produced an annualized return of 18.77 percent and a profit of $15,209,502 compared with a $1,273,310 gain for buy-and-hold—thus producing an additional profit of $13,936,192 over buy-and-hold.

There were a total of 94 trades over the 32-year test period, averaging about 2.94 trades per year. However, only 54.3 percent of the trades were winners, but the ratio of average winners to losers was 2:1, and the profit factor was 2.37, both reasonable ratios. The long trades had a profit factor of 1.41 versus 2.78 for the short side. There were 59.6 percent profitable trades on the long side and 48.9 percent on the short side.

The only negative performance years were 1973 (–3.3 percent), 1984 (–0.1 percent), and 1994 (–11.8 percent). In 90 percent of the years tested, there was a profit. And there were gains in the bear market years of 1974 (34.2 percent), 1987 (11.3 percent), 2000 (9.8 percent), 2001 (39.5 percent), and 2002 (22.4 percent). This is what market timing is all about—protecting you from bear market devastation while making positive returns. This strategy was very successful in accomplishing this feat.

Figure 11-1 provides the equity curve for this strategy. As you can see, the slope of the curve is upward and to the right, with drops between trades 73 and 91 and then a resumption of the trend to new highs in November 2002. Figure 11-2 shows the buy and sell

**FIGURE 11-1**

Nasdaq composite 6% weekly, February 1971–November 2002.

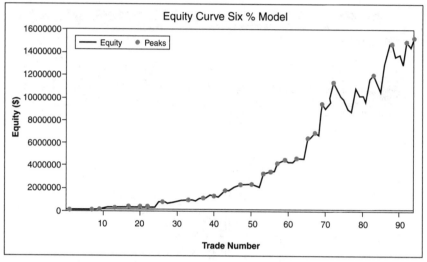

signals (up and down arrows) of this strategy during the 2000–2002 bear market. You can see how well the signals caught the market turns in that volatile period.

### Original Test 2: Weekly Nasdaq 100 Index 6 Percent Strategy (NDX6%): 1971–2002

Next, the Nasdaq 100 Index (NDX6%; contains only 100 nonfinancial stocks) strategy was tested over the 12-year period from November 11, 1990 (first date data were available), through November 29, 2002. This weekly strategy produced an annual return of 43.64 percent, with a net profit of $607,828, for a cumulative return of 6,078 percent. This compares with buy-and-hold's cumulative return of 191.4 percent. Although only 47.17 percent of the 53 trades were profitable, the ratio of winning trades to losing trades was 2.41, and the profit factor was 2.15, making this strategy a winner. All the years produced positive returns, and the equity curve parallels the NC6% curve.

**FIGURE 11-2**

Nasdaq composite 6% weekly TradeStation chart analysis, 2000–2002.

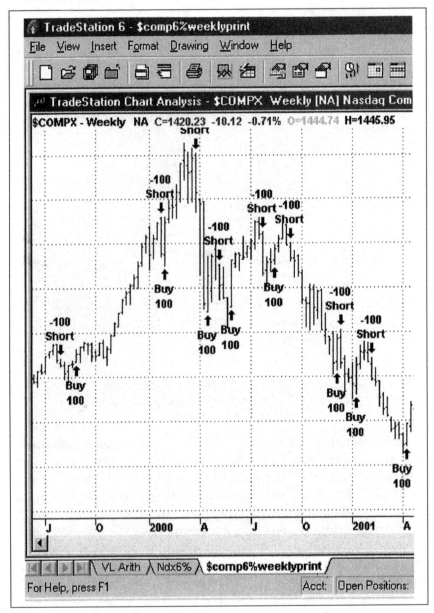

*Source:* Created with TradeStation. Printed with permission.

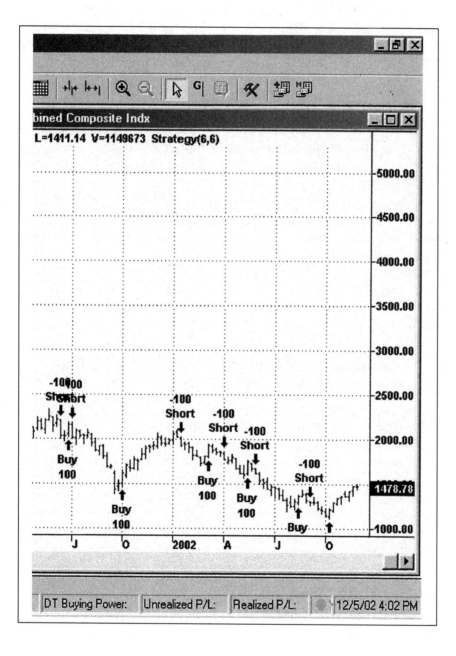

I was curious to see how the NDX6% did in comparison with the NC6% over the same time period and found that the NC6% earned $132,969 more in profit than the NDX6% strategy ($740,797 compared with $607,828). I also ran the actual VL4% *daily* strategy over the exact time period, and it came out with a profit of only $363,682, and the VL3% weekly had a profit of only $204,235.

### Original Test 3: Daily Nasdaq Composite Index 6 Percent Strategy (NC6%): 1971–2002

Based on the exceptional results of the NC6% weekly strategy, I decided to run the same strategy on a daily basis for comparative purposes. This change produced a meager total profit of only $15,040 over the entire 13-year period. Profits started slowly, reached a nice peak, and then deteriorated. Therefore, using daily data instead of weekly data produces very poor results. Using the optimization feature of TradeStation, the optimal daily parameters for both the buy and sell signals turned out to be 11 percent, and that strategy produced a total profit of only $341,411 over the 13 years, still not a good showing. In conclusion, the *NC6% daily strategy does not cut the mustard and should be discarded.*

### Original Test 4: Daily Nasdaq 100 Index 6 Percent Strategy (NDX6%): 1971–2002

I also tested the daily NDX6% data over the same period (1990–2002). The results were disastrous, with a *loss* of $88,806 for the entire period, or a –17.4 percent annual return. The optimal parameters turned out to be 12 percent for both the buy and sell sides, producing a gain of $75,436. This strategy is completely unstable because a 1 percentage point change drastically altered the results. Also, the equity curve is downward-sloping right from the start, a bad sign. In conclusion, this daily strategy also should be avoided.

## PART 2. LATEST TESTS: RESULTS THROUGH OCTOBER 2010

Four more tests covering through 2010 are summarized here.

## Latest Test 5: Weekly Nasdaq Composite Index 6 Percent Strategy (NC6%): 1971–2010

This latest test of the strategy added almost eight years of data from November 29, 2002, the last date in the prior test. These additional years resulted in an overall net profit of $24,772,616 from 1971 forward, for an annual rate of return of 20.7 percent. This compares very favorably with the previous annualized return of 18.77 percent and a profit of $15,209,502 for the prior test period. Overall, the return on capital was 247,726 percent compared with 2,201 percent for buy-and-hold, quite an astonishing difference.

There were a total of 126 trades over the 37 years and 9 months of the test period, averaging 3.15 trades per year. However, only 48.4 percent of the trades were winners, but the ratio of average winners to losers was 1.93:1, and the profit factor was 1.81, both reasonable ratios. The long trades had a profit factor of 2.03 versus only 1.52 for the short side. There were 54 percent profitable trades on the long side and 42.9 percent on the short side.

The only negative performance years since the original test were 2004 (−9.21 percent), 2007 (−5.23 percent), and 2010 (−5.9 percent). Overall, 84 percent of the years tested turned a profit. And there was a gain in the big bear market year of 2008 of 9.1 percent. This is what market timing is all about—protecting you from bear market devastation while making positive returns. Table 11-1 provides the performance statistics, and Table 11-2 shows the annual returns.

Looking at the equity curve in Figure 11-3, there was some volatility along the way and a few fair-sized drawdowns but, overall, an upward-sloping curve with top-notch performance.

## Latest Test 6: Weekly NDX 6 Percent Strategy, 1990–2010

This test substituted the Nasdaq 100 Index (NDX6%) for the Nasdaq Composite Index. This weekly strategy produced an annual return of 25.0 percent, with a net profit of $753,685, for a cumulative return of 7,536.9 percent. This compares with buy-and-hold's cumulative return of 449.5 percent. Although only 44 percent of the 89 trades were profitable, the ratio of winning trades to losing trades was 1.96, and the profit factor was 1.53, making this strate-

## TABLE 11-1

### TradeStation Performance Summary Nasdaq Composite Index, 6% Weekly: 1971–2010

| All Trades | | | |
|---|---|---|---|
| Total net profit | $24,772,616.24 | Profit factor | 1.81 |
| Gross profit | $55,252,751.53 | Gross Loss | ($30,480,135.29) |
| Rollover credit | $0.00 | | |
| Open position P/L | $2,304,711.68 | | |
| Select total net profit | $12,084,930.07 | Select profit factor | 1.43 |
| Select gross profit | $40,352,213.16 | Select gross loss | ($28,267,283.09) |
| Adjusted total net profit | $13,917,630.84 | Adjusted profit factor | 1.41 |
| Adjusted gross profit | $48,178,361.62 | Adjusted gross loss | ($34,260,730.78) |
| Total no. of trades | 126 | Percent profitable | 48.41% |
| Winning trades | 61 | Losing trades | 65 |
| Even trades | 0 | | |
| Average trade net profit | $196,608.07 | Ratio average win/ average loss | 1.93 |
| Average winning trade | $905,782.81 | Average losing trade | ($468,925.16) |
| Largest winning trade | $9,001,097.90 | Largest losing trade | ($2,212,852.20) |
| Largest winner as % of gross profit | 16.29 | Largest loser as % of gross profit | 7.26% |
| Net profit as % of largest loss | 1,119.49% | | |
| Selected net profit as % of largest loss | 546.12% | Adjusted net profit as % of largest loss | 628.95% |
| Maximum consecutive winning tables | 3 | Maximum consecutive losing trades | 5 |
| Average bars in winning trades | 25.61 | Average bars in losing trades | 7.62 |
| Average bars in total trades | 16.33 | | |
| Maximum shares/contracts held | 1,543,300,000 | Account size required | $5,409,114.54 |
| Total commission | $0.00 | Total slippage | $0.00 |
| Return on initial capital | 247,726.16% | Annual rate of return | 20.70% |
| Buy/hold return | 2202.55% | Return on account | 457.98% |
| Average monthly return | $136,690.87 | SD of monthly return | $1,436,260.11 |
| Return retracement ratio | 0.21 | RINA index | 26.77 |
| Sharpe ratio | 0.12 | K-ratio | 1.75 |
| Trading period | 37 years, 9 months | Percent of time in market | 98.68% |
| Time in the market | 37 years, 3 months | Longest flat period | n/a |
| Maximum equity run-up | n/a | | |
| Date of maximum equity run-up | n/a | Maximum equity run-up as % of initial capital | n/a |

Source: Created with TradeStation. Printed with permission.

**TABLE 11-2**

TradeStation Periodical Returns: Annual 1971–2010
Nasdaq Composite Index 6% Weekly Strategy

| Period | Net Profit | % Gain | Profit Factor | No. of Trades | % Profitable |
|---|---|---|---|---|---|
| Last 12 months | ($77,267.07) | (0.28%) | 0.97 | 5 | 20.00% |
| 1/1/2010 | ($1,697,929.93) | (5.90%) | 0.58 | 5 | 20.00% |
| 1/1/2009 | $8,041,607.62 | 38.77% | 3.84 | 5 | 40.00% |
| 1/1/2008 | $1,724,846.71 | 9.07% | 1.32 | 8 | 25.00% |
| 1/1/2007 | ($1,050,008.77) | (5.23%) | 0.43 | 4 | 25.00% |
| 1/1/2006 | $2,207,624.30 | 12.36% | 24.59 | 3 | 66.67% |
| 1/1/2005 | $38,151.05 | 0.21% | 1.03 | 3 | 33.33% |
| 1/1/2004 | ($1,808,286.01) | (9.21%) | 0.58 | 7 | 28.57% |
| 1/1/2003 | $2,454,330.59 | 14.29% | 1.74 | 4 | 25.00% |
| 1/1/2002 | $2,168,382.55 | 14.45% | 1.68 | 10 | 60.00% |
| 1/1/2001 | $4,276,145.24 | 39.84% | 2.49 | 8 | 50.00% |
| 1/1/2000 | $937,207.87 | 9.57% | 1.21 | 12 | 33.33% |
| 1/1/1999 | $3,823,979.31 | 64.04% | 8.93 | 5 | 60.00% |
| 1/1/1998 | $1,653,929.31 | 38.31% | 3.46 | 8 | 50.00% |
| 1/1/1997 | $922,754.01 | 27.18% | 31.14 | 4 | 75.00% |
| 1/1/1996 | $540,923.97 | 18.96% | 10.78 | 3 | 66.67% |
| 1/1/1995 | $763,818.91 | 36.55% | 12.57 | 2 | 50.00% |
| 1/1/1994 | ($291,097.27) | (12.23%) | 0.01 | 4 | 25.00% |
| 1/1/1993 | $96,605.17 | 4.23% | 1.61 | 3 | 33.33% |
| 1/1/1992 | $415,100.43 | 22.21% | 100.00 | 3 | 100.00% |
| 1/1/1991 | $477,141.82 | 34.27% | 6.07 | 3 | 66.67% |
| 1/1/1990 | $203,946.71 | 17.17% | 3.31 | 4 | 75.00% |
| 1/1/1989 | $147,890.86 | 14.22% | 5.26 | 3 | 33.33% |
| 1/1/1988 | $52,441.57 | 5.31% | 2.32 | 2 | 50.00% |
| 1/1/1987 | $109,422.26 | 12.46% | 1.65 | 6 | 50.00% |
| 1/1/1986 | $201,829.60 | 29.83% | 100.00 | 2 | 100.00% |
| 1/1/1985 | $40,278.20 | 6.33% | 1.48 | 4 | 50.00% |
| 1/1/1984 | ($717.24) | (0.11%) | 0.98 | 3 | 33.33% |
| 1/1/1983 | $198,356.29 | 45.22% | 100.00 | 2 | 100.00% |
| 1/1/1982 | $113,736.31 | 35.00% | 4.61 | 5 | 40.00% |
| 1/1/1981 | $43,425.81 | 15.43% | 13.94 | 4 | 75.00% |
| 1/1/1980 | $95,470.19 | 51.32% | 5.06 | 4 | 50.00% |
| 1/1/1979 | $36,785.78 | 24.65% | 4.35 | 4 | 50.00% |
| 1/1/1978 | $42,584.26 | 39.93% | 100.00 | 2 | 100.00% |
| 1/1/1977 | $13,493.94 | 14.49% | 100.00 | 1 | 100.00% |
| 1/1/1976 | $21,677.78 | 30.33% | 3.84 | 2 | 50.00% |
| 1/1/1975 | $31,684.11 | 79.62% | 4.29 | 3 | 66.67% |
| 1/1/1974 | $33,052.90 | 490.27% | 5.62 | 5 | 60.00% |
| 1/1/1973 | ($3,258.29) | (32.58%) | 0.78 | 4 | 25.00% |

Source: Created with TradeStation. Printed with permission.

**FIGURE 11-3**

Equity curve—Nasdaq Composite Index, weekly (02/19/71–10/22/10).

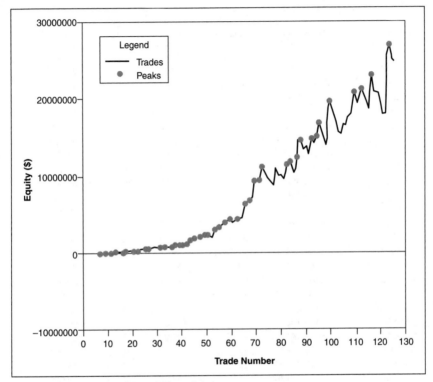

*Source:* Created with TradeStation. Printed with permission.

gy a winner. All the years but four produced positive returns, and the equity curve parallels the NC6% curve.

I also used TradeStation to run an optimization of the parameters and found that the 6 percent buy and sell signals actually provided one of the most profitable combinations. Only two strategies did better than the 6 percent strategy. The 5 percent off the low and 6 percent off the high strategy earned a profit of $770,317, and the 5 percent off the low and 8 percent off the high strategy earned a profit of $721,387.

I was curious to see how the NDX6% did in comparison with the Nasdaq Composite Index (NC6%) over the same time period and found that the NDX6% earned about $200,353 more in profit than the NC6% strategy ($954,038 compared with $753,685), with a

26.34 annual rate of return. I also ran the actual VL4% daily strategy over the exact 13-year time period, and it came out with a profit of only $363,682. The VL3% weekly, though, had the largest net profit of all at $1,325,253.

## Latest Test 7: Daily Nasdaq Composite Index 6 Percent Strategy (NC6%): 1990–2010

Based on the exceptional results of the NC6% weekly strategy, I decided to run the same strategy on a daily basis for comparative purposes. This change produced a *loss* of $25,547 over the period. Profits started slowly, reached a nice peak, and then deteriorated. Therefore, using daily data instead of weekly data produces very poor results. In conclusion, the *NC6% daily strategy does not cut the mustard and should be discarded.*

## Latest Test 8: Daily Nasdaq 100 Index 6 Percent Strategy (NDX6%): 1990–2010

I also tested the daily NDX6% data over the same time period. The results were disastrous, with a *loss* of $95,372 for the entire period, or a –12.1 percent annual return. The optimal parameters turned out to be 12 percent for both the buy and sell sides, producing a gain of $75,436. This daily strategy is completely unstable because a 1 percentage point change in either direction drastically altered the results. Also, the equity curve is downward-sloping right from the start, a bad sign. In conclusion, *this daily strategy also should be avoided.*

# COMPARISON OF THE NASDAQ WEEKLY WITH THE VL3% WEEKLY: 1992–2010

Let's compare the Nasdaq 6% weekly performance with the best performing Value Line strategy—VL3% weekly (Table 11-3).

Clearly, the VL3% weekly strategy is superior to both Nasdaq weekly strategies in eight of the nine metrics. This strategy had 111 trades during the test period compared with 85 and 73 for the Nasdaq strategies. This is really not a large difference in the number of trades over a 17-year time frame. Its Sharpe ratio also was the highest of all, which is a positive indication of its lower risk.

**TABLE 11-3**

Value Line 3% Weekly versus the NC6% and NDX6% Weekly: 1992–2010

| Metric | VL3% Weekly | Nasdaq Composite 6% Weekly | NDX 6% Weekly |
|---|---|---|---|
| Total net profits | $885,293 | $653,814 | $553,442 |
| Profit factor | 2.06 | 1.73 | 1.52 |
| Total no. of trades | 111 | 73 | 85 |
| % profitable trades | 42.34% | 41.10% | 43.53% |
| Ratio average win/average loss | 2.81 | 2.48 | 1.97 |
| Return of initial capital | 8,852.9% | 6,538.1% | 5,534.4% |
| Annual rate of return | 29.50% | 27.47% | 26.49% |
| Buy/hold return | 382.4% | 398.83% | 270.84 |
| Sharpe ratio | 0.29 | 0.25 | 0.01 |

## CONCLUSIONS

Insofar as the Nasdaq indexes are concerned, the weekly 6 percent signals are clearly superior to the daily 6 percent signals. The daily signals are much more frequent because of the volatility of their respective indexes. Moreover, both weekly strategies—NC6% and NDX6%—significantly beat the VL4% strategy's performance but were inferior to the VL3% weekly performance.

I also backtested the Standard & Poor's (S&P) 500 Index with various buy and sell filters, but the results were poor for both the weekly and daily signals because that index does not have the volatility and large percentage moves as does the Nasdaq. Based on the backtest results shown in this chapter, I recommend that you use either the NC6% (Nasdaq Composite Index) or the VL3% strategy for market timing because of their exceptional performance compared with buy-and-hold.

Regarding the use of these strategies for market timing, the same approach can be used as mentioned in the other strategy chapters using appropriate exchange-traded funds (ETFs) and proper stop-loss controls.

## CHAPTER 12

# Market Timing Resources: Newsletters, Web Sites, and Advisors

*Ignorance is not knowing something; stupidity is not admitting your ignorance.*

—Daniel Turov (*Turov on Timing*)

*If we don't change the direction we're going, we're going to end up where we're headed.*

—Chinese Proverb

**T**here is a plethora of market timing newsletters ready to take investors' money. The problem is that the vast majority are worthless and dangerous to your wealth. One way to engage in market timing without doing the work yourself is to subscribe to a market timing newsletter or timing service and scrupulously follow its buy and sell signals.

The first part of this chapter will cover market timing newsletters, and the second part will focus on other related resources. Today, there are hundreds of market timing newsletters or services published in hardcopy or on the Web. New ones appear all the time, and old ones with miserable track records disappear into the night. The problem is determining which, if any, meet your specific needs with a long-term track record.

## MARKET TIMING NEWSLETTERS AND SERVICES

In general, to locate market timing newsletters or services, if you did a search on www.google.com or www.bing.com, you would come up with hundreds of thousands of entries. You will find not only advertisements for a number of the newsletters but also the good, the bad, and the ugly. You then can go to specific sites to see what they offer and get a sample issue or perhaps a 30-day free trial. Each newsletter's or service's performance record should be available for viewing against a comparable benchmark. Be aware that some unscrupulous individuals provide inaccurate track records, and some services have only backtested and optimized a trading system that has minimal real-time performance statistics. And the advertising claims of some of the purveyors are outrageous. *Caveat emptor!*

Another option is to use the services of the Select Information Exchange, which has a Web site (www.stockfocus.com) that provides trial subscriptions to over 200 newsletters and advisory services, of which 30 focus on market timing. You then can decide if you are interested in a trial of four newsletters for five months for $69. The exchange also can be reached at (800) 743-9346.

## INDEPENDENT MARKET TIMING NEWSLETTER TRACKING SERVICES

After scrutinizing Google's offerings and reviewing those of the Select Information Exchange, you still may find yourself unsure of what to do because neither provides an analysis of the performance of their product offerings. The marketing hype and testimonials of many newsletters are often grossly misleading. Fortunately, three independent tracking services are available that verify the performance of market-timers. They publish their results at least monthly for subscribers, and one service provides daily access. Having these services is just like having *Consumer Reports* for timing newsletters—getting the facts rather than the hype. You need the truth, not the baloney sandwich.

### *Timer Digest*

The *Timer Digest* newsletter, edited by Jim Schmidt since 1987, tracks the performance of over 100 market timing models published in newsletters. Schmidt follows the timing signals in each newsletter, as would a typical subscriber, including those provided by e-mail or a telephone hotmail service. All newsletter signal changes are benchmarked against the Standard & Poor's (S&P) 500 Index. All market timing newsletters are ranked against each other, and the timers are listed in each issue of *Timer Digest*. The newsletter focuses only on the timing of their signals, not on their investment recommendations.

*Timer Digest* is published every three weeks in newsletter format (hardcopy or a .pdf file that can be downloaded from the Web site, www.timerdigest.com). This information is supplemented with a biweekly hotline service (accessed via the Web site or telephone) that is updated on Wednesday and Saturday nights. The hotline reports any signal changes from the timers as well as their latest opinion. The newsletter ranks the top stock, bond, and gold timers based on their latest 52-week performance.

The top timers are those with the best stock market performance over the past 52 weeks compared with the S&P 500 benchmark. The latest market call (bullish or bearish), performance data, and signal date from each of these timers is printed in the newsletter, along with the timer's latest market commentary (one to two lines). Over time, since the evaluation encompasses a rolling 52-week period, there are different top timers. Thus only those with the best performance out of the 100-odd timers are highlighted. In addition, the "top 5" bond and gold timers are shown, with their performance, buy and sell signals, and brief market comment.

The "Top 10 Consensus" tells the current recommended position of the majority of these stock timers—that is, either a bullish or bearish call on the market. In addition to providing the top timers for the past 52 weeks, *Timer Digest* also lists the stock timers for the most recent six and three months, along with their timing performance compared with the S&P 500 benchmark and the date of their most recent signal. Additionally, the "top 5" bond and gold timers are ranked, and a consensus reading (bullish or bearish) is also provided with the same information just mentioned.

How have the 100 timers tracked by *Timer Digest* performed recently? Publisher Jim Schmidt indicates that about 25 percent of the timers beat or matched the S&P 500 Index in 2007, which was up 3.53 percent, and approximately 60 percent beat that benchmark in 2008 (S&P –38.5 percent). Only 22 percent beat it in 2009

(S&P +23.5 percent), and through September 30, 2010, 30 percent beat or matched the index (S&P +2.34 percent). The relative performance of all the timers monitored versus the benchmark was strong during the volatile bear market period. This doesn't necessarily mean that the timers actually had positive returns but that they lost less than the S&P 500.

For the year ending in 2008, the "Top 10 Consensus" as a group had a performance index of 122.15 compared with the S&P performance index of 61.51. The performance index is set at 100.0 at the beginning of each year for each timer and for the index. And timing signals assume either long or short positions in the S&P 500. Thus, for the one-year period ending in 2008, the "top 10" timers performed 60 percentage points better than the benchmark, certainly an outstanding performance and one of the record variances for a one-year period since *Timer Digest*'s inception.

Thus far in 2010, the "Top 10 Consensus" as a group had a performance index of 107.31 (base reading is 100) compared with the S&P performance index of 102.34. Thus, for the current nine-month period, the top timers performed almost 5 percentage points better than the benchmark.

Table 12-1 shows the performance of the top timers relative to the S&P 500 benchmark at year end 2009. Overall, the "Top 10 Consensus," designated as "T.D. Consensus" in the table, beat the S&P 500 Index in all but the one-year time period. In strongly positive years, timing does not usually beat buy-and-hold. However, over longer, range-bound periods containing fewer predictable bull and bear cycles (as in the recent decade), timers tend to excel. Also provided is the same table but for the period ending at year end 2002 for comparison purposes (Table 12-2).

In Table 12-1, the more recent period, the "T.D. Consensus" performance was more than double the benchmark for 10 years and between 60 and 85 percentage points higher for the three-, five-, and eight-year time frames.

Timers who can maintain such consistent standings, year after year, are exceptional. The longer they remain as top performers on the three-year lists and longer, the more credibility their forecasting recommendations have. As I pointed out earlier, the timers may not beat buy-and-hold in all time frames, but they are worth their weight in gold during bear markets.

**TABLE 12-1**

Top 10 Timers' Performance versus S&P 500 Index, Years Ending December 31, 2009

|  | 1-Year Performance Index | 3-Year Performance Index | 5-Year Performance Index | 8-Year Performance Index | 10-Year Performance Index |
|---|---|---|---|---|---|
| T.D. Consensus | 116.43 | 145.50 | 151.63 | 183.12 | 192.57 |
| S&P 500 | 123.45 | 78.62 | 92.01 | 97.13 | 75.90 |
| Top Timer | 169.37 | 191.15 | 215.63 | 286.04 | 352.38 |
| Tenth Top Timer | 128.08 | 136.45 | 143.56 | 131.96 | 131.90 |

Source: "Special Annual Report," *Timer Digest*, January 25, 2010. Information printed with permission of *Timer Digest*.

**TABLE 12-2**

Top 10 Timers' Performance versus S&P 500 Index, Years Ending December 31, 2002*

|  | 1-Year Performance Index | 3-Year Performance Index | 5-Year Performance Index | 8-Year Performance Index | 10-Year Performance Index |
|---|---|---|---|---|---|
| T.D. Consensus | 126.23 | 132.74 | 155.59 | 317.47 | 306.65 |
| S&P 500 | 76.63 | 59.88 | 90.66 | 191.57 | 201.93 |
| Top Timer | 178.64 | 223.91 | 246.20 | 285.19 | 267.48 |
| Tenth Top Timer | 126.84 | 130.89 | 126.76 | 128.14 | 102.10 |

*Only four timers beat S&P 500 in eight-year performance, and only three did so over 10 years.

Source: "Special Annual Report," *Timer Digest*, January 27, 2003. Information printed with permission of *Timer Digest*.

# One-, Three-, Five-, Eight-, and 10-Year Lists

Christopher Cadbury, *Cadbury Timing Service*
Dale Woodson, *Woodson Wave Report*
Joseph Granville, *The Granville Market Letter*

## Three-, Five-, Eight-, and 10-Year Lists

Dan Sullivan, *The Chartist*

Ike Iossif, *Aegean Capital*

Steve Hochberg and Pete Kendall, *Elliott Wave Financial Forecast*

## Five-, Eight-, and 10-Year Lists

Mark Leibovit, VRTrader.com

## Three-, Five-, and 10-Year Lists

William Corney, *No-Load Portfolios*

## One-, Three-, and Five-Year Lists

George Slezak, Stockindextiming.com

## Five- and Eight-Year Lists

William Ferree, *Ferree Market Timer*

## Three- and Eight-Year Lists

Holly Hooper, *Mutual Fund Strategist*

## One- and Five-Year Lists

Carl Swenlin, *Decision Point Alert*

How has the *Timer Digest* "Top 10 Consensus" performed? According to the *Hulbert Financial Digest*, an independent newsletter rating service, for the 10 years ending June 30, 2010, *Timer Digest*'s average annual return for the "Top 10 Consensus" was 8.1 percent compared with –0.8 percent for buy-and-hold (Hulbert uses the Wilshire 5000 as the benchmark, not the S&P 500). Schmidt's Fidelity Select program (buying the strongest single Select fund based on a proprietary evaluation) was up an average of 3.6 percent for this same period (but had more risk). On an overall basis for the 15-year period ending May 31, 2010, the average investment portfolio recommended by *Timer Digest* has risen 191.1 percent compared with 178.3 percent for the Wilshire 5000.

*Timer Digest* is a comprehensive newsletter and timing service that offers investors unbiased information at a reasonable price ($225 annual subscription cost). For more information, contact the newsletter at (203) 629-3503 or on its Web site at www.timerdigest.com.

### *Hulbert Financial Digest*

Another publication that tracks the performance of investment and timing newsletters on an apples-to-apples basis is the *Hulbert Financial Digest (HFD)*. Mark Hulbert founded this monthly newsletter in 1980. The *HFD* became part of MarketWatch in April 2002. Its goal was to provide investors with an unbiased investment newsletter rating service. The focus of *HFD* is not strictly on market timing newsletters. Instead, it encompasses a broader spectrum of investment advisor newsletters. However, market timing newsletters make up a subset of the universe covered by Hulbert. Currently, about 180 newsletters (relating to mutual funds, stocks, sectors, timing, and so on) and 500 portfolios are tracked against the Wilshire 5000 Index (a broad-based index of the entire market).

Every monthly issue of the newsletter ranks the top seven performing newsletters for total return and risk-adjusted return over the last 5-, 10-, and 15-year periods. There is also information on the most- and least-recommended mutual funds and stocks based on mentions among all letters tracked by the *HFD*. Another section of the newsletter provides the average market exposure to stocks, gold, and mutual funds for the market-timers tracked. In addition, profiles of newsletters show their performance since 1980 to the present time compared with the Wilshire 5000 benchmark. The profiles describe the newsletter, its objectives, strategies, and performance. Each issue also contains a lead article covering a subject of current interest and two newsletter profiles. Twice a year, the newsletter provides a 16-page report on the track record of each newsletter's portfolio over the last 5-, 10-, and 15-year period, if available. Also, the performance over the past year is shown in the January edition of the next year.

In the January 2010 issue of *HFD*, there is an analysis of the top 15 newsletters in 2009 and their performance over prior periods compared with the Wilshire 5000 Total Return Index. This analysis indicated that the top 15 newsletters had an average annualized return in 2009 of 99.1 percent compared with the benchmark's 28.3 percent return. Six newsletters returned more than 100 percent, and the worst performer was up 60.9 percent. Eleven of these newsletters outperformed the benchmark of a five-year period. Over 10 years (only 10 of these newsletters had data), they averaged an annualized return of 5 percent compared with –0.3 percent for the benchmark, and 9 of the 10 newsletters beat the benchmark. Over a 15-year period (9 of these funds had data), they averaged equal performance to the benchmark, although three funds had a better performance. Among the best-performing newsletters in these four periods were the *Turnaround Letter*, *Global Investing*, *The Investment Reporter*, *The Ruff Times*, and *The Dines Letter*.

For more information on the *HFD* ($69 annual subscription cost via mail and $49 via e-mail), contact *HFD* at (866) 428-6568 or www.marketwatch.com.

## *TimerTrac.com*

TimerTrac.com tracks and ranks the performance of approximately 700 market timing strategies offered by hundreds of market-timers from the United States and abroad. TimerTrac independently verifies the performance of market timing services by receiving their real-time signals and measuring them against other timers and against specific index benchmarks and updates its database daily. In the case of trading through Rydex or ProFunds, the signals are verified through group trading data. Some of the timing strategies are based on using the Rydex or ProFunds, index funds, exchange-traded funds (ETFs), closed-end funds, sector funds, and mutual funds. Asset classes tracked include growth stocks, small- and mid-cap stocks, high-yield bonds, precious metals, Treasury bonds, and leveraged and unleveraged funds.

TimerTrac.com tracks long, intermediate, and short term, as well as fast timing, as defined in Table 12-3, but does not track trading.

### *Sample Report of Top Performers*
The partial report presented in Table 12-4 contains the top performers over the five-year period from August 31, 2005, through Tuesday, August 31, 2010, compared to the S&P 500 Index (–13.20% over this

## TABLE 12-3

### TimerTrac.com Typical Timing Periods*

| | |
|---|---|
| Long term | Investors who hold securities longer than one year or more. (This is the IRS definition.) |
| Intermediate term | Investors trading anywhere from about 3 to 12 times per year. |
| Short term | Investors trading anywhere from about 12 to 50 times per year. |
| Fast timing | Investors trading a few times a week or less. |
| Trading | Investors trading multiple times per day. |

*These definitions were created by TimerTrac.com.

## TABLE 12-4

### Top Performers: Five-Year Period Ending August 31, 2010

| Rank | Strategy Name | % Gain/ Loss | Difference to % S&P 500* | Trades in Time Frame |
|---|---|---|---|---|
| 1 | Market Systems II-DD | 120.05% | 133.25% | 629 |
| 2 | Index Trades.net Short Term | 64.67% | 77.87% | 76 |
| 3 | KT QQQ-a | 49.16% | 62.36% | 506 |
| 4 | KT QQQ-crude | 48.19% | 61.39% | 372 |
| 5 | Trend-Chart.com S&P 500 Aggr. Market Timing | 41.71% | 54.91% | 147 |
| 6 | Premium Trust NDX Trader | 37.78% | 50.97% | 137 |
| 7 | Premium Trust XPX Trader | 28.42% | 41.62% | 135 |
| 8 | Premium Trust RUT Trader | 21.15% | 34.35% | 97 |
| 9 | PrimeMarketTrader Alpha AT-L | 17.62% | 30.81% | 218 |
| 10 | Q5TrackerST | 13.27% | 26.46% | 84 |
| 11 | TimingStock | 12.18% | 25.38% | 35 |
| 12 | PrimeMarketTrader ATX | 10.54% | 23.74% | 199 |
| 13 | PrimeMarketTrader Alpha QQQQ | 8.37% | 21.57% | 224 |
| 14 | FitzpatrickForecast.com Nasdaq 100 | 6.46% | 19.65% | 55 |
| 15 | PrimeMarketTrader Alpha Index | 6.06% | 19.26% | 291 |
| 16 | Performance Signal Short Term | 3.17% | 16.37% | 84 |
| 17 | Indextrades.net Equity | 2.78% | 15.98% | 74 |
| 18 | Trend-Chart.com S&P 500 Standard Market Timing | −1.95% | 11.24% | 159 |
| 19 | Timing Cube | −2.12% | 11.07% | 29 |

*Difference between strategy and the S&P 500 Index.
Source: TimerTrac.com.

same time period). You can see that all 19 beat the benchmark, although the last two shown had a negative performance. However, on a relative performance basis, they both beat the benchmark by 11 percentage points. Subscribers can determine any time frame for measuring performance, as well as selecting the benchmark.

Looking at the trades during the five-year period, there is a wide variance among the top performers. Interestingly, Market Systems II had the best performance by a wide margin, with a gain if 120.05 percent, but it also had the largest number of trades at 629. The next-best performer, IndexTrades.net short term, had only 76 trades and a 64.67 percent gain. This was compared with a –13.2 percent performance of the S&P 500 Index.

Shown in Figure 12-1 is a TimerTrac.com chart of the market timing performance of three strategies AccuFundTrader.com measured against the S&P 500 Index. Two of the strategies (ultra-

**FIGURE 12-1**

Market timing performance of three strategies, measured against the S&P 500 Index.

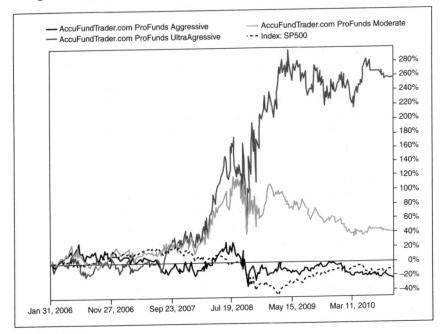

*Source:* TimerTrac.com.

**TABLE 12-5**

TimerTrac.com Strategy Summary

| | S&P | Aggressive | Moderate | Ultra-Aggressive |
|---|---|---|---|---|
| | | **Annual Returns** | | |
| Part year 2006 | 10.80 | 9.74 | 17.82 | −6.08 |
| Year 2007 | 3.53 | −8.75 | 14.77 | 53.11 |
| Year 2008 | −38.49 | −18.91 | 10.01 | 105.91 |
| Year 2009 | 23.45 | 10.68 | 21.19 | 5.10 |
| YTD 2010 | 4.09 | −21.85 | −20.71 | −34.42 |
| | | **Total Returns** | | |
| Total return | −9.32 | −29.77 | 42.95 | 104.09 |
| Annual return | −2.07 | −7.27 | 7.94 | 16.47 |

aggressive and moderate), the two top lines on the chart, respectively, easily beat the benchmark, whereas the aggressive strategy underperformed as of October 5, 2010.

A TimerTrac.com summary of the returns of the three strategies (aggressive, moderate, and ultra-aggressive) is provided in Table 12-5.

A typical description of AccuFundTrader.com's ultra-aggressive strategy is provided in Table 12-6.

Subscribers to TimerTrac.com can

- Research performance and information on 682 timing signals
- Find real-time market timing signals
- Compare one timing signal with others
- Contact market-timers directly
- Rank timing signals over different time periods—six months, one year, or any custom time period
- Apply a timing signal to many indexes to determine which one performs the best
- Apply a timing signal to the Rydex or ProFunds family of funds to determine which funds and signals work best

## TABLE 12-6

## AccuFundTrader.com ProFunds Ultra-Aggressive Strategy

| | |
|---|---|
| Strategy name | AccuFundTrader.com ProFunds Ultra-Aggressive |
| TimerTrac.com tracking start date | Thursday, July 31, 2008 |
| Asset class | Sector |
| Trades/year | 132 |
| Method | This is a very aggressive absolute-return strategy designed to make profits regardless of market conditions or direction. The model usually holds just two leveraged funds, making it very volatile but historically very profitable. It selects from a universe of approximately 30 to 35 ProFunds mutual funds composed of 2x beta long and short major market index funds and 1.5x beta sector funds. The model generally remains 100 percent invested and does not use a stop-loss strategy. |
| Comments | The trade signals for this model are available via subscription to www.AccuFundTrader.com. A managed account program for several of our models is available through our business partner, Scott Daly, Comprehensive Capital Management, LLC, 121 Hollywood Ave., Douglas Manor, NY 11363; phone: (718) 428-2261; fax: (718) 428-8472; e-mail: TimeItNow@AOL.com. |
| Developer | AccuFundTrader.com (Gary Bozlinski) |
| Address | P.O. Box 2320 |
| | Fraser, CO 80442, USA |
| Phone | (970) 531-4523 |
| E-mail | info@AccuFundTrader.com |
| Web site | www.AccuFundTrader.com |
| Years experience | 11 |
| Philosophy | I believe that using our "absolute return" strategies, we can make money regardless of market conditions or direction. There's always a bull market somewhere. |
| Background | Gary Bozlinski was formerly a senior-level computer programmer for United Airlines. He has been developing trading strategies since 1998. |
| Tracking time | AccuFundTrader.com ProFunds Ultra-Aggressive has been tracked since July 31, 2008, 2:16:00 p.m., by TimerTrac.com, in which time we've received 467 trade signals for this strategy. |

For more information, contact

TimerTrac.com
59 Canterbury Lane
Logan, UT 84321
Phone (888) 697-3577 or (435) 245-1711
E-mail: support2010@timertrac.com
www.timertrac.com

Subscription cost: Quarterly: $89.95; semiannually: $129.95; and annually $179.95

## THREE MARKET TIMING NEWSLETTERS

Three newsletters that offer different perspectives on market timing are included in this section. Other newsletters that you've located by using the independent rating services mentioned previously also may provide you with the type of information that you are looking for.

### *Formula Research* Newsletter

For investors interested in learning about the latest in *timing models*, one newsletter—*Formula Research*—provides unique, time-tested, profitable models. Since October 1991, Nelson Freeburg has been its editor and publisher and is an active trader and investor. Freeburg is a master systems builder and developer of systematic timing models and trading systems for stocks, bonds, commodities, and ETFs. He provides research to over 1,000 clients—institutional and individual—in over 25 countries. As you will recall, Freeburg's extensive model testing was frequently referenced in prior chapters. Freeburg is a popular speaker in the United States and abroad.

Formula Research is neither a stock tip sheet nor a market timing service. It offers neither investment advice nor opinions on where the markets are going. Freeburg's sole objective is finding, developing, and rigorously testing market timing models and strategies using standard statistical testing routines. His extensive research, published over many years, has produced a large number of timing models that produce consistent performance while outperforming the S&P 500 Index. All timing models are strictly mechanical and fully disclosed.

Each issue of the newsletter provides a proprietary trading system with high performance and limited risk. Freeburg's writing is crisp and to the point. If he is testing a system developed by someone else, he provides complete attribution and credits the individual for his work and then does his own research using different sampling periods and other variations to improve on the originator's work. For more information on the newsletter, contact:

Formula Research
4646 Poplar Avenue, Suite 401
Memphis, TN 38117
(800) 720-1080
(901) 756-8607
E-mail: FormulaResearch@comcast.net
Subscription: $295 for 12 issues

Past issues are available for $30 for subscribers and $45 for nonsubscribers.

## Sy Harding's Street Smart Report

Sy Harding, mentioned previously for his contribution to seasonal investing, also provides investment and market timing advice via his online eight-page newsletter *Sy Harding's Street Smart Report*, published every three weeks since 1988. The information provided covers:

- *Markets:* U.S. and global stock markets, gold, bonds, and the dollar.
- *Two strategies:* The seasonal market timing strategy described in this book and a nonseasonal market timing strategy based on technical and fundamental analysis.
- *A specific active portfolio:* This is provided for each strategy, with periodic recommended holdings and ongoing buy, sell, and hold signals on each. Holdings may include ETFs, mutual funds, and stocks, including short sales and "inverse" ETFs on sell signals.

*Sy Harding's Street Smart Report* can be obtained online and is also available in the following formats:

- The hardcopy newsletter is published and mailed every three weeks and is available for .pdf download or printing. Included are telephone hotline updates and online Internet access.

- The online Internet newsletter alone includes updates, additional commentaries, and other educational materials from the Street Smart School and the Street Smart Library.

- Both subscriptions include a copy of Sy Harding's book, *Beat the Market the Easy Way*. Annual subscriptions cost $275. Monthly subscriptions cost $25.95.

For further information on the newsletter, contact:

Asset Management Research Corp.
505 East New York Avenue, Suite 9
DeLand, FL 32724
Phone: (386) 943-4081
www.StreetSmartReport.com

### *Mutual Fund Prospector*

Eric Dany has published the *Mutual Fund Prospector (MFP)* newsletter since December 1998. His goal is to provide a simple mutual-fund timing strategy that provides solid long-term returns. He has accomplished this goal because the MFP model portfolio from January 1999 through September 2010 has risen 110.6 percent versus the benchmark return (Vanguard Total Stock Market Index Fund) of only 26.6 percent. His MFP aggressive portfolio had an even better return of 188.7 percent. His research indicated that "equity-style timing" is a strategy that produces excellent returns. Rather than focusing on the more traditional market timing approaches, Dany concentrates on selecting actively managed mutual funds that are performing well not only in the large-cap, midcap, and small-cap areas and international areas but, more important, where "value" or "growth" is the dominant theme. Then he selects the appropriate funds to take advantage of the situation.

Each month, Dany publishes his 12-page newsletter that is sent to subscribers over the Internet. It contains his current recommended portfolios, his view on the market, latest news about the mutual funds that he follows, and a detailed six-page listing of the top-performing funds in all the asset classes mentioned earlier. He then assigns a score to each one that he refers to as "nuggets." The higher the nugget rating, the better is the potential for a positive return.

The *Mutual Fund Prospector*'s model portfolio active core consists of 11 funds, with one core broadly based market fund accounting for about 31 percent (as of September 30, 2010) of the weighting, with 69 percent invested in actively managed funds (seven equity-based funds and three bond funds). The percentages in the active funds can vary based on Dany's analysis of market conditions and which equity styles are outperforming the market. Dany also offers an aggressive portfolio for investors with a higher risk tolerance. The *Hulbert Financial Digest* tracks the performance of these portfolios.

For more information about this newsletter, contact the firm at: customerservice@prospectornewsletters.com or at (866) 541-5299. The newsletter costs $129 a year or two years at $199 in North America.

## SPECIALIZED ONLINE WEB SITES

Discussed below are four Web-based services that provide a unique stock market perspective.

### www.haysadvisory.com

The Hays Advisory Group offers www.haysadvisory.com, a Web site that provides twice-weekly financial commentary and investing strategy for individual investors and professionals. Each commentary explains and interprets the current economic and financial news, the short- and long-term stock market outlook, and the impact of news affecting the stock market.

In addition to the commentary, the Web site contains numerous updated charts so that subscribers can observe the current situation. Some of the indicators tracked in chart form are sentiment indicators, market breadth and overbought/oversold indicators, market trends in major averages, market valuation, and monetary indicators. The Web site also provides subscribers with sector and industry analysis with weekly updates and a list of recommended stocks in top-performing industries.

A yearly premier subscription costs $250 and includes the following:

- Market commentaries posted to the Web site three times a week.
- Access to proprietary market research and studies, including
  - Charts of over 60 market indicators
  - Asset-allocation recommendations
  - Studies of industries and sectors
- Global valuation reports

For additional information, contact the firm at:

Hays Advisory Group
301 Seven Springs Way, Suite 150
Brentwood, TN 37027
(615) 467-6070
www.haysadvisory.com
www.fundadvice.com

## www.Merriman.com

Merriman, Inc., offers a complementary online research center that contains in-depth and comprehensive information on investing. Over 100 articles are on the site (in the archives, and articles are updated as needed with the latest annual statistics) on all aspects of investing, including market timing, buy-and-hold, and investment psychology. The following information is available at this information-packed site:

- Over 90 Paul Merriman videos from Sound Investing TV
- Sample ETF and Vanguard portfolios for conservative, moderate, and aggressive investors
- Audio archives of the weekly *Sound Investing* radio show podcast
- 401(k) Help Center
- Ask Merriman questions and answers
- Latest articles on investing
- Library of archived articles—market timing

By signing up on the site, investors will be sent an e-mail message whenever new articles are published and whenever a new timing signal occurs. Additionally, Merriman writes an investing column, which can be found at www.cbs.marketwatch.com.

For more information, contact the firm at:

Merriman, Inc.
800 Fifth Avenue, Suite 2900
Seattle, WA 98104-3108
Phone: (800) 423-4893
E-mail: info@merriman.com
Web site: www.Merriman.com

## www.decisionpoint.com

The www.decisionpoint.com site contains a myriad of technical stock market information that can be used for market timing. Carl Swenlin is the site's president and founder, and he originally developed it for his own stock market research. He has been researching and investing in the stock market since 1981. This is one of the most comprehensive sites that I've come across as far as the depth of technical information and charting are concerned. There are over 800 pages of current and historical charts of market indexes and indicators.

Among the components of this site are the following:

- Sector and market indexes
- Periodic updates from top advisors
- Over 25 technical market indicators (e.g., TRIN, new highs/new lows, stocks above 200-dma, put/call ratios, VIX, McClellan oscillator, and overbought/oversold)
- Sentiment indicators (e.g., bullish percentage indexes, AAII Investor Sentiment, Investor's Intelligence Sentiment)
- Long-range historical charting, with some charts going back to 1926
- Intraday charting
- Chart books of Rydex Funds, ProFunds, Fidelity Select Portfolios, ETFs, and more
- Charts of the relative strengths of various indexes

- Basic course on technical analysis in the Learning Center
- Glossary of terms

This site also has a comprehensive charting capability. Except for a few free items on the site, this is a subscription-based service. The service costs $19.95 a month and covers all the information just mentioned and more. For more information about the site, contact Decision Point at the Web address above or send an e-mail to DPService@decisionpoint.com. To reach the firm by phone, call (714) 692-1630.

## David Korn's Advisory Service

The last item in this section is an unusual Web-based service that is neither a market timing newsletter nor a market timing advisory service. However, it offers interesting market insights, and it tracks the recommendations and commentary of *Bob Brinker's Moneytalk* weekly radio show that can be heard on radio stations across the country on weekends. Brinker is a long-time market-timer and publisher of *Bob Brinker's Marketimer*, which has been around for over 23 years.

David Korn, an attorney by profession and an avid stock market buff, decided in 1998 to offer a fee-based commentary service on the stock market and, in particular, on *Bob Brinker's Moneytalk*. For 15 years, Korn has been reading Brinker's newsletter and listening to his radio show. Korn's Internet-based service came about because of demand from investors who wanted his interpretation of Brinker's comments. Korn's service, known as David Korn's Stock Market Commentary, contains interpretations of *Bob Brinker's Moneytalk*, financial education, helpful links, guest editorials, a special alert e-mail service, Korn's own market insights, and a model portfolio. He also follows other market-timers and keeps his subscribers apprised of the changing financial and economic environment.

In the year 2000, Korn's subscribers wanted a Web site where they could meet to discuss the stock market, Bob Brinker, and whatever other financial topics were of interest. Thus Korn's discussion threads sprung up on his Web site, www.begininvesting .com. Subscribers post questions on all aspects of investing, including the workings of the stock market, technical analysis, market timing, bonds, real estate, and anything else they can think of. Korn responds to all subscribers' questions with detailed answers. Korn is also the coeditor of the *Retirement Advisor*, whose Web site is www.theretirementadvisor.net.

For more information on Korn's services, contact him at:

David Korn, LLC
P.O. Box 58076
New Orleans, LA 70158-8076
E-mail: david555@earthlink.com
Web site: www.begininvesting.com

# Epilogue

*You can observe a lot just by watchin'.*

—Yogi Berra

*Odds are you don't know what the odds are.*
—Gary Belsky and Thomas Gilovich,
*Why Smart People Make Big Money Mistakes*

**N**umerous stock market "experts" fill the airwaves, twitter, magazines, and newsletters with the assertion that market timing doesn't work. They profess, until they are blue in the face, that buy-and-hold is a far superior strategy over the long run. Of course, we all know that a bull market makes geniuses out of everyone who follows the buy-and-hold approach. But what about the consequences of the inevitable, recurring bear markets? This book has provided you with the facts on both sides of the argument, so that you can decide for yourself whether or not market timing has merit.

The purpose of *All About Market Timing* is not to provide a comprehensive statistical compilation of the performance of a myriad of market timing models and strategies. But rather, the purpose is to provide you with several step-by-step, time-tested, easy-to-use strategies to time the market successfully so you can protect your investments and enhance your investment performance. These strategies include seasonality, presidential year cycles, moving averages, and fixed-percentage entry-and-exit systems. I have also provided a few market indicators so you can know when the market is about to change and can keep on the right side of the trend. You may want to embrace market timing, but you may not have the time, skill, or temperament to do it yourself. For those investors, detailed information was provided on numerous market timing resources.

To be a successful investor, you must decide on your investing objectives, get a strategy that will work for you, and, most importantly, establish rules for limiting your losses that you will adhere to. Don't leave it to chance or you'll be left with chump change. Don't rely on gurus, brokers, or financial advisors to maximize your returns. They have already set the stage and are just waiting for you to come along. And they won't be there to tell you when it's time to get out.

Instead, think long and hard about selecting a mechanical, nonemotional market timing approach that you can master so you can make your own independent selection of investment vehicles and your own buy-and-sell decisions. You should feel comfortable with the strategy you select. Make sure you use it with the proper risk-control measures, which means cutting losses quickly and always placing stop-loss and trailing stops.

No one but you has your best interests at heart. You didn't depend on someone else to tell you how to earn your money, and you don't need to depend on some disinterested "expert" to tell you how to manage it. Remember that the overwhelming majority of financial advisors pay little heed to the market's health, and they hardly ever tell you when to sell and never, ever tell you to go into cash. They don't believe in market timing or technical analysis but rather focus exclusively on the buy-and-hold long-term story and the fundamentals (i.e., current earnings, the forecasted earnings, and revenues) that don't work and can frequently backfire on you.

Over the long run, the key to investment success is to protect your capital in the short run by cutting your losses and having a strict sell discipline so that small losses don't cascade into monstrous losses. I would bet that fewer than 5 percent of all investors follow this approach. Hardly any of the mutual fund managers follow buy-and-hold for their funds portfolio. According to Morningstar, the average portfolio turnover of a domestic stock mutual fund is 89 percent a year (*Morningstar Mutual Funds,* October 6, 2010). That means that on average almost every stock in the portfolio is sold each year and replaced by new ones. So, if it looks like market timing and smells like market timing, then it is market timing and should be acknowledged as market timing as practiced by the mutual fund managers. And, what's good for the goose should be good for the gander.

Some critics of market timing point out that unless your winning percentage is 70 percent or more, you have no chance of equaling or beating buy-and-hold. That is not true. You should cut your losses to a maximum of 7 to 8 percent below your purchase price, according to Bill O'Neil, the founder of *Investor's Business Daily.* Many of the strategies presented in this book only have winning percentages around 40 to 45 percent or less, and they still beat buy-and-hold by a mile. Remember the sage advice of financier Bernard Baruch, who said: "Even being right three or four times out of 10 should yield a person a fortune if they have the sense to cut losses quickly."

The market timing strategies I have presented all have, as the centerpiece of their performance, the concept of being out of the market (or short) when the market begins to fall. The main concern is to protect your capital and to cut your losses. Investors will always be moved by fear and greed. When the market is rising, they look for more and more profits. When the market is falling they become so fearful that they freeze and do nothing. They rationalize it by saying that it is only a "paper" loss, and that history shows that the market "always comes back." They stay the course when they should have acted and acted fast. They put their heads in the sand and pretend that the mounting losses are not happening to them. They think this will blow over and that everything will be fine.

But the losses are very real, not just on paper. For the day comes when investors get so frightened or so tired of waiting for the turnaround or they become so enamored of the latest "fad" stock that they simply must get in on before it gets away from them that they bite the bullet and "take" the loss that had actually been incurred all along. That is the psychological nature of the investor and that is how it has always happened.

Market timing attempts to avoid all that. Be true to your timing principles and be true to yourself, and market timing can work for you. If by now you are convinced that market timing is the way to go, you have three options:

1. Consider using one or more of the strategies in this book, if you are comfortable that the strategy works and will work for you. Be sure to use stop-loss orders to prevent your drawdowns from getting out of hand. Protecting your principal and reducing your risk should be your main goals.

2. Subscribe to a market timing newsletter and follow the signals given religiously. But first you should check the newsletter's performance from independent sources that have been provided to you and request the complete actual real-time buy and sell signals that occurred in the past.

3. Use a market timing advisory service to time the market and invest in appropriate index funds or ETFs.

In summary, if you use a reliable, time-tested, unemotional market timing approach, then the odds will be in your favor that you can avoid the brunt of future bear markets. Additionally, you can retain your profits during bull markets while reducing your risk. These benefits are hard to beat. And over the long term, you will substantially outperform the outdated, and potentially lethal, buy-and-hold strategy.

I hope that this book will help you to think and invest for yourself. May your time be well spent, and may you enjoy many successes in the future. The next step is yours!

I'd like to hear from you with questions, comments, and descriptions of your experiences with market timing. You can e-mail me at lesmasonson@yahoo.com. For more information on other investing strategies, go to my Web site, www.buydonthold.com, and my new e-book *Profitable ETF Rotation Strategies for Any Market*.

# The Capitalism Distribution
## Observations of Individual Common Stock Returns, 1983–2006

**W**hen most people think of the stock market, they do so in terms of index results such as the S&P 500 or the Russell 3000. They are unaware of the massive differences between successful stocks and failed stocks "under the hood" of their favorite index.

- 39 percent of stocks were unprofitable investments.
- 18.5 percent of stocks lost at least 75 percent of their value.
- 64 percent of stocks underperformed the Russell 3000.
- 25 percent of stocks were responsible for all of the market's gains.
  - High-performance stocks all tended to have one thing in common.

In this appendix, we make the case for the Capitalism Distribution, a nonnormal distribution with very fat tails that reflects the observed realities of long-term individual common stock returns.

Our database covers all common stocks that traded on the NYSE, AMEX, and Nasdaq since 1983, including delisted stocks. Stock and index returns were calculated on a total return basis (dividends reinvested). Dynamic point-in-time liquidity filters were used to limit our universe to the approximately 8,000 (due to index reconstitution, delisting, mergers, etc.) stocks that would have qualified for membership in the Russell 3000 at some point in their lifetime. The Russell 3000 Index measures the performance of the largest 3,000 U.S. companies representing approximately 98 percent of the investable U.S. equity market. Figure A-1 shows the total lifetime returns for individual U.S. stocks between 1983 and 2006.

Figure A-2 shows the *lifetime* total return for individual stocks relative to the *corresponding* return for the Russell 3000 (stock's return from X-date to Y-date, minus index return from X-date to Y-date).

The fat tails in this distribution are notable. A total of 494 (6.1 percent of all) stocks outperformed the Russell 3000 by at least 500 percent during their lifetime. Likewise, 316 (3.9 percent of all) stocks lagged behind the Russell 3000 by at least 500 percent.

Figure A-3 shows the *lifetime* annualized return for individual stocks relative to the *corresponding* return for the Russell 3000.

**FIGURE A-1**

Total lifetime returns for individual U.S. stocks, 1983–2006.

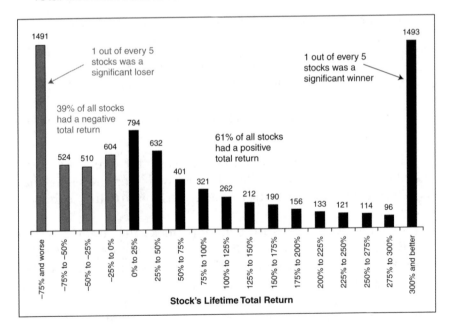

**FIGURE  A-2**

Total returns of individual stocks versus the Russell 3000
index, 1983–2006.

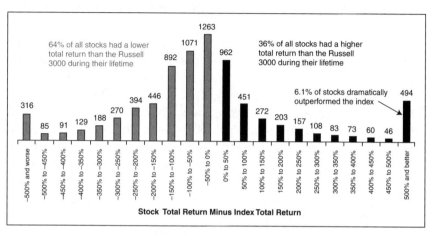

**FIGURE  A-3**

Annualized returns of individual stocks versus the Russell
3000, 1983–2006.

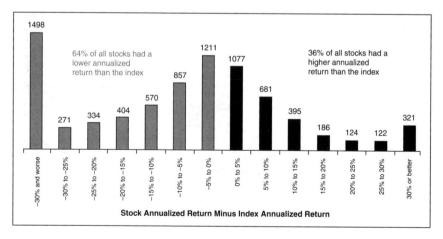

The left tail in this distribution is significant. A total of 1,498 (18.6 percent of all) stocks dramatically underperformed relative to the Russell 3000 during their lifetime.

Figure A-4 shows the cumulative distribution of the annualized returns of all stocks.

You may be wondering how the Russell 3000 Index can have an overall positive rate of return if the average annualized return for all stocks is negative. The answer is mostly a function of the index construction methodology. Like the S&P 500, the Russell 3000 is market-capitalization weighted. This means that successful companies (with rising stock prices) receive larger weightings in the index. Likewise, unsuccessful companies are removed from the index (delisted), making way for growing companies. In this way, market-capitalization-weighted indexation is like a simple trend-following system that rewards success and punishes failure.

It's also important to point out that stocks with a negative annualized return had shorter life spans than their successful coun-

**FIGURE A-4**

Annualized returns for individual stocks, 1983–2006.

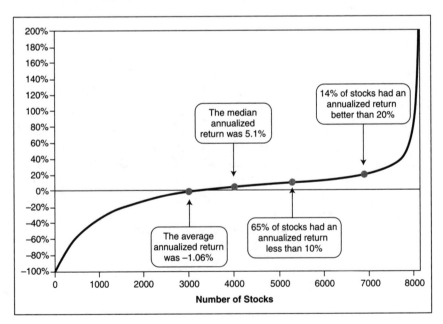

terparts. The average life span of a losing stock was 6.85 years versus 9.23 years for winning stocks (many of which are still living right now), meaning that losing stocks have shorter periods of time to impact negatively on index returns. For these reasons, the average annualized return is probably a somewhat deceptive number for the purposes of modeling the "typical" stock, but interesting nevertheless.

The astute reader at this point is probably wondering if outperforming large-capitalization stocks explain the observed distributions. Mathematically this would make sense. Small-cap stocks certainly outnumber large-cap stocks, while large-cap stocks dominate the index weightings. However, while large-cap stocks (Russell 1000) have outperformed small-cap stocks (Russell 2000) over the long term, it has been by less than 1 percent per year, certainly not enough to explain our observations.

Figure A-5 shows how stocks, when sorted from least profitable to most profitable, contributed to the total gains produced

## FIGURE A-5

Attribution of collective return, 1983–2006.

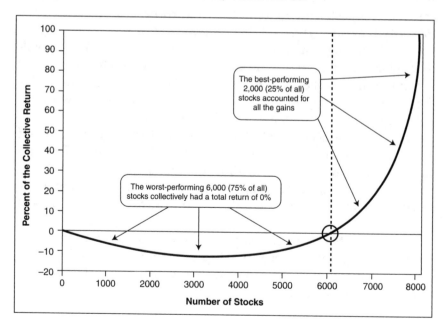

from all stocks. The conclusion is that if an investor was somehow unlucky enough to miss the 25 percent most profitable stocks and instead invested in the other 75 percent, his or her total gain from 1983 to 2007 would have been 0 percent. In other words, a minority of stocks are responsible for the majority of the market's gains.

We identified the best-performing stocks on both an annualized return and a total-return basis, and studied them extensively. The biggest-winning stocks on an annualized-return basis had a moderate tendency to be technology stocks, and most (60 percent) were bought out by another company or a private equity firm—not surprising.

Some of the biggest winners on a total-return basis were companies that had been acquired. Examples include Sun America, Warner Lambert, Gillette, Golden West Financial, and Harrah's Entertainment. However, most (68 percent) are still trading today. Not surprisingly, they are almost exclusively large-cap companies. In addition, further research suggests that they weren't large companies when they were enjoying the bulk of their cumulative returns. Becoming a large-cap company is simply the natural result of significant price appreciation above and beyond that of other stocks in the market. We were not able to detect any sector tendencies. The biggest winners on a total-return basis were simply the minority that outperformed their peers.

Both the biggest winners on an annualized-return and total-return basis tended to have one thing in common while they were accumulating market-beating gains: Relative to average stocks, they spent a disproportionate amount of time making new multiyear highs. Stock ABC can't typically travel from $20 to $300 without first crossing $30 and $40 levels. Such a stock is going to spend a lot of time making new highs. Likewise, the worst-performing stocks tended to spend zero time making new multiyear highs while they were accumulating losses. Instead, relative to average stocks, they tended to spend a disproportionate amount of time at multiyear lows.

Mathematically it makes perfect sense. Stocks that generate thousands of percent returns will typically hit new highs hundreds of times, usually over the course of many years. See Table A-1 for examples of such stocks.

## TABLE A-1

Representative High-Performing Stocks

| Stocks | On the Way Up | | After the Peak | |
| --- | --- | --- | --- | --- |
| | Number New Highs | Gain (%) | Number New Highs | Loss (%) |
| Cisco Systems | 488 | 99,975 | 0 | −81 |
| General Electric | 1,011 | 25,316 | 0 | −71 |
| Ford Motor | 348 | 5,484 | 0 | −94 |
| General Motors | 384 | 3,151 | 0 | −95 |
| Citigroup | 353 | 5,519 | 0 | −90 |
| Microsoft | 424 | 62,188 | 0 | −61 |
| Fannie Mae | 342 | 8,531 | 0 | −99 |
| Intel Corp | 304 | 16,898 | 0 | −81 |
| American International Group | 348 | 3,974 | 0 | −98 |
| Bear Stearns | 285 | 4,691 | | −95 |

Could it be this simple, long-term trend-following on stocks? That's our conclusion. For detailed results of the trading system that was inspired by this research, see the paper "Does Trend Following Work on Stocks?"

—Eric Crittenden and Cole Wilcox

*Note:* This Appendix is included with permission of the authors. Contact information for the authors and Blackstar Funds is as follows:

Eric Crittenden and Cole Wilcox
Blackstar Funds, LLC
4725 N Scottsdale Road, No. 110
Scottsdale, AZ 85251
Tel: 602-910-6957
Fax: 602-910-6956
eric@blackstarfunds.com
cole@blackstarfunds.com

# BIBLIOGRAPHY AND WEB SITES

## BOOKS

Alexander, Colin. *Street Smart Guide to Timing the Stock Market.* New York: McGraw-Hill, 1999.

Arnold, Curtis M. *Timing the Market: How to Profit in Bull and Bear Markets with Technical Analysis,* rev. ed. New York: McGraw-Hill, 1995.

Bulkowski, Thomas N. *Encyclopedia of Chart Patterns.* New York: Wiley, 2002.

Colby, Robert W. *The Encyclopedia of Technical Market Indicators,* 2nd ed. New York: McGraw-Hill, 2003.

Dorsey, Thomas J. *Point and Figure Charting: The Essential Application for Forecasting and Tracking Market Prices,* 2nd ed. New York: Wiley, 2001.

Faber, Mebane T., and Eric W. Richardson. *The Ivy Portfolio: How to Invest Like the Top Endowments and Avoid Bear Markets.* Hoboken, NJ: Wiley, 2009.

Duarte, Joe. *Market Timing for Dummies.* Hoboken, NJ: Wiley, 2009.

Ferri, Richard A., Jr. *All About Index Funds: The Easy Way to Get Started.* New York: McGraw-Hill, 2002.

Harding, Sy. *Riding the BEAR: How to Prosper in the Coming Bear Market.* Holbrook, MA: Adams Media Corporation, 1999.

Headley, Price. *Big Trends in Trading: Strategies to Master Major Market Moves.* New York: Wiley, 2002.

Hirsch, Jeffrey A., and Yale Hirsch. *Stock Trader's Almanac 2011.* Hoboken, NJ: Wiley, 2010.

*Investment Company Fact Book 2010,* 50th ed. New York: Investment Company Institute, 2010.

Kaeppel, Jay. *Seasonal Stock Market Trends: The Definitive Guide to Calendar-Based Stock Market Trading*. Hoboken, NJ: Wiley, 2009.

Masonson, Leslie N. *Buy—DON'T Hold: Investing with ETFs Using Relative Strength to Increase Returns with Less Risk*. Upper Saddle River, NJ: FT Press, 2010.

McDonald, Michael. *Predict Market Swings with Technical Analysis*. New York: Wiley, 2002.

Merriman, Paul. *Live It Up without Outliving Your Money! 10 Steps to a Perfect Retirement Portfolio*. Hoboken, NJ: Wiley, 2008.

Merriman, Paul, and Merle E. Dowd. *Market Timing with No-Load Mutual Funds*. Mercer Island, WA: Backwater Books, 1985.

Murphy, John J. *Technical Analysis of the Futures Markets*. New York: New York Institute of Finance, 1986.

O'Neil, William J. *How to Make Money in Stocks: A Winning System in Good or Bad Times*. New York: McGraw-Hill, 2002.

Pring, Martin J. *Technical Analysis Explained*, 4th ed. New York: McGraw-Hill, 2002.

Sosnowy, John K. *Lasting Wealth Is a Matter of Timing*. Cheyenne, WY: 21st Century Publishers, 1997.

Wild, Russell. *Exchange-Traded Funds for Dummies*. Hoboken, NJ: Wiley, 2007.

Zweig, Martin. *Martin Zweig on Timing*. New York: Warner Books, 1986.

## ARTICLES ON MARKET TIMING

Basso, Thomas. "Timing the Market Revised." *Financial Planning* 31(2):104–110, 2001.

Brinson, Gary, Brian D. Singer, and Gilbert L. Beebower. "Determinants of Portfolio Performance: II. An Update." *Financial Analysts Journal*, May–June 1991.

Dare, William H. "To Hold or Not to Hold." *Journal of Financial Planning*, July 1995, pp. 123–126.

Droms, W. G. "Market Timing as an Investment Policy." *Financial Analysts Journal*, January–February 1989, pp. 73–77.

Merriman, Paul. "Market Timing's Bad Rap." Available at www.fundadvice.com or www.fundadvice.com/FEhtml/MTStrategies/0208.htm.

Sy, W. "Market Timing: Is It a Folly?" *Journal of Portfolio Management*, Summer 1990, pp. 11–16.

Wagner, Jerry C. "Why Market Timing Works." *Journal of Investing*, Summer 1997.

## PAPERS ON MARKET TIMING

Bollen, Nicolas P. B., and Jeffrey A. Busse. "On the Timing Ability of Mutual Fund Managers." *Journal of Finance*, June 2001. Available at http://papers.ssrn.com/sol3/papers.cfm?abstract_id=2457 90.

Chance, Don M., and Michael L. Hemler. "The Performance of Professional Market Timers: Daily Evidence from Executed Strategies." *Journal of Financial Economics* 62(2):377–411, November 2001.

Kumar, Alok, and Vicente Pons-Sanz. "Behavior and Performance of Investment Newsletter Analysts." Paper presented at the EFA 2002 Berlin Meetings, November 2002. Available at http://papers.ssrn.com/sol3/papers.cfm?abstract_id=302888.

## WEB SITES

### Charting and Technical Analysis Sites

www.bigcharts.com

www.decisionpoint.com

www.dorseywright.com (point-and-figure charting)

www.freestockcharts.com

www.investorsintelligence.com (point-and-figure charting)

www.stockcharts.com

### Advisory Service or Newsletters

www.begininvesting.com

www.elliottwave.com
www.fundadvice.com
www.haysmarketfocus.com
www.investorsintelligence.com
www.robertwcolby.com
www.streetsmartreport.com
www.stocktradersalmanac.com
www.timerdigest.com

## Funds for Market Timers

www.direxion.com
www.invesco.com
www.powershares.com
www.profunds.com
www.proshares.com
www.rydex-sgi.com

## Sector Funds and Index Funds

www.indexfunds.com
www.fidelity.com
www.vanguard.com

## ETFs

www.amex.com
www.indexfunds.com
www.etfconnect.com
www.ishares.com
www.NASDAQ.com
www.etfreplay.com
www.etftrends.com
www.etfscreen.com

## Independent Ratings of Market Timers

www.timerdigest.com
www.timertrac.com
www.hulbertdigest.com (now part of www.cbs.marketwatch.com)

## Other Useful Sites

www.aaii.com
www.bankrate.com
www.bloomberg.com
www.businessweek.com
www.cnbc.com
www.icifactbook.org
www.kirkreport.com
www.mfea.com
money.cnn.com
www.moneycentral.com
www.morningstar.com
www.sec.gov/investor.shtml
www.wilshire.com

# INDEX

**Leslie N. Masonson** is president of Cash Management Resources, a financial consulting firm based in Monroe, New York, that he founded in 1987. Masonson's 40-year working career has spanned financial advisory services, investing/trading, banking operations, management, teaching, and cash/treasury management consulting. Previously, he worked for three banks—Citibank, Bank of America, and Irving Trust Company—before starting his own firm. In the past six years ending in April 2010, he was a financial advisor.

In April 2010, Masonson authored *Buy—DON'T Hold: Investing with ETFs Using Relative Strength to Increase Returns with Less Risk* (FT Press). Previously, he authored *All About Market Timing* (McGraw-Hill, 1st ed., 2003), *Day Trading on the Edge: A Look-Before-You-Leap Guide to Extreme Investing* (AMACOM, 2001), and *Cash Cash Cash: The Three Principles of Business Success and Survival* (HarperBusiness, 1990). And in 1985, he coauthored *Corporate Cash Management: Techniques and Analysis*, published by Dow-Jones Irwin. Since November 1998, Masonson has been editor of the *Corporate Treasury Management Manual*, published by Sheshunoff Information Services.

Masonson has been interviewed on business radio stations, as well as on the Financial News Network and CNBC. He has been interviewed by the *Las Vegas Review Journal, Boardroom Reports*, and *Pensions & Investment Age*. Furthermore, he has written over 60 articles, including trader interviews and product and book reviews for numerous financial publications, such as *Technical Analysis of Stocks & Commodities, Active Trader, Futures Magazine*, and *Pensions & Investment Age*. In November 2000, he was a speaker at the Online Investor Expo, where he gave a speech entitled, "Successfully Trading Stocks for a Living."

Masonson has been studying the stock market for over 50 years. He has invested and traded ETFs, mutual funds, stocks, options, futures, and commodities. He has read over 500 books on investing and trading and is proficient in technical analysis. Masonson has used many investing and trading software programs over the years, including TradeStation, High Growth Stock Investor, VectorVest, Telescan, OmniTrader, DTN, ULTRA, and many other charting, investing, and trading sites on the Internet.

Masonson has a BBA in finance and investments from the City College of New York and an MBA in operations research from the Bernard M. Baruch College. The title of his master's thesis was, "A Statistical Evaluation of the Relative Strength Concept of Common Stock Selection." His Web site is www.buydonthold.com.